INDIAN EXPLORERS OF THE 19th CENTURY

ACCOUNT OF EXPLORATIONS IN THE HIMALAYAS, TIBET, MONGOLIA AND CENTRAL ASIA

INDRA SINGH RAWAT
FORMERLY OF THE SURVEY OF INDIA

PUBLICATIONS DIVISION
MINISTRY OF INFORMATION AND BROADCASTING
GOVERNMENT OF INDIA

First Published July 1973 *(Asadha 1895)*
Reprint 2002 *(Saka 1924)*

© Publications Division

ISBN : 81-230-1041-9

Price : Rs. 95.00

Published by The Director, Publications Division,
Ministry of Information and Broadcasting,
Government of India, Patiala House, New Delhi-110 001

Sales Emporia • Publications Division

- Patiala House, Tilak Marg, New Delhi - 110 001
- Super Bazar, Connaught Circus, New Delhi - 110 001
- Commerce House, Currimbhoy Road, Ballard Pier, Mumbai - 400 038
- 8, Esplanade East, Kolkata - 700 069
- 'A' Wing, F Block, Ground floor, Rajaji Bhawan, Besant Nagar, Chennai - 600 090
- Press Road, Thiruvananthapuram - 695 001
- Block-4, 1st Floor, Gruhakalpa Complex M.J. Road, Nampally, Hyderabad-500 001
- 1st Floor, 'F' Wing, Kendriya Sadan, Koramangala, Bangalore - 560 034
- Bihar State Co-operative Bank Building, Ashoka Rajpath, Patna - 800 004
- 27/6 Ram Mohan Roy Marg, Lucknow - 226 001
- Ambica Complex, 1st Floor, Above UCO Bank Paldi, Ahmedabad
- Naujan Road, Uzan Bazar, Guwahati-781 001

Sales Counters :

- C/o PIB, C.G.O. Complex, 'A' Wing, A.B. Road, Indore (M.P.)
- C/o PIB, 80, Malviya Nagar, Bhopal - 462 003 (M.P.)
- C/o PIB, B 7, Bhawani Singh Marg, Jaipur - 302 001 (Rajasthan)

Typeset at : Quick Prints, Naraina, New Delhi - 110 028
Printed at : Tara Art Press, New Delhi - 110 002

INDIAN EXPLORERS
OF THE 19th CENTURY

To
JAWAHARLAL NEHRU
The Lover of Mountains

FOREWORD

From the days of Ptolemy, the Greek philosopher of 1800 years ago, knowledge of the earth's surface had advanced by fits and starts through the zeal of men imbued with curiosity and a sense for geography and with the enterprise to go forth and see the world themselves. But only one hundred years ago there were still large blanks in the maps of all the great continents and Central Asia was one of these blanks. Perhaps worse than these blanks were the distortions and inventions scattered by the cartographers in their efforts to fit together the tales of the more adventurous travellers.

By 1860 the surveys of India had been brought up by accurate survey on the ground to her northern borders, following generally the natural barrier of the Himalayan Mountains, and the British surveyors responsible were bitten by the urge to find out something of the lands beyond, the same urge that has led our astronomers and cosmonauts of the present day to know what lies beyond their ken.

But the people of Asia were quite naturally most suspicious of intruders and especially of surveyors and map-makers and British at that. Had not the British surveyors always been well forward in their advance? It was, moreover, the Government of India's strict order that none of its servants should venture into foreign territory beyond the recorded borders.

And so, to satisfy their craze for knowledge of the unknown, the British surveyors conceived the plan of training suitable Indians in the elements of survey — the measurement of distance by pacing and the fixing of bearings and positions by observation of the stars, and then sending these hardy enthusiasts to make their secret ways in various guises away in the blue. The plan prospered and for some thirty years these trained explorers brought back records that were worked up into maps at the headquarters of the Trigonometrical Survey of Dehra Dun. The technical results are all on records with the Survey of India and a general account has been written and published by Kenneth Mason in Chapter II of his "Abode of Snow". And now Indra Singh Rawat has given us this fascinating story of the adventures of these marvellous men. His story is alive with personal touches and intimate detail, inspired with a sense of filial duty; he is the nephew of Pundit Kishen Singh, the great A.K. and thus closely related to the Chief Pundit Nain Singh. He was born and bred near Milam in Johar Valley, the home of the Rawat family. He enlisted in the Kumaon Regiment in 1919 and was brought into Survey of India by Harry Meade. After 41 years service in the Department as a practical surveyor, he is giving his years of retirement to writing up the stirring story of the devotion of his kinsfolk and their comrades to the cause of Geography.

"The Club"	COLONEL R.H. PHILLIMORE
Dehra Dun (UP) India	CIE, DSO
The 16th February 1964	*Late Acting Surveyor General of India*

PREFACE

In my childhood I used to hear the legendary songs of the travels of explorers Nain Singh and Mani Singh to Ladakh during fairs and festivals in Johar valley of Kumaon. I also heard from uncle Kishen Singh interesting stories of the Grand Lama of Great Tibet, the robbers' battle cry of Ullul-lullul-lu-u-u, the black and white tent-dwellers and jet-black wild yaks of Chang-tang (the heart of pastoral life in Tibet) and various other events during his exploration in Tibet, Mongolia and other parts of Central Asia. All these left a deep impression on my young mind and created a great desire in me to follow in their footsteps.

The circumstances and environments in which a child is born and brought up in the Himalayas prepare him for active life. His daily gaze at the snow-capped peaks, the surrounding grandeur and the scenic beauty fill his heart with joy and love for the Himalayas. From time immemorial, our sages have sung songs in its praise and the Hindu mythology is full of the Himalayan legends. Here in the peaceful atmosphere, Lord Shiva used to meditate, sing and dance in his *tandav* mood to the glory of the Almighty God. The dales and valleys still echo and re-echo with the legendary songs. There entwine our fondest recollections and wherever we may go, our eyes always turn towards it with deep love and respect. To the western people, the Himalayan peaks are just giants to be conquered, but to the Himalayan people these are holy places to the worshipped. The Himalayas feed the great perennial rivers of India, halt the northward march of the moistureladen monsoons and shield us from the piercing winds blowing from the other side. For centuries, it was a barrier to invasions from the north. Thus it will be seen that much of God's blessing reaches us through the holy Himalayas.

Thus born and brought up in the Himalayas and after being

educated, I enlisted myself in the Kumaon Rifles in 1919 and was brought into the Survey of India in 1920 by Major H.R.C. Meade. As a surveyor, I had an active and tough life for 41 years in the high Himalayas, deserts, wild and malarious jungles and other parts of the Indian sub-continent, among various colourful, rural and romantic, tribal people, including the valiant Pathans of the North Western Frontier Province and the head-hunting Nagas of NEFA.

The surveyor in India is still maintaining the old tradition of hard work and discipline of the Survey of India, working from daybreak to sunset to complete the allotted work within the fixed period and leading tent-life during the field season. Considering its vast area, comprising different and varied features from the high Himalayas to Cape Comorin and from the eastern to western frontiers, India is one of the best mapped countries in the world and the Survey of India is one of the best scientific departments of the Government of India.

Being interested in mountaineering and travels in Central Asia, I read such books as "The Abode of Snow" by Kenneth Mason, "The Scottish Himalayan Expedition" by W.H. Murray, "The Man of Everest" by James Ullman, "Beyond the Himalayas" by William O. Douglas and various other works and geographical journals. This spurred me in my ambition to write an account of the historical work of the Indian explorers of the nineteenth century.

On my retirement in 1961, I changed over from sports and active life to research and literary work. With the permission of the then Surveyor General of India, I used to visit the Survey library at Dehra Dun to consult the old Survey records. I also visited the National Archives of India at New Delhi and consulted the original diaries of the Indian explorers, the Memoirs of the Indian Survey by Markham and various other old records. My own family records gave me valuable informations about the Pundit explorers.

I made Colonel Phillimore (a distinguished Survey Officer and a great Survey historian) my Guru (teacher). I used to contact him often during the winter from 1961 to 1964 at his residence in "The Club", Dehra Dun for help and guidance. Even in his advanced age, he used to give me sufficient time. He was a strict critic and advised me to be true to facts and to avoid vagueness. In 1964 he wrote the Foreword for my book before proceeding to Gulmarg, Kashmir where he died at the age of 85.

LANDOUR VIEW INDRA SINGH RAWAT
COTTAGE NO. 4
MUSSOORIE (U.P.) INDIA
The 4th September 1969

ACKNOWLEDGEMENT

I am indebted to Colonel R.H. Phillimore, CIE, DSO, one time acting Surveyor General of India, a great Survey historian and the author of the five volumes of "The Historical Records of the Survey of India" for his help and guidance. I thank Brigadier Gambhir Singh, MIS, MIE, the first Indian Surveyor General of India and the Director of the National Archives of India for the facilities given for the research work; Colonel J.A.F. Dalal, MIS, MIE, now Surveyor General of India, for his help and encouragement; Mr. Taring, the Principal of the Tibetan School, Mussoorie, for his verification of the meanings of the words in the Tibetan language as given in the Glossary and Colonel Kenneth Mason, MC, formerly of the Survey of India and Professor of Geography in the University of Oxford, for his interest in and sympathy for my literary endeavour.

CONTENTS

INTRODUCTION	
SECTION ONE	1
Nain Singh	3
SECTION TWO	73
Kishen Singh	75
SECTION THREE	173
Kalian Singh	175
Hari Ram	183
Lala	205
Nem Singh	212
Kinthup	217
Rinzin Namgyal	226
Ugyen Gyatso	240
Mirza Shuja	250
Ata Mohammad	251
Abdul Subhan	251
APPENDIX	252
Kailas • Manasarowar	
GLOSSARY	257

INTRODUCTION

THE YEARS 1865 to 1885 were the most fruitful for Indian explorers who, trained by the Great Trigonometrical Survey* of Dehra Dun, explored the uplands of Tibet, Mongolia and Central Asia. They were inspired by the professional spirit to fill in the blanks in the map of the continent, to discover remarkable places, to put every town and village in its right place on the great globe, to trace the course of every river, lake, mountain and road and also to discover the customs and manners of the people they came across, with no ill-will for any one.

Before 1864, the maps of this region were either blanks or based on travellers' tales and vague pictorial Chinese maps. Here and there were gleanings from the redoubtable Marco Polo and the devoted Jesuit priests. Chilas, Chitral and Gilgit in the northwest were unexplored; Yarkand, though explored, was a hundred miles out of position on the map; Central Tibet was quite unknown; the position of Lhasa in longitude was largely doubtful; only one point on the Tsangpo, Shigatse, had been fixed with any accuracy by Samuel Turner in 1783.

It was in 1863 that Colonel Walker, the Superintendent of the Great Trigonometrical Survey and Captain Montgomerie set about to train Indian explorers who might explore the uplands of Central Asia. Through Major Smyth, the British Education Officer in Kumaon, himself a great traveller in his district, Nain Singh, a bright intelligent youth, 33 years of age and Mani Singh, a little older were selected.

The two cousins were called to Dehra Dun in 1863 and were given two years' training in practical survey. They were

---

* A section of the Survey of India, then called by this name and assigned the task of fixing the cor-ordinates of points on earth and their elevation

taught to take latitudes by sextant and directions by compass, to recognize the stars and observe them, to determine heights by observing a thermometer in boiling water, to count paces and keep accurate notes. All this had to be done without attracting attention. They had to pass as simple travellers and be everybody's friend.

To help them in their disguise, they carried a rosary and a prayer wheel like all good Tibetans. But instead of the 108 beads, their rosaries had exactly 100 with every tenth a big one. A bead was counted after a hundred paces, a large one reading a thousand. With due piety, the disguised Lamas murmured the Buddhist prayer "*Om mani Padme hum*" (Oh Jewel of the Lotus), turned the prayer wheel and dropped a bead to count the distance. This helped the accurate counting of the paces, while preserving an air of devotion. The prayer wheel was fitted to take long stripes of paper on which they jotted their survey notes. Very few strangers would venture to speak to a Tibetan devotedly twirling the wheel. So the explorers could count the paces with the least amount of interruption. These very wheels have been exhibited in the Dome of Discovery at the Festivals of Britain.

To hide their identity, the explorers worked under various pseudonyms that were as a rule devised by inverting the first and final letters of the full name. Nain Singh was No. 1 or the 'Chief Pundit' or simply 'the Pundit'; his cousin Kalian Singh was GK, and his cousin Kishen Singh, enlisted as Krishna, became AK. Kishen Singh's first cousin Mani Singh was GM.

Pundit Nain Singh was born in 1830 in the village of Milam in Johar Valley in the upper border region of Kumaon in Uttar Pradesh. He was the first of the Pundit explorers. His first famous journey of 1200 miles from Kathmandu to Lhasa and thence to the Manasarowar Lake and back to India, which he performed in 1865-66, was a great pioneering feat. He brought back details for a map of the southern trade route of Tibet and of the Tsang-po's course for 600 miles., This journey won the applause of European geographers, and was recognised by the Royal Geographical Society by the award of a gold watch which, **alas**, was stolen by one of his pupils.

Nain Singh's last and greatest journey was from Leh in Ladakh via Lhasa to Assam in the years 1873-75. This really magnificent achievement has yielded rich and valuable geographical results. He displayed qualities which place him high in the rank of geographical explorers, combining extraordinary hardihood, endurance and perseverance with prudence and skilful diplomacy, while his observations were remarkable for accuracy and precision. It is not often that such splendid services have been performed for geography by one man, and the greatest scientific traveller that India has produced was not to be allowed to retire from service wihtout some special recognition by geographers of his achievements.

In the proposal for an award, Nain Singh is described as "a man who has added a greater amount of positive knowledge to the map of Asia than any individual of our time". In concurring with the application for bestowal of a village in Rohilkhand with a revenue of Rs. 1,000, Lord Salisbury, Secretary of State for India, wrote to the Viceroy of India as follows:

"The successful travels of the Pundit, crowned as they have been recently by the most remarkable journey from Ladakh by way of Lhasa to Assam have for many years past attracted attention not only in England but among geographers all over Europe. I concur with your Excellency in the high value you set upon these services and have much pleasure in expressing my approval of the manner in which you propose to recompense them."

Besides the gold watch from the Royal Geographical Society, Nain Singh was later honoured by a second gold watch by the Paris Geographical Society and by the Founder's Gold Medal of the Royal Geographical Society in 1877. He was later appointed "Companion of the Indian Empire" (CIE).

Pundit Kishen Singh, son of Deb Singh who was also born in September 1850 at Milam, was destined to gain almost greater fame than his master, Pundit Nain Singh. He was known as Krishna in the earlier documents of the Survey and AK in Tibetan Exploration. He was called to Dehra Dun by Colonel Walker in

1867 and was given practical training in route survey under Captain Montgomerie and Pundit Nain Singh.

His first important journey was performed in 1872, when he made a route survey from Shigatse, north of Tsang-po, round the shores of Tengri Nor and reached Lhasa from the North.

His last journey in Tibet and Mongolia during 1878 and 1882, full of long preserving adventure, set the seal on his labour and won him applause from the geographers in Europe.

In India, all trace of him was lost and because of his long absence hope of his return was abandoned. After nearly four years, he made his way back by the confines of China and reached India in 1882. His robust health, subjected to so many hardships, had broken under the strain and it was doubted at first whether he would survive. He too was forced to abandon future exploration work. In his absence, he had been awarded a First Class Medal of the Geographical Society of Italy and on his return the Government of India granted him the title of Rai Bahadur. On his retirement in 1885, he was granted the village of Itarhi in Sitapur district with a gross rental of Rs. 1,850, a reward which he had the great fortune to enjoy for nearly 36 years.

He was the last survivor of the old Indian explorers and died in February 1921.

Our story would not be complete without reference to Chhumbel, the redoubtable and faithful companion of the Pundit explorers, Nain Singh, Kishen Singh and Kalian Singh. Chhumbel was engaged as a cook and porter. He hailed from Zaskar village in Ladakh. Going on an exploration is like getting married; a man has to live with his companions for months and years in the worst of circumstances. It is not like meeting people at social rounds at home or going out on weekends when everyone is at his best. It is essential that companions shoould start liking each other. It is praiseworthy that the explorers and Chhumbel were in perfect harmony. Chhumbel was true and faithful and stuck to his masters throughout the hazardous jouney, enduring hardships cheerfully and willingly. Even in difficulties, he never divulged the secrets of the explorers. When Pundit Kishen Singh was robbed by bandits in the Chang-tang anmd was deserted by another follower, Chhumbel stood firm as a rock and enabled the explorer to complete his work. In the last stage of his journey, when Kishen Singh had run completely out of cash, Chhumbel did not hestitate to take the begging bowl in his hand and follow his master. He fell sick, lost his toe, suffered from frost-bite and sun-blindness but never left his leader. It is hard to find such a faithful companion. Though Chhumbel's services have not been worthily recognised, we pay our affectionate homage to his memory.

Explorer Kalian Singh also hailed from Milam in the Johar valley and he was the second cousin of Pundit Nain Singh. He added a great deal to knowledge of the mineral products of Tibet and explored a large part of unknown areas of that country.

Hari Ram, "No. 9" or MH was also a resident of Kumaon. He surveyed 844 miles, of which 550 may be said to be entirely new ground.

Valuable contribution to knowledge was made by the other explorers mentioned in the book, Lala of Sirmur near Simla, and Kinthup and Nem Singh of Sikkim. Rinzin Namgyal (RN) was the uncle of Sirdar Bahadur Laden La, a well known police officer and member of the Himalaya Club of Darjeeling. The explorer Ugyen Gyatso of Pemayangtse monastery and a Darjeeling schoolmaster, the Lama or UG of the Records, was also the uncle of Sirdar Bahadur Laden La.

the Mohammedan explorers, Mirza Shuja (the Mirza), Ata Muhammand (Mullah) of Peshawar and Munshi Abdul Subhan, who surveyed mostly on the north west frontier and beyond, also desrve mention. Unfortunately, full accounts of their work are not available.

The explorer Sarat Chandra Dass (the Babu) or SCD worked from 1879 to 1881 between northern Sikkim and Lhasa which he reached in 1881. Unfortunately, the full account of his work is also not available.

The narrative account of the activities of explorers Mani Singh and Kala of Pundit Nain Singhs's family could not be found in the Records.

A casual visitor with a superiority complex will never be able to understand other people. To know their religion, customs and manners, a traveller should spend sufficient time among them, taking part in their domestic, social and cultural activities. He should consider himself as one of them and then alone will he be able to give their true picture.

The Indian explorers, whose narrative accounts are given in the following pages, spent weeks, months and years among the colourful and romantic people of the uplands of Tibet, Mongolia and other parts of Central Asia, donning the local dress, speaking the local language and taking part in their domestic, social and cultural activities. So, whatever they have described is based on vast experience and intimate knowledge.

The explorations were carried out under adverse conditions. Hurried notes were taken by the explorers which were later complied and translated into English. Due to this, and the obvious limitations of the journey it is quite possible that certain discrepancies may be found in the narrative.

All the heights mentioned in the book are approximate and based on boiling water observations.

SECTION ONE

NAIN SINGH

1. *Kathmandu • Lhasa • Manasarowar • Mussoorie • 1865-66*

2. *Leh • Lhasa • Assam • 1874-75*

NAIN SINGH

Pundit Nain Singh was the most successful of the Indian explorers between the year 1865 and 1885. Son of Lata Burha, he was born in 1830 in the village of Milam in the Johar valley in the upper border region of Kumaon in Uttar Pradesh. The village, 11,200 feet above the sea-level, is situated at the foot of the Milam glacier from which the Goriganga river emanates. It is tucked away north-east of the great snow mountain Nanda Devi.

The Johar valley is acclaimed as one of the most beautiful parts of Kumaon. Between Mansiari and Rilkot, the gorge of the Goriganga is very deep and precipitous. From Rilkot village, the valley broadens and the slopes become gradual. The tree line ends and alpine pastures begin. Rhododendron trees which are huge in the south become dwarfed from here. The place marks the beginning of the beautiful valley.

During the summer, these alpine pastures glow with velvet-green grass and multi-coloured sweet scented flowers and are studded with dwarfed junipers. Horses, cows, *jobos*, sheep and goats graze merrily and it is a pleasure to look at these animals after their stay in these pas-tures when they get into their natural shape. The hill ponies of the region are famous.

Milam and other villages of the upper Johar valley are inhabited only for a few months from June to October. Barley, buck-wheat, *phanper*, *sarson* and vegetables are grown.

During the season, the men folk of the valley used to go to Tibet and visit Gyanima, Gartok and various other trade markets in Ngari Khorsum, the upper basin of the Sutlej river in Western Tibet. These markets were dependant on Indian trade for cereals, cotton cloth, *gur*, sugar, tobacco and all kinds of hardware and exported wool, borax, salt, butter, horses, sheep, goats and also gold to India.

Each Indian trader of Johar had a *mitra* or colleague in Tibet. Initially their partnership in trade was marked by the splitting of a stone, each keeping one half. Henceforth the Indian trader or his representative would carry the token and sell his goods in the Tibetan market only to his *mitra* or the *mitra's* representative who could fit his half of the stone to the Indian's. Some Tibetans also visited the Johar valley with their sheep caravans laden with wool, borax and salt and took back cereals and other Indian commodities.

As the journey to Tibet through Unta Dhura pass (height 17,640 feet above the sea-level) and the Kingri Bingri La (pass) is hazardous and as Tibet was infested with robbers, the relatives of the traders gave them touching send-offs and on their return a befitting welcome. They were happy and proud of their menfolk returning home safely with their horses, *jobos,* sheep and goats fully laden with valuable Tibetan goods. In the caravan, there were seen newly bought fine Tibetan horses with bright coloured ribbons on their manes and little sweet ringing bells around their necks. This happy and carefree atmosphere is no more seen in this border region due to the dislocation of the Indo-Tibetan trade.

After leaving the school, Nain Singh helped his father in trade. He used to visit the different centres in Tibet with his father, learnt the Tibetan language, customs and manners and became familiar with the people.

From 1855 to 1857, Nain Singh and his first cousin, Mani Singh, son of Deb Singh, were in the service of the German scientists. Schla-gintweit brothers, who travelled in the Himalayas during that period. The Pundits were found to be resourceful and intelligent. Afterwards Pundit Nain Singh joined the Education Department, being head-master of a Government vernacular school in his village from 1858 to 1863.

Way back, the Rajput ancestors of the Pundit explorers, Nain Singh, Kishen Singh, Mani Singh, Kalian Singh and Kala, migrated to Garhwal from Rajputana during the invasions of Mohammed Ghori between 1191 and 1193 and settled down at a place known as Jwala Bagarh. In about 1680, one of the family members by the name of Hiroo Dham Singh went on pilgrimage to Kailas and Manasarowar and entered Tibet with his party. In those days the pilgrims used to move in big parties and were all armed to protect themselves from robbers. About that time, bandits from China entered Tibet and they were after cattle, sheep and horses. Hiroo Dham Singh helped the Tibetans against the marauders and taught them new guerilla tactics. Eventually the bandits were defeated. In appreciation of this help, Hiroo Dham Singh received the honour of a "Pradhan" from the Government at Lhasa and also other trade concessions in Tibet. His family enjoyed the privileges upto 1951 when the Chinese attacked Tibet and occupied Lhasa.

Hiroo Dham Singh returned from pilgrimage through the Johar valley which he liked and settled down there. By his bravery and diplomacy, he became the leader of the valley. During the period of the Chand dynasty in Kumaon, the Rawats ruled over the Johar valley, after paying a part of the revenue to the Chands. In 1790, the Chands were defeated by the Gurkhas. During the Gurkha period also, the Rawats ruled over the Johar Valley. The Gurkhas were defeated by the British in 1816. Quithi village was the headquarters of the Rawats where the sites of old courts are still in existence. Recently during excavations for building new houses, bows, arrows and other warlike implements were discovered in this village. The family members were great traders and spread their trade to north and south. They were rich and philanthropic. The *dharmashalas* (charitable rest-houses for travellers) built by the millionaire Mani Singh, a relation of the explorer of the same name, are still in existence in Kumaon and at Almora proper.

It was in 1863 that Colonel James Walker and Capt. Montgomerie of the Great Trigonometrical Survey set about to train Indians for exploring the uplands of Tibet, Mongolia and Central Asia. Through Major Smyth, the British Education Officer in Kumaon-a great traveller, Captain Montgomerie selected Nain Singh, a bright intelligent youth and his cousin, Mani Singh, son of Deb Singh.

The two cousins were called to Dehra Dun in 1863 and were given two years' training in practical survey. Nain Singh proved particularly intelligent and rapidly learnt the use of sextant, compass and other instruments and recognised all the large stars without difficulty.

Kathmandu • Lhasa Manasarowar • Mussoorie

Pundit Nain Singh and Pundit Mani Singh were instructed to make for Lhasa. While in Kumaon, they came across some Johari merchants who had been robbed whilst trading near Gartok in Ngari Khorsum district in Tibet. These merchants thought that, if the matter was properly represented, they might get redress from the Lhasa government, and hearing that the Pundits were going to Lhasa, asked them to be their agents *(vakils)* in order to recover what they could. The Pundits consented. This furnished a plausible reason for the journey.

The Pundits attempted to go direct from Kumaon to Lhasa via Manasarowar but they found it impracticable. It appeared that the best chance of reaching Lhasa would be through Nepal as there was frequent intercourse between Lhasa and that country. The explorers started from Dehra Dun in January 1865 and crossed the frontier at Nepalgunj and reached Kathmandu on the 7th March, 1865 by the Sisagarhi road.

In Kathmandu, they made enquiries as to the best route to Lhasa. They found that the direct one by Kuti (or Nilam) across Dingri plain (or Ting-ri Maidan) was likely to be very difficult, if not impossible, owing to the snow at that early season (March-April). The explorers consequently determined to try the route by Kerun Shahr, a small town in the Lhasa territory, as that route was said to be possible.

Departure from Kathmandu

Having made their arrangements, the two explorers started on the 20th March, 1865 with great hopes, accompanied by four men whom they hired as servants. On the 25th, the party arrived at Shabru village, situated near the junction of the streams Gandak and Lendu Chu. This was a customs post where all goods were taxed and travellers had to pay a toll. On the 26th, they reached Meadongpodo village and there they changed their dress to one better known to the people of Lhasa in order to prevent any suspicion about the object of their travels. On the 27th, they arrived about noon at Temure, a Nepalese police and customs post, where officials forced them to undergo a strict examination. Their boxes and baggage were closely searched but they failed to discover anything suspicious as the survey instruments had been hidden. They however compelled the explorers to pay toll 'tax, after examining their passports. The Pundits then proceeded on their way and by night-fall arrived at Rasulgarhi, a fort built by the Nepalese ruler Jang Bahadur in 1855 during the war between him and the Lhasa Raja. This fort is situated near the junction of the Gandak and Lendi Chu streams.

On the 28th, the party arrived at noon on the left bank of the Gandak river at Paimunesa, a halting place near a police post of the Kerun Shahr district. There they were stopped and interrogated as to who they were. The customs officials told them that they must be detained till the Kerun Shahr official gave them the sanction to pass. Acting on their decision, the officials sent word to Kerun Shahr, mean-while searching the explorers' boxes. But the same good fortune attended the party; the customs people failed to discover anything suspicious. They however made the Pundits pay toll tax.

After detaining them for two days, the expected answer from the Kerun Shahr governor arrived and was read to the explorers. It stated that they were forbidden to continue their journey by way of Kerun Shahr, because this was not the ordinary route from Kathmandu to Lhasa, the proper route being via Nilam or Kuti.

Turned back to Kathmandu

In view of this order, the Pundits made a detour to Rasulgarhi With heavy hearts and gloomy forebodings about the ultimate success of their enterprise. On the 31st March, 1865, the party left Rasulgarhi fort early in the morning and arrived at nightfall at Shabru. On the 2nd April, starting early in the morning from Shabru, they reached the Dongkhang halting place. On the way the explorers discovered that the Kerun Shahr governor had known Pundit Mani Singh personally when he had been the governor of Taklakhar or Purang near Manasarowar and the Chief official of Gartok, and had in fact been frequently in close and friendly relations with him. On the 7th April, they arrived at Khinchat Bazar situated on the bank of the Trisuli Gandak river. Here they discharged two of their servants who knew very little of Tibetan language. Pundit Nain Singh made over to them the papers relating to the work already finished, with instructions to deposit them at a safe place till his return. They themselves marched back and arrived at the Batar Bazar by nightfall. Resuming their march the next morning, they arrived at Kathmandu on the 10th Aprils 1865.

Suffering from anxiety and losing nearly all hope of ever accomplishing his design. Pundit Nain Singh again rose to the occasion and determined to overcome his despondency and make one more effort. In Kathmandu, they made fresh enquiries about some more promising way of getting to Lhasa. At last, they beard of two opportunities, the first by accompanying the camp of a new agent (vakil) that the Nepalese ruler Jang Bahadur was about to send to Lhasa and the second by accompanying a Bhot merchant. To increase the chances of success, they decided that one of them should go with the Nepal agent and the other with the merchant. The Nepal agent at first agreed to take one of them along but ultimately refused. It was impossible for Mani Singh to go with the Bhot merchant who intended to take the Kerun Shahr route. This was because he was personally known to the Kerun Shahr governor.

Mani Singh consequently decided to try a more circuitous route by Muktinath in Nepal but he was unsuccessful due to bad health. After a long journey through the upper parts of Nepal territory, he returned to Hindustan.

Pundit Nain Singh was at first not more successful with the Bhot merchant than his cousin had been with the Nepal agent. The merchant, Dawa Nangal, promised to take the Pundit to Lhasa and on the strength of that proceeded to borrow money from him- Dawa Nangal, how-ever, put off starting from day to day and eventually the explorer had to start with one of the merchant's servants, the merchant himself promising to follow in a few days. The Pundit wore the dress of a Ladakhi and to complete his disguise added a pig-tail to his head. This change was made because he was afraid that the Kerun Shahr officials who stopped him the first time, might recognise him.

Departure again from Kathmandu

Starting on the 3rd June, 1865 with his trusted servant Chhumbel and Dawa Nangal's man, Nain Singh reached Shabru on the 20th of June, having been delayed for six days by an attack of fever. At Shabru he was received by Dawa Nangal's family with kindness but Dawa Nangal himself never made his appearance and it became evident that he did not intend to keep his promise. In his perplexity, the Pundit appealed to Dawa Nangal's uncle, a man of some authority and told him how he had been treated. The uncle sympathised with him. He gave him a pass to Kerun Shahr and a letter to Dawa Nangal's brother, who had just returned to Kerun Shahr from Lhasa. In the letter, he mentioned that the Pundit's claim against Dawa Nangal was just, and, in consequence, requested him to arrange for the Pundit's journey to Lhasa and, if necessary, to stand surety for him.

Starting on the 6th July, accompanied by a relative of the Shabru official, Nain Singh reached Temure, On the 7th, he arrived at Paimanesa post where, as on the first occasion, the officials attempted to stop him, but the person who accompanied him from Shabru opened the way and the same evening they arrived at Kerun Shahr.

Kerun Shahr, a small town, possessed fifteen to twenty shops, some kept by the Nepalese and some by Bhotias who sold a variety of articles. It had a fort and a good-sized temple. Its population was estimated at about 3,000 or 4,000 souls. Rice was imported and salt was exported. Three crops were raised here. Wheat and barley were sown in October and two other grains, *phanpar* and *sarson*, in May. A number of edible herbs were cultivated.

On arriving at Kerun Shahr, the Pundit lost no time in seeing

Dawa Nangal's brother, Chung Chu and after offering a few trifling presents explained his business with him. The latter promised that all in his power would be done to enable him to travel onwards to Lhasa, but as regards the money, he could not refund it as his brother, Dawa Nangal, was a bad man and it was not his intention to pay his debts. Chung Chu proved himself a better man than his brother for though permission to travel by the direct route was, at first, refused, he ultimately succeeded in getting the Pundit permission to travel onwards.

On August 13, the Pundit left Kerun Shahr and passed through the villages of Ramka, Todang and Mun. On the 17th, he crossed Juktumba pass and arrived at Kolung Chuksa. After progressing through Jong-hil and Chantan-phuk villages he arrived on the 20th half way up Lachumu Phurphur mountain. Tradition has it that a priest rose to heaven on wings from the top of this mountain; hence its name. Travelling further through villages of Namdul and Loha, he arrived at Babuk village.

Babuk

At this place, a spicy plant called nirbisi or *jadwar* (somewhat like ginger in its leaves but of a sweet scent) grows wild and abundantly. Its roots are held in very great esteem throughout India as possessing great healing powers when applied to cuts, scars, bites of venomous serpents and insects. From Kathmandu to Loha village, jungles and forests were generally abundant, but at this place there were none visible, and onwards to Lhasa the mountains were very bare and rocky.

Babuk was a large mart for the exchange of goods. Bhotias from all parts met there. Salt, wool, felt and borax were brought from Tibet, prior to being carried into Nepal. Cereals, sugar, hardware and cloth came from Nepal, destined for Tibet.

The Pundit learnt that on the 25th August, Baro Thele Dureha, with a large party and about 200 yaks, laden with goods, intended to start from Babuk towards Tradon. Having told these people that he was a Bashahri, a countryman of theirs, Nain Singh enjoyed every one's favour and consequently received no opposition to his wish to accompany them.

The caravan accordingly started and arrived in the evening at Galasatang camp. On the 26th, crossing the Gala mountain and after pass-ing Sang-jomba village, they arrived by evening at Sonmath Camp.

On the 27th August, he crossed No La (pass) and arrived at Baruduksam camp. On the 29th, he was at Zangra Dung or Rebo grazing ground (at that time full of herds) and then passed through Tala and Mala Labrang.

On the 2nd September he arrived at Rela monastery on the right bank of the Brahmaputra; on the 3rd he was at Muna Ghat on the bank of the river, where boats, formed of a framework of wood and covered with leather, conveyed people and goods across. On this occasion, one boat was lost with three people. On the 4th, he arrived at Jang Thakdong grazing grounds and on the 5th, the Lik-tse monastery situated on a low hill on the right bank of the river. He crossed the river by ferry at Lik-tse on the sixth and arrived at Tra-don monastery.

Tra-don

Tra-don (14,200 feet) possessed a large monastery surrounded by eight or nine *ta'sams* (post houses). At this place there are extensive plains, stretching seven miles by four miles to the east and fifteen miles by about fifteen miles to the west. Grain and food, generally imported, were very dear. Grain was not raised at all at the place.

At Tra-don, Pundit Nain Singh learnt that once in two years the Maharaja of Kashmir used to send a merchant called Lopchak with a caravan consisting of 270 horse or yak-loads to Lhasa, carriage being supplied by the Tibetan Government while within its territory. The goods from Ladakh were dried apricots, saffron, currants, chintz, and piece goods and the articles brought back were shawls, wool and tea. Lopchak, the leader of the caravan, must be a Ladakhi and was always chosen from a family of rank. The profits of the undertaking were shared between the Kashmir Government and the leader's family. Lopchak, by the order of the Lhasa Raja, was shown great attention and treated with great distinction as he passed along the road.

The Tibetan Government also used to send a similar venture of the same number of loads to Kashmir under a Tibetan merchant called Jang Chongpon, the Maharaja conveying it at his own expenses, when within his borders.

Hearing that Lopchak with his caravan was to be sent that year, it occured to the explorer that he had better try to accompany this party. On the 8th of September, 1865, a traveller came into Tra-don from Gar-tok and on questioning him, Pundit Nain Singh was delighted to hear that Lopchak would be there within thirty days. He accordingly rented a house, and made up his mind to wait. To avoid suspicion, he pretended that illness prevented him from joining the party on the way to Manasarowar.

Lopchak's headman, named Chiring Nirpal, accompanied by about twelve men and seventy laden yaks, reached Tra-don on the 2nd October. Pundit Nain Singh sent for him and made friends with him. On hearing the Pundit's story, Chiring Nirpal at once consented to take him to Lhasa.

Starting the next morning with the Ladakhi camp he marched eastward along the great road called the Jong-lam or Whar-lam. From Tra-don, the road follows the Brahmaputra, sometimes close to it, some-times several miles away. Eighty miles east of Tra-don, it leaves the river and crossing some higher ground, descends into the Ra-ga river, which is a great tributary of the Brahmaputra. Leaving the Rakas valley, the road crosses over the mountains and again reaches the Brahmaputra at about 180 miles below Tra-don. About ten miles further down, it changes from the left bank to the right bank, travellers having to cross the great river by ferry boats near the town of Janglache. Below Janglache, the road follows, the river closely to a little below its junction with the Ra-ga river. From this point it runs some ten miles south of the river, crossing the mountains to the large town of Shigatse.

On the 5th October, he arrived at Nyuk-ku *ta-sam* (a staging place) where Chiring Nirpal dismissed the porters from Tra-don and engaged fresh men. After crossing the Charta Sengpo river, they arrived at Jhalung camp on the 8th.

Marching along the bank of the Chaka river, the party arrived at Sa-ka *ta-sam*. This place was presided over by two *Jongpons*, residing at Sar Dzong and Nub Dzong. Grain was not raised at Sa-ka *ta-sam* but was brought all the way from Kerun Shahr and Jong-kha fort.

So far everything had gone smoothly, but here the enquiries made by the authorities rather alarmed the Pundit and as his funds (owing to the great delays) had begun to run short, the two things combined made him very uneasy. However he resolved to continue his journey He became a great favourite with Chiring Nirpal and the whole of the Ladakhi camp.

He travelled further through the camp of Naguling, Se-mo-ka to-sam, Tar-Chung, Gangbiako, Ruan, Sang-sang *ta-sam* and Kukap and on the 19th October arrived at Ra-tung camp. The porters and packs were changed at the *ta-sams*.

Cultivation was found from this place onwards and willow trees made their appearance. From Tra-don to Ra-tung, there were no signs of cultivation and the population was very scant.

The party reached Ngap-ring *ta-sam* to the north-west of which place lies a lake, eight miles long and three miles broad. On the bank of this lake was situated Ngap-ring village ruled by a *Jongpon*.

The yaks between Ngap-ring and Lhasa are very small. So the goods which had been carried on large yaks from Tra-don were trans-ferred to asses at Ngap-ring.

On the 21st October, after passing a small lake called Lang-cho-gonak, four miles by two miles, they arrived at Burkha village, lie water of this lake is very salty and is reported to be 162 feet in depth.

The next day the party reached the town of Janglache, with a fort and a fine monastery on the Nari-chu (Brahmaputra River). There a number of shops were run by the Nepalese. The Kerun Ting-ri Maidan road passed through this place. On the 23rd they were joined by a second portion of Lopchak's men and 105 yaks conveying goods.

From this point, people and goods were frequently transported by boats to Shigatse, five days' march (85 miles*), lower down the river. Most of the Pundit's companions went by boat, but he, having to survey and count paces, went by land. He passed through the village of Tashiling and reached Pin-dzoling village with a fine monastery on the 26th October. It was ruled by a *Jongpon*. The river was spanned there by a bridge, formed by iron chains and ropes. Then he passed through Si-lung and Chiari villages.

Shigatse : Panchan Lama

On October 29, they arrived at Digarcha or Shigatse city (11,700 feet) on the Pen-nang Chu near its junction with the great Nari Chu. At Shigatse, Chiring Nirpal had to wait for his master, Lopchak. The Pundit and his companions remained in a large caravan-sarai called *kunkhang*, built by the Government. At the north-west end of the city, on a low hill, stood a strong fort, called Gang Mar Dzong, which, as tradition has it, was built by a *Deo* (deity). About half a mile to the south-west of the city, stood a very well-built monastery, called Tra-shi-Lhun-po, surrounded by a wall about a mile in circumference. Numerous houses and temples rose within this enclosure. Four of the larger temples among these were superior to the rest and had gilded spires.

The idols in the temples were studded with precious stones, gold and silver and there were about 3,300 priests in the monastery, the Chief being the Great Lama, called Panjan Ring-bo-che, (The Panchan Lama), considered throughout Tibet as an incarnation of the Deity, who can read thoughts of men and who is supposed never to die.

The only incident during their long stay at Shigatse was a visit that Nain Singh and the Ladakhis paid to the great Tra-shi-lhun-po monastry. The Pundit would rather not have paid the Lama a visit but he thought it imprudent to refuse and therefore joined the Ladakhis who were going to offer their respects to him. The Pundit confesses that the proposed visit rather frightened him, as the Lama was supposed to know the secrets of all hearts.

---

* 1 mile = 1.6 kilometre.

However, putting a boldface on the matter, he went and was much relieved to find that the Lama, a boy of eleven, only asked him three simple questions.

They formed a small party and on the 1st November went to pay homage to Panjan Ring-bo-che and were conducted to the presence of a lad seated on a high throne covered with rich silks. He was surrounded by a number of priests, standing in reverential attitude and bearing the insignia of their calling. The worshippers uncovered their heads and made a low obeisance and presented offerings of pieces of silk. Panjan Ring-bo-che then placed his hand on each of their heads and beckoned to his priest to have them seated. Upto this time he had preserved a profound silence, but on seeing that they were seated, he asked only three questions, as he did to every worshipper, viz., "Is your king well ?", "Is your country prospering ?" and "Are you in good health ?". The priest then placed a small strip of silk aound the neck of each worshipper and from a silver kettle poured a little tea into their cups. After this were dismissed.

The city of Shigatse was three quarters of a mile in length and half a mile in breadth. The Kon-Kialing monastery was situated on the left bank of the Pen-nang-chu, in the centre of a garden about three quarters of a mile north-east of Shigatse. A market (*bazar*) was daily held on the space called Thom between the city and the Tra-shi-lhum-po monastery, where every saleable article was displayed throughout the day, the vendors retiring to their homes in the evening. The population of the city was estimated at 9,000 souls, exclusive of the 3,300 priests. The rich earth yielded fine crops of grains. The city was ruled by two *Jongpons*.. A force of 400 Tibetan soldiers was quartered there and gold was found in Ma-u-ri hill, about fifteen miles south of the city but a strict order prohibited the people from digging for it.

Whilst Pundit Nain Singh was at Shigatse, he noted the atmospheric temperature several times. In November, the thermometer always fell below the freezing point at night, even inside a house. The lowest temperature recorded was 25^0F and during the day it hardly ever rose to 50^0. The snowfall in Shigatse was never more than twelve inches, but the cold in the open air was intense. The water of running streams froze if the current was not very strong. A good deal of rain fell during July and August around Shigatse, accompanied by lightning and thunder. The wind throughout Tibet is generally very strong on the table-land but at Shigatse it did not seem to have been in any way remarkable. The sky duirng the winter was generally clear.

At Shigatse, the Pundit took to teaching Nepalese shopkeepers the Hindustani method of keeping accounts and thereby earned a few rupees.

On the 16th November, the Kashmir Maharaja's merchant, Lopchak, for whom the party was waiting, reached Shigtse and Pundit Nain Singh waited on him with a few presents, requesting permission to accompany his men, as he had done from Tra-don. He told Lopchak the story of his illness. Lopchack saw no objection to the Pundit continuing with the party and promised to assist him at Lhasa.

The Nepalese agent *(vakil)* at Lhasa, who was recalled by his ruler Jang Bahadur, arrived at Shigatse city on the 28th November, but Nain Singh was sorry not to discover his cousin Mani Singh among his followers.

From Shigatse, the road runs considerably south of the river. It ascends the Pen-nang Chu and, crossing the Kharo La (17,000 feet), descends into the basin of the Yam-drok Tso. For two long stages, it goes along the great lake (13,700 feet), then rising sharply crosses the lofty Kam-pa pass and descends to the Brahmaputra again, now only 11,400 feet above the sea-level. Following the great river for one stage more, the road, which has hitherto been running from west to east, leaves the Brahmaputra and meets its tributary, the Kyi Chu. Lhasa is three stages further away north-east. The total distance is about 800 miles from Gartok to Lhasa.

On the 22nd December, the party left Shigatse city and marched to Gang village. On the 23rd, it arrived at Pen-nang town governed by a *Jongpon* who resided in the fort, and reached Takse village the following day.

Gyantse

On the 25th, the group arrived at Gyantse city, which was about the size of Shigatse and had a fort on a low hill in the heart of the town, and also a large gilded temple. The city was ruled by two *Jongpons*. A force of 200 Tibetan soldiers was quartered there. The boundary between the Lhasa and Loh (Bhutan) territories is three days' journey from Gyantse.

Rice and tobacco were imported from Bhutan. Wheat, barley, oil, radish, peas and ghee produced in this place were sold very cheap. The city was famed for its woollen products, *getha*, *nambu*, *chuktu* and *purik nambu*, the last one being very superior. It is also known for the manufacture of a kind of small bell called *yarka*, with which they adorn their horses. To the south-west, north-west and south-east of the city are plains stretching from six to ten miles through which the Pen-nang Chu flows. At that time of the year, the river became frozen, and people passed over it on foot.

Crossing the lofty Kha-ro la (pass) (17,000 feet), the party arrive on the 31st December, 1865 at Nang-kar-tse village on the Yam-drok Tso or Lake Palti, with a usual fort on a small hill. The Pundit moved for two days along the great lake, the periphery of which was frozen. On the second day, he nearly fell a prey to a band of robbers but, being on horse back, managed to escape and reached Demalong village safely. This village is situated at the northern angle of the lake. The paces of this portion and of one or two other parts were counted on the return journey, while travelling from Lhasa to Manasarowar.

From Tram-lung, the lake of Yarn-drok Tso was seen to stretch some twenty miles to the south-east. Nain Singh estimated the circumference of the lake to be forty five miles, but as far as he saw, it was only two to three miles wide. The lake encircled a large island which rose into low rounded hills about 2,000 or 3,000 feet above the surface of the lake. Between the hills and the margin of the lake, several villages and a white monastery were visible on the island. The villagers communicated with the mainland by means of boats.

The Pundit was told that the lake had no outlet but as the water was perfectly fresh, he thought the outlet may be on the eastern side where the mountains appeared to be not quite so high as those on the other sides. The existence of an island with a very large area as compared to the lake in which it stands is a curious topographical feature; no similar case is known to exist elsewhere. The lake (from the Pundit's observations) appears to be about 13,500 feet above the sea-level. It contains quantities of fish. The water is very clear and deep. The island in the centre was estimated to be 16,000 feet above the sea-level, an altitude at which coarse grass is found in most parts of Tibet.

From the basin of the Yam-drok Tso, the party crossed over the lofty Kam-pa pass, reaching the great Nari Chu (the Brahmaputra) at Kam-pa-par-tse village. Taking a boat from there, they were rowed down the river at the foot of a hill and alongside an old bridge, formed of iron chains and ropes. The bridge was insecure and was seldom used, ferries being preferable.

From the lofty Kampa pass, the Pundit got a capital view. Looking south, he could see over the island in the Yam-drok Tso and made out a very high range to the south of the lake. The mountains to the east of the lake did not appear to be quite so high. Looking north, he had a clear view of the Brahmaputra but all the mountains in that direction were comparatively low and in no way remarkable.

The Kam-pa mountain forms the boundary between the two districts and Utsang.

After a three day stay at a fort situated on a low hill, on the bank of the river, the party reached Chabanang village on the 8th January, 1866 and on the 9th, marching along the right bank of the Kyi Chu, they reached Netang village.

The Kyi Chu comes from the direction of Lhasa and falls into the Brahmaputra at Chu-shul village. The Brahmaputra from there flows to the east.

Lhasa

On the 10th January, the party arrived at Lhasa (the abode

of God). It is a compound word: *Lha* being God and *sa*, place. The chief divinity worshipped in this part is the Buddha. Soon after their arrival, Pundit Nain Singh took two rooms in a building. One of the rooms was well adapted for taking observations of stars from within.

The Pundit had been there for some ten days when the Lopchak's men told him they were going to visit the Gaden monastery and asked him to go with them. Accordingly he left Lhasa in their company on the 21st and arrived at Se-ra monastery, about three miles away at the foot of the Topiphu mountain.

The circumference of this hill is a little more than one mile. Numerous temples with gilded spires, and of all sizes, were seen in the enclosure. The idols within were studded with gold, silver and precious stones. Some had horns although the limbs and lower portion of the figures were generally those of men. The Pundit was informed that there were about 5,500 priests in this monastery.

On the 24th, the party arrived at Gaden monastery, situated at the top of a low hill. The circumference of this monastery is about three-quarters of a mile. There are numerous well-built temples, with idols much the same as those at Se-ra. It is reported to be a very wealthy monastery and was occupied by about 3,300 priests.

They returned to Lhasa the next day. It was the Pundit's wish to follow the course of the Brahmaputra river, but he was informed that, unless he went with a well-armed party of at least a dozen, it would be dangerous.

The city of Lhasa (11,400 feet) is circular with a circumference of two and a half miles. In the centre of the city stands a very large temple called by three different names, Machindranath, Jo and Phokpochengra. The idols in it were richly inlaid with gold and precious stones. The temples were surrounded by *bazars* (markets) and shops, kept by Lhasan, Kashmiri, Ladakhi, Azimabadi and Nepali merchants, a number of them being Mohammedans. There were numerous Chinese tradesmen.

The city stands on a tolerably level plain surrounded by mountains. The ridge to the east of the Lhasa river is formed of sandstone. The level or open ground extends about six miles to the east, seven miles to the west, four to the south and three to the north. At the northern end of the city, there are two monasteries called Muru and Ramoche. At the north west corner stands the Chumuling monastery and at the west end the Tankyaling monastery. The monastery called Kontyaling is about a mile west of the city, at the foot of a low isolated hill called Chapochi which has a house on its summit.

Po-ta-la Palace

About three-quarters of a mile west of the Ramoche monastery, there is, on a low hill, a large and strong fort called Po-ta-la, which was the residence of the Lama Guru, also called Gewaring-bo-che (the Great Lama of Tibet). The term "Dalai Lama" by which Lama Guru is known to outsiders is never used in Tibet. The Mongolian ruler, Altan Khan, who embraced Buddhism, gave the title of "Dalai Lama" to the incarnations, meaning "Broad Ocean". He was also called Da Lama in China. His head minister was called Raja.

The fort is one and a half miles in circumference and about 300 feet above the surrounding level. Steps lead up to the fort on every side. The village Jol lies under the fort. Four miles west of the city stands the Dre-phung monastery at the foot of a hill. It was occupied by about 7,700 priests who were held in great veneration by all classes of the Lhasa people.

The Dalai Lama

Pundit Nain Singh, accompanied by the Ladakhi merchant, Lopchak, went on the 7th February, 1866 to pay homage to the Gewaring-bo-che, a fair and handsome boy of about thirteen years, seated on a throne six feet high, attended by two of the highest priests, each holding a bundle of peacock feathers. To the right of the Gewaring-bo-che and seated on a throne three feet high, was the Raja Gyalbo-Khuro-Gyago, his chief minister. Several priests, in reverential attitudes, were standing at a respectful distance from them.

The party of the Pundit was ordered to be seated and after making offerings of silks, sweets and money, the Lama Guru asked them three questions, placing his hand on each person's head. "Is your king well?", "Does your country prosper?" and "Are you in good health?" They were served with tea, which some drank and others poured on their heads. After having a strip of silk, with a knot in it, placed by the priest round their necks, they were dismissed. But many were invited to inspect the curiosities that were to be seen in the fort. The walls and ceilings of all the chief houses in the fort and all the temples that contained images of gold were covered with rich silks.

The Lama Guru is the Chief of all Tibet but he does not interfere with the state business. He is looked upon as the guardian divinity and is supposed never to die but transmigrate into anybody he pleases The dead body from which the Lama Guru's soul has departed is placed in a gold coffin studded with the finest gems and kept in the temple with great care. The belief of the people is that the soul of one Lama Guru is privileged to transmigrate thirteen times. The Lama Guru was then in his thirteenth transmigration. *Churtans* are placed over the coffins containing the Lamas' bodies and it is said that these dead bodies diminish in size, while the hair and nails grow.

The Raja or *Gyalbo* was next to the Lama Guru in rank. Below him there were four ministers called *Kaskaks* who conducted all business and carried out his orders. The Chinese agent at Lhasa was called *Amban*.

The general belief of all the Tibetans is that no sooner is the Lama Guru born, than he speaks and all withered plants and trees about his birth place at once begin to bear green leaves. The moment news of such an occurrence gets to the Lhasa court, the four ministers repair to the house in order to ascertain the truth.

Articles of all descriptions are placed before the child and he is requested to tell which belonged to the late Lama Guru and which did not. Should he be able to select from the articles those that belonged to the Lama Guru, then he is pronounced to be the True Lama and is forthwith carried away to the fort of Po-ta-la and placed upon the throne of the Lama Guru.

Of all the monasteries in these parts, the largest apparently were Se-ra Dre-phung and Gaden and were occupied likewise by the largest number of priests. But in former times the monasteries held in the greatest esteem were Kontyaling, Tankyaling, Chumuling and Chocholing. On the death of the Po-ta-la Raja, the successor was chosen from the Dre-phung monastery only. This is because, not very long ago, Sata Safade, allied with the 7,700 Dre-phung priests and also with the people, and aided by the Chinese agent, managed to remove the then reigning Raja, Gyalbo Riting from the throne and drove him to Peking where he died shortly afterwards. Sata Safade then assumed the position of the Raja and since then the head Lama of the Dre-phung monastery had held that position.

The Samaye monastery is situated on the left bank of the Brahmaputra river, about thirty six miles east of Lhasa. It was the seat of the Jam Raja, who was believed to possess the power and authority to punish or reward the souls of the departed. The State treasury of Lhasa was also at this place, and in the event of a war, the four ministers went there and after a little ceremony received the amount they solicited with the injunction to return the same within a certain period. Chetang city, rivalling in size the city of Shigatse, is situated on the right bank of the Brahmaputra river, about forty miles east of the Samaye monastery. The Brahmaputra river flows from here in an easterly direction for a distance of 120 miles and then flows to the south.

New Year Celebrations

The New Year commenced with the new moon appearing on about the 15th of February. They called it Lohsar, On the new year's eve, an order from the Court went round to have every house in the city cleaned. The houses were swept and whitewashed and the streets were cleaned. On the following day, each house hold displayed as many flags from the house top as it could afford. Throughout the day and at night, singing dancing and drinking went on.

On the second day of their new year, all the people of the city assembled before the Po-ta-la to witness a feat performed generally by two men. A strong rope was fastened from the fort walls to strong rivets in the ground, one hundred yards away from the base of the fort. The two unfortunate men had to slide down this rope, which very often proved fatal. Should they however survive, they were rewarded by the Court. The Lama Guru was always a witness to the performance.

From the commencement of the new year, whoever paid the highest sum was considered the Judge of the Raja's Court and for twenty-three days exercised his authority in the most arbitrary manner possible for his own benefit. All fines collected were his. The purchaser of such authority must be one of the 7,700 priests attached to the Dre-phung monastery. The successful priest was called *Jalno* and he announced the fact through the streets of Lhasa in person, bearing a silver stick.

The priests attached to all the temples and monasteries in the neighbourhood assembled in the fort and offered homage. The assembling of the priests was called *Molam Chambo* and the holidays went by the same name. The *Jalno's* men then went about the streets and places in order to discover any conduct in the inhabitants that might be found faulty. Every house in Lhasa was taxed at that time and heavy fines were levied for the slightest fault. The severity of the *Jalno* drove all the working classes out of the city till the twenty three days were over. The profit gained by the *Jalno* was about ten times the purchase-money.

During the twenty three days, all the priests of the neighbourhood congregated at the Machindranath temple and performed religious ceremonies. On the fifteenth day of the new year, they displayed hundreds of idols in form of men, animals, trees, etc., and throughout the night burned torches which illumined the city. The day on which the authority of the *Jalno* ceased, the Raja's troops paraded through the streets and proclaimed that power had again been assumed by him. Twenty four days after the *Jalno* ceased to have authority, he again assumed it for ten days and acted in the same arbitrary manner as on the first occasion. These ten days were called *Chok-chut-Molam*.

On the first day, the Lamas assembled at Machindranath temple and, after a religious ceremony, invoked the assistance of their deities the prevent sickness among the people, and as a peace-offering sacrificed one man. The man was not killed purposely but the ceremony often proved fatal. Grain was thrown against his head and his face was painted half white, half black.

On the tenth day, all the troops quartered at Lhasa marched to the temple and formed a line before it. The victim, who had his face painted, was then brought forth from the temple and received small donations from all the populace assembled. He then threw the dice with the *Jalno* and if the latter lost, it was considered a great evil. If the *Jalno* won, it was believed that the victim, who was to bear the sins of all the inhabitants of Lhasa, had been permitted by the gods to do so. He was marched to the walls of the city, followed by the entire populace and troops, hooting and shouting and the victim was carried to the Samaye monastery. If he died shortly after this, the people said it was an auspicious sign; if not, he was kept a prisoner at the monastery for a whole year, after which he was released and was allowed to return to Lhasa.

The day following the banishment of the man to Samaye, all the State jewels and gold and silver plates were brought out from Po-ta-la and carried through the streets of Lhasa, protected by the armed troops and followed by thousand of spectators. Towards evening everything was taken back to the fort and kept as before.

The next day, immense images of the gods, formed of variegated paper, on wooden frames and escorted by soldiers were dragged by men through the city. About noon, the whole populace, high and low, assembled on the plain, north of the city, caroused, raced and practised rifle shooting. Nain Singh was informed that the *Molam Chambo* and *Chokchut Molam* vacations, with all the religious ceremonies and observances, were instituted from time immemorial. But the business of auctioning the office of the Chief Magistrate dated from the tenth transmigration of the soul of the present Lama Guru.

Life in Lhasa

The food of the inhabitants of Lhasa consisted chiefly of

salted butter-tea, mutton, beef, pork and fowl. Owing to its high price and also because it was considered a frightful source of disease, rice was not eaten. Other edibles, such as wheat and barley, were cheap.

The people used ornaments of coral, pearls, precious stones, and occasionally of gold and silver, which were more especially worn by women on their heads. Coats lined with skins of sheep were generally worn.

A few houses of the rich were built of brick and stone; all others were of mud.

Lhasa manufactured woollen cloth and felt, Cows, sheep, goats, yaks, horses, and asses were the main cattle. Pigs and dogs were also reared, the latter being very big. There were also domestic cats, mostly black and a few white and red. Fowls, pigeons, kites, crows, ducks and pheasants, together with a variety of small birds were in plenty. Snakes, reptiles and scorpions were not known.

Lhasa received its supply of water from wells for the use of which a monthly tax of two *annas* was imposed on every house.

The current coin of the country was a silver piece called *naktang*, two and a half *naktangs* being the equivalent of one Indian rupee. The silver pieces were cut into halves or into three pieces. The half piece was called *chikyah*, one third *karma* and two thirds *shokang* or *miscal*. There was also a large lump of silver called *dojah* or *kuras*, bearing the seal of the Government, the value of which was equal to 333 *naktangs*.

Whilst the Pundit was at Lhasa, he took a series of thermometer obversations to determine the temperature. In February, the thermometer generally fell below 32^0F during the night. The lowest observed temperature inside a house was 26^0. From September to the end of June, when the Pundit was in the Lhasa territory, it never rained, and snow fell ony thrice. Nain Singh did not recollect seeing lightning or hearing thunder. The wind throughout Tibet is generally very strong on the table-land but at Lhasa it did not seem to have been in any way remarkable. The sky duirng the winter had been generally clear.

Only one crop was raised in the year. Sown in April, it was harvested in September. The grains produced were *sua, ne, dau, sama* and *youkar*, (i.e., barley, a kind of wheat, peas and mustard). Radish, carrots, onions, potatoes, beans, garlic and various other edibles were also cultivated. There were two kinds of trees called *changma* and *jawar* but these were not indigenous and were to be seen only in gardens. There was no jungle. Excepting one thorny bush called *sia*, hills were absolutely barren.

During the month of December, merchants from China, Tartary, Ta-Chien-lu, Chiamdo, Kham, Tawang, Bhutan, Sikkim, Nepal, Darjeeling, Azimabad and Ladakh brought their merchandise. From China came silks of all varieties, carpets and chinaware, from Liling in Tartary gold-lace, silks, precious gems, carpets of a superior manufacture, horse saddles and a very large kind of *dumba* sheep and also valuable horses and from Ta-Chien-lu immense quantities of tea. Ta-Chien-lu is situated north-east of Lhasa at about two months' journey. From Chiamdo city in the Kham territory an enormous quantity of musk was brought, which eventually found its way to Europe through Nepal. Rice and other grain that were foreign to Lhasa, were brought from Tawang and Bhutan. From Sikkim, rice and tobacco and from Nepal, Darjeeling and Azimabad, broad-cloth, silks, satins, saddles, precious stones, coral, pearls, sugar, spices and a variety of Indian commodities were brought. *Charas* and saffron (*kesar*) came from Ladakh and Kashmir. The merchants who came in December returned in March before the setting in of rains which rendered the rivers impassable.

Fossils were plentiful in the Lhasa district. They were supposed to possess great healing properties when applied to wounds in a powdered form. The Pundit saw fossils on sale in the Lhasa market. One fossil particularly struck him. It consisted of a skull about two and a half feet long and equally broad. The jaws were elongated but the sharp points had been broken off.

About four miles to the north of Lhasa there is a long hill called Totiphu, stretching from east to west. It was reported to contain immense quantity of silver. But a Government order prohibited any one from exploiting its wealth. The Government itself refused to work the mine, for the general belief was that the country would be impoverished and the men degenerate, should the metal be obtained from that source. A Chinese, not many years ago, gathered a large quantity of silver from there but, on Government being informed, he was seized and his hands were cut off.

It is also reported and believed that gold exists in Totiphu hill and near the monasteries of Dre-phung and Ramoche but it was not exploited. Gold was, however, extracted to a very slight extent near the monasteries by the priests but should they, in their search, discover a nugget of large size, it was immediately replaced in the earth under the impression that the large nuggets had life and germinated in time.

At Sa-ka or Thok, which is about one and a half months' journey to the north of Lhasa, gold was extracted in large quantities, there being no bar to it. This gold was carried to Lhasa, Gar-tok and Shigatse.

The strength of the standing force in Lhasa was about 1,000 Tibetan soldiers, armed with long flint guns. Of late, seven small pieces of ordnance had been introduced. During the war between the Gurkhas and the Lhasa Government in 1854, order was given for a census of the inhabitants. Exclusive of the military and the priests, Lhasa was found to contain about 9,000 women and some 6,000 men. This preponderance of females over males is easily explained. A large number of males became priests and were compelled to vow celibacy. One reason for the population of Lhasa being scanty was the custom of one family, consisting say of four or five brothers, keeping one wife.

The Nepalese residents of Lhasa, though believing in the same divinity—Buddha, differed from the Lhasans in many minor points.

Having made such a long stay in Lhasa, Pundit Nain Singh had completely exhausted his funds, and to support himself took to teaching book-keeping, to some Nepalese merchants. The explorer was one day questioned as to who he was by two Mohammedan merchants of Lhasa, who appeared to be of a better class than the generality of the people. He told them as he told every one, who asked him the same question, that he was a Bashahri but they said they were convinced he was no Bashahri. At last they forced him to confess the truth, but solemnly swore to keep the secret. By this confession, the Pundit was able to borrow from them a sum of money on pledging his watch. After borrowing another small sum, he made up his mind to leave Lhasa at the first opportunity that presented itself.

At about this time the explorer was very much alarmed on seeing the Kerun Shahr *Jongpon* in the streets of Lhasa one day and he was still more alarmed on seeing the summary manner in which treachery was dealt with in those parts. A Chinese who had raised a quarrel between the priests of Se-ra and Dre-phung monasteries, was brought out before the people and beheaded with very little hesitation. Alarmed, he changed his residence and seldom appeared in public again.

At that time Nain Singh learnt that the Ladakh merchant, Lopchak, with whose servant he had travelled, was sending his party back to Ladakh with large quantities of tea that he had purchased. Hearing this, the Pundit went to see him and after making a few presents, preferred his request to be allowed to return to his country along with the merchant's party. The merchant assented and ordered that the Pundit should be well provided for and that he could return any loans on arrival at Manasarowar.

Return from Lhasa : the diary

21st April 1866-Left Lhasa early this morning and arrived at eve at Netang village ; 22nd April—Arrived at Chu-shul; 23rd—Arrived at Kam-pa-par-tse village; 24th-Crossed Kam-pa pass and arrived at Pe-de village ; 25th—Arrived at Nang-ka-tse village ; 26th—Crossed Ka-ro pass and arrived at Ra-lung village; 27th-Arrived at Gyantse city, halted for the 28th ; 29th—Arrived at Takse village ; 30th-Arrival Pen-nang village.

May 1st-Arrived at Shigatse city, made a stay of six days while collecting provisions for the road; 8th-Left Shigatse and passed through the villages of Shap-ge-ding, Shilkar, Tamcheding, Pin-dzo-ling, Chap-trang, and on the 14th Arrived at Janglache town and halted there for one day, seeking provisions for the road as far as Manasarowar; Crossed the Brahmaputra river and arrived at Sen-ge-lung village; 17th-Arrived at Larcha, village; 18th-Arrived at Gnapring *ta-sam*; 19th—Arrived at foot of Qigu Tapjang monastery, situated on the hill. Then he proceeded through the *ta-sams* of Sang-sang, Gang-biako, Raga, Semo-ku, Sa-ka and camps of Jagung and Shricarpo. After passing Syuk-ku-ta'sam, he arrived at Thuku camp on the 31st.

June 1st—Arrived at Tra-don monastery. Just after leaving Tra-don, the great road crosses a big tributary, a little interior to the main river itself. Near Tra-don, it adheres very closely to the left bank. The road is for the first time actually on the river at about fifty miles from its source. To reach the Ma-yum pass, the road ascends gradually, following close to the north of the main course of the Brahmaputra and within sight of the gigantic glaciers, which give rise to the great river. The road descends gradually from the Ma-yum pass (15,500 feet), the water-shed between the Sutlej and the Brahmaputra, then coasting along a long lake, the Manasarowar and Rakastal, passes through Ngari Khorsum, the upper valley of the Sutlej and crosses the Kailas range by a very high pass and reaches Gartok (15,500 feet) on the Indus.

June 2—Left Tra-don and after crossing the Chachu stream, arrived at Barmalung camp on the left bank of the Brahmaputra. The Brahmaputra river is called by the people in these parts by three names: Tamjan Khamba, Mar-tsang and Nari-Chu; 3rd-Arrived at Totu camp; 4th-Arrived at Truk-sum *ta'sam*. Sheep, goats, yaks and horses are seen here in large numbers. Salt, which is obtained from Chaba, is bartered for grain, brought from Muktinath and Jumla. This place produces no grain; 5th—Arrived at Demar camp; 6th-Arrived at Lahro camp; 7th-Arrived at Tamjan *ta-sam*. Sheep, goats and yaks are seen here in large numbers and salt is bartered for grain brought from Jumla. Halted here one day; 9th-Arrived at Tha Kabjor. The explorer's servant fell sick here and he was compelled to ask the assistance of his Ladakhi companions for the prosecution of his work; 10th-Arrived at Gyamzar camp, halted here one day; 12th-Crossed Ma-yum pass (the watershed between the Brahmaputra and the Sutlej) and arrived at Uk-rung *ta-sam*. situated near the Gun-Chu lake. This lake is about ten miles in length and two miles in breadth; 13th-Arrived at Nyuk-chu camp; 14th—Arrived at Tok-chen ta-sam on the right bank of a stream. Halted for one day; 16th—Arrived at Sarniah Uniah camp, half a mile from the bank of Manasarowar lake; 17th—Travelling fast arrived at Tar-chen, a large village.

At Tar-chen (14,485 feet), Pundit Nain Singh met Supia Shopol, an inhabitant of Kumaon, through whose assistance he was enabled to discharge his debts which had been accumulating since he left Lhasa. The Pundit and his Ladakhi companions parted with mutual regret, the Ladakhis going north to Gar-tok while Nain Singh, in company of two of Supia's sons, started for Kumaon. The Pundit left his servant who was ailing at Tar-Chen as earnest of his promise to return and pay Supia all he had borrowed. He could not however redeem his watch and told the man with whom it had been pledged to leave it at Gar-tok where he would send the money.

On the 20th June, 1866, Pundit Nain Singh left Tar-chen and arrived at a camp; 21st-Arrived at Gya-ni-ma market. During the rains Tar-chen and Gya-ni-ma were frequented by many traders from Kumaon and other places who came to dispose of' their merchandise; 22nd-Arrived at the right bank of Nagu stream; 23rd-Arrived at Lam Thazing camp. The Pundit was surprised to see the low hills in the vicinity covered with snow in a way he had never seen before. The road over Kingri Bingri La pass was covered with snow and rendered quite impassable. This caused him to journey on to Niti pass. But even this road was so much covered with snow that on crossing over a hill, he slipped and the thermometer which he was carrying fell and broke. He left Lam Thazing the same day and arrived at Shipchalam camp; 24th—Arrived at Nak-tsok camp on the bank of Sag stream ; 25th—The Sag stream was not fordable. So the Pundit travelled alongside it till he arrived at Dongpu village. At Dongpu, he had some difficulty with the local officials but he tactfully managed to proceed further and arrived at Lhamlong camp. From Dongpu to Lhamlong he was unable to continue his route survey.

26th—Arrived at Lapthal camp; 27th—Arrived at Khingur camp, where he met Major Brereton. The Pundit halted here for a part of the next day and was very kindly treated by Major Brereton; 28th—Arrived at Topi Dhunga camp where the Pundit left his servants in consequence of one of them having been taken suddenly ill; 29th June, 1866-the Pundit crossed Unta-Dhura pass and made his way through Kumaon and Garhwal to Mussoorie. His faithful servant, Chhumbel, whom he had left at Tar-chen, rejoined him on the road, having quite recovered from his illness.

Nain Singh's cousin, Mani Singh, who had returned to the British territory some time before him, had been instructed to cross the passes in order to assist him. Pundit Nain Singh gave him his sextant and told him to carry the route survey back to Dongpu, where he was forced to leave off and thence to Gartok in order to fix that position and at the same time to redeem his watch which the Ladakhis had left for him. Pundit Mani Singh was successful in both these operations

Lhasa-Gartok Road

Between Lhasa and Manasarowar lake, Pundit Nain Singh travelled by the great road called the Jong-lam or Whor-lam by means of which the Tibetan officials keep up their communications for a length of 800 miles along the top of the Himalayan range from Lhasa to Gar-tok. This road is generally well defined, but it is not metalled. The natural slopes over which the road is carried are, however, wonderfully easy. The Tibetans, as a rule, had simply to clear away the loose stones, and only at three or four places some road building had been necessary for a few miles.

In many parts, there appears to have been considerable danger of losing the road in the stretches of the table-land, the whole surface looking very much like a road. But this danger was guarded against by the frequent erection of piles of stones, surmounted with flags on sticks. These piles, called *lapcha* by the Tibetans, were found exceedingly handy for the survey. The quick eye of the Pundit generally caught the forward pile thus securing a capital object on which to take his compass bearings. The Tibetans look upon these piles partly as guide-posts and partly as objects of veneration. Travellers generally contribute a stone to them as they pass, or if very devout and generous, add a piece of rag. Consequently on a well-used road, these piles grow to a great size and form conspicuous objects in the landscape. Over the tableland, the road is broad and wide enough to allow several travellers to go a abreast. In the rougher portions the road generally consists of two or three narrow paths, well worn by horses, yaks and men following one another. In two or three places, these dwindle down to a single track but are always passable by horsemen and indeed only in one place, near Pin-dzo-ling, is there any difficulty about laden animals. A man on horseback need never dismount between Lhasa and Gar-tok except to cross rivers.

The road was in fact wonderfully well maintained, considering the very elevated and desolate mountains over which it was carried. Between Lhasa and Gar-tok, there were twenty two staging places or ta-*sams* where the baggage animals were changed. The ta-*sams* were from twenty to seventy miles apart. At each, shelter was available and effi-cient arrangements existed for the onward journey of officials and messengers. The ta-*sams* generally consisted of a house or houses made of dried bricks. The larger ta-sams were capable of holding 150 to 200 men at a time but some of the smaller ones could only take a dozen people. In the latter case further accommodation was provided in tents. At six ta'*sams*, only tents were available. Each *ta-sam* was in charge of an official called ta-sampa who was obliged to have horses, yaks, and porters in attendance whenever notice was received of the approach of a Lhasa official. From ten to fifteen horses and as many men were always in attendance night and day. Horses and beasts of burden, yaks in the higher ground and donkeys in the lower, were forthcoming in great numbers when required. They were supplied by the nomadic tribes whose camps were pitched near the halting houses.

Though the iron rule of Lhasa kept this high road in order, the difficulties and hardships of the Pundit's march cannot be fully realised without bearing in mind the great elevation on which the road is carried. Between the Manasarower lake and the Tra-don monastery the average height of the road above the sea must be over 15,000 feet or about the height of Mount Blanc in Europe. Between Tra-don and Lhasa, its average height is 13,500 feet and only for one stage does the road descend as low as 11,000 feet whilst on several passes it rises to more than 16,000 feet above the sea-level. Ordinary travellers with laden animals make two to five marches between the staging-houses. Only special messengers go from one staging-house to another without halting. Between the staging-houses, the Pundit had to sleep in a rude tent that freely admitted the biting Tibetan wind and on some occasions he had to sleep in the open.

The camp was without creature comforts. The yaks and donkeys carried a good supply of ordinary necessities such as grain, barley-meal, tea and butter. Sheep and goats were generally procurable at the halting places. A never failing supply of fuel, though not of the pleasantest kind, was generally forthcoming from the *argols*, dried dung of the baggage animals. Each camp was supposed to leave behind at least as much dried dung as it burnt. At most of the halting places, there was generally a very large *accumulation*.

Between the Manasarowar and *Sa-ka ta-sam*, nothing in the shape of spirits was to be had, but to the east of the latter place, a liquor made from barley could generally be obtained in every village. This liquor, called *chhang*, varies in strength, according to the season of the year, being in summer something like sour beer and in winter approximately closer in taste and strength to the strongest of smoked whisky. The good natured Tibetans are constantly brewing *chhang* and they never grudge any one a drink. Thirsty travellers, on reaching a village, soon find out where a fresh brew has been made; their drinking cups are always handy in their belts and they seldom fail to get them filled at least once. The Pundit stoutly denied that this custom tended to drunkenness among his Tibetan friends, and it must be allowed that in Ladakh, where the same custom prevails, the people never appeared to be much the worse for it. Guides had however to be rather closely watched if the march took them through many villages, as they seldom failed to pull out their cups at each one.

A good deal of fruit was grown on the banks of the

Brahmaputra, between Shigatse and Chu-shul. The Pundit only saw it in a dried state.

When marching along the great road, Nain Singh and his companions rose very early. Before starting they sometimes made a brew of tea. The Tibetans stew their tea with water, meal and butter; the tea leaves are always eaten. Another brew was always made about the middle of the march or a mess of stirabout (*sattoo*) made in their cups, with barley meal and water. On arriving at the other end of the march, they generally had some more tea at once to stave off the pangs of hunger, until something more substantial was got ready in the shape of cakes and meat, if the latter was available. Their marches generally occupied them from dawn till 2 or 3 p.m., but sometimes they did not reach their camping ground till quite late in the evening,

Rushing Messengers

On the march they were often passed and met by special messengers, riding along as fast as they could go. The Pundit said these men always looked haggard and worn. They had to ride the whole distance continuously, without stopping either by night or day except to eat food and change horses. In order to make sure that they never took off their clothes, the breast fastening of their overcoat was sealed and no one was allowed to break the seal except the official to whom the messenger was sent. The Pundit says he saw several of the messengers arrive at the end of 800 miles of ride. Their faces were cracked, eyes bloodshot and sunken and bodies with large wounds eaten by lice.

It is difficult to understand why the Lhasa authorities were so particular about the rapid transmission of official messages but it seemed to be a principle that was acted upon throughout Tibet as one of the means of government. Ordinary letters had a feather attached to them and this simple addition was sufficient to carry a letter from Lhasa to Gar-tok, 800 miles, in a little over 30 days. A messenger arriving at a village with such a letter was at once relieved by another, who took it on to the next village.

If a very special message was in preparation and if time

permitted, an ordinary messenger was sent ahead to give notice. Food was then kept ready and the special messenger only remained at each staging-house long enough to eat his food and then started on a fresh horse. He rode day and night as fast as his horses could carry him. The road throughout was negotiable at night. If there was no moon, the bright starlight of Tibet gives sufficient light. The starlight in Tibet, as in all high regions, is particularly bright. Tibet is rarely troubled by dark nights, but in case it should be cloudy or a horse should break down, two mounted men always accompanied the messenger. These men were changed at every stage and were thoroughly acquainted with their own piece of road. Each of these two men took along at least two spare horses. If a horse became tired, it was changed at once and left on the road to be picked up on the return of the men to their own homes. By this means the messenger made great progress where the road was good and was never stopped entirely even on the rougher portions. A special messenger did the 800 miles in twenty-two days on an average and in two or three days less on very great occasions.

With the assistance of Mr. W.H. Johnson, who is well known for his adventurous journey to Khotan in 1864 and who was then the Wazir or governor of Ladakh under the Maharaja of Kashmir, arrange-ments were made for Pundit Nain Singh's journey from Leh to Assam. To carry the baggage, twenty-six sheep were bought from Tankse, a village five days' march east of Leh and on the border with Tibet. It was given out that Nain Singh was destined for Yarkand as the route to that town also lay through Tankse. The *Kardar* or headman of the village co-operated with the arrangements.

The Pundit was accompanied by four attendants, two of whom were natives of Tibet, and had been with him on former explorations. The third was the faithful Chhumbel of Leh, and the fourth, Kunchu Dunduk, belonged to the village of Chushul in the Tankse district and was a nominee of the *Kardar*.

It was arranged that the Pundit and three of his servants should enter Tibet as Lamas going on a pilgrimage to a temple in

Rudok white Kunchu Dunduk who was well known in the frontier district would purchase wool as an agent of the *Kardar*.

Provision was thus made for the first great difficulty which might have to be encountered while crossing the frontier. Once well inside Western Tibet, the Pundit would have to depend on his own devices to reach Lhasa. It was, however, indispensable that he should be well provided with funds. It was clearly impossible for him to carry a large sum of money or even valuable merchandise as tribes of wandering robbers might have to be encountered *en route*.

It so happened that just about the time the Pundit was making his preparations from Leh, the usual mission, half mercantile and hall political, was being despatched to Lhasa under the command of the *Kahlon*, a high official at Leh.

For years it had been customary for a large caravan to leave Leh for Lhasa once in every two years. The leader had the honorary title of Lopchak. While in Tibetan territory, the districts through which they marched were bound to furnish gratuitously three hundred yaks for carrying merchandise as well as supplies and food for the trading party under the order of the Lhasa government. As the quantity of merchandise sent with the caravan was rarely enough for the allotted yaks, the Lopchak in charge carried goods for others on the way and made considerable profit. At the start of the journey he was provided by the Kashmir authorities goods worth fifteen thousand rupees, chiefly silks, *shawls* and saffron. On return he was expected to pay into the treasury double the amount of the advance made to him. This he did from the sale proceeds of the tea, wool, turquoises and silver bullion which he obtained from Tibet in exchange of the wares taken from Ladakh.

With the aid of Mr. Johnson, the Ladakhi official, the *Kahfon*, was prevailed upon to take charge of a considerable s.um of money on the understanding that an equivalent amount waste be paid by him to Nain Singh in Lhasa, whenever he would make personal application for it. It was hoped that want of money would not stand in the way of exploration after arrival at Lhasa. Most unfortunately the *Kahlon* died during the journey and the Pundit did suffer at Lhasa for want off funds.

The journey begins

These preliminary arrangements having been made, a suit of Lama's clothing was made in Leh and carefully packed so as to be available when the occasion required. On the 15th July, 1874, the Pundit and his companions left Leh in their ordinary costumes. On the 2lst they reached Tankse where they remained for two days in the house of the *Kardar* who accompanied them to Chugra, three marches further on. At Chugra they found a summer encampment of shepherds, the last inhabited spot on the road to Yarkand. At night, under cover of darkness, the Pundit and his three men cast off their old garments and donned their Lama clothes. Before morning, they were all well on the road.

For the first day, they followed the Chang Chenmo route to Yarkand, halting at the foot of the Landar or Marsmik pass. On the following day, they crossed the pass (18,420 feet) and then quit the Yarkand road. Turning off to the east, they crossed the Kiu pass still higher than the Marsmik and encamped for the night at Pangur Gongina after a march of nine miles.

The versatile sheep

The Pundit was obliged to travel slowly as all his worldly possessions, including tents, beddings and commissariat for the party had to be carried on the backs of sheep. It is astonishing what admirable beasts of burden these animals make in a pastoral country. The Pundit started with twenty-six sheep from Tankse. Of these, some were eaten on the way, some became ill and were exchanged for fresh ones but four or five of the original lot reached Lhasa, having in less than four months carried loads from 20 to 25 lbs. each, over a distance of more than a thousand miles. Throughout the journey they never received a Single ounce of food beyond what they could pick up for themselves on the road and the camping grounds.

On the 28th July, the party descended from the Kiu pass to Ningri, a camp which takes its name from a large heart-shaped m which overhangs it. Continuing, the next day they encountered a large party of Tankse villagers returning from Rudok with wool and salt. Our Lamas, somewhat nervous lest their identity should be discovered, concealed themselves in a jungle of willow trees while Kunchu and a companion in charge of the sheep met the traders and narrated how they were travelling alone to Noh to purchase wool for the *Kardar*. This anxiety over, they had tense moments again on arriving at the camp and finding some half a dozen natives of Rudok collecting saltpetre. The travellers were somewhat reassured, however, at finding that there were no suspicions raised as to their being anything else but Lamas.

The men, who were collecting saltpetre stated that the *Jongpon* or Governor of Rudok had ordered them to pay their taxes for the current year in that article. To obtain saltpetre, the soil is dug and placed in brass vessels. Hot water is poured over it. The water dissolves the saltpetre and is then decanted off into another vessel. After a time the saltpetre is precipitated. One can manufacture a sheepload or about 20 lbs. in as many days.

A day's halt was made here to rest the sheep and the Pundit made an excursion a few miles up the Rawang stream to Rawang Yokma, a winter encampment belonging to the men of Tankse, in the neighbour-hood of a favourite grazing ground where in addition to abundant supplies of grass there was also a large supply of jungle wood which is rare in Ladakh. The wood is of three kinds: *changma* (willow), *shukpa* (pencil cedar) and *womphu* (tamarisk).

From Nlagzu, six short marches brought our travellers to Noh. The country through which they passed was almost uninhabited. A few solitary tents belonging to Noh shepherds and a single hut in Gunnu Chauki, occupied by a small frontier guard were the only habitations they came across.

Noh is a small village in the Rudok district and contained about twenty huts, built of stones, cemented by mud. It had a small permanent population, which grew large in the winter months with the advent of numerous shepherds who during the summer are scattered intents in two's and three's in whichever parts of the district grass and water are to be found in abundance for their numerous flocks of sheep and goats. The Chiefman of Noh, Changkep by name, whose official title was *Lhamba*, was at the time of the Pundit's visit at a camp called Pangda, about three days' journey north west from Noh. Kunchu Dunduk had been despatched to him for obtaining the requisite *lhamik* and for permission to proceed. *Lharnik* would appear to be the literal Tibetan equivalent for the Persian *rahdari* which is much the same as the English word passport. The *Lhamba* of Noh and the *Kardar* of Tankse occupied similar positions on their respective frontiers and appeared to respect each other even to the extent of remitting taxes of all goods exported or imported by either party. The Pundit thus not only obtained his passport without difficulty but also escaped the usual duty of ten per cent, which would otherwise have been levied on the valuables he had with him.

The *Lhamba* was immediately under the *Jongpon* or Governor of Rudok whose jurisdiction extended over that portion of North-western Tibet which lies to the north of the Singh-gi branch of the Indus far east as the Thok Jalung gold-fields. The *Jongpon* of Rudok-was in his turn subordinate to the *Garpon* of Gar-tok, who had under his orders the *Jongpons* of the large districts of Guge (Duba) and Purang as well as other independent Pons or Rajas of Western Tibet The *Garpan* took his orders from the *Gyalbo* or Raja of Lhasa. The ofiice af *Garpon* was tenable only for three years and was always held by a native of Lhasa who was appointed by the *Gyalbo*. The *Jongpons* were generally changed every three or four years.

The province of Western Tibet is frequently termed Ngari Khorsum, The inhabitants of the northern portion, i.e., the district through which the Pundit travelled, are called by the settled population to the south, Champas or Changpas, literally northmen. They are called Taghliks or mountaineer by the inhabitants of Turkistan. The Champas encountered by the Pundit were, contrary to the general opinion, quite inoffensive like the people of Rudok and the more civilised districts further south. They were all Buddhists, but religious edifices were scarce in their country. On the Pundit's route through this portion of Tibet, became across no *gom-pa* or monastery although he occasionally encountered *manis* and *churtans*.

A *churtan* or *chhartan* is a "holy receptacle or offering repository". It is a pyramidal shaped building erected in honour of some of the holy Buddhas. A *mani* is an oblong dyke or pile of stones four or five feet high and ten to twelve feet broad, varying in length from twenty feet to nearly a mile. It is composed entirely of stones deposited one by one by travellers passing by. The surface of each stone is generally inscribed with the well-known Buddhist formula "*Om mani padmi hom*".

The road near Noh skirts the Pangong lake, which at Noh is joined by a stream from the north-east beside which runs a good road to Khotanivia Polurand Kerya.

The distance to Khotan by the road is about 450 miles. For a length of forty miles from Noh, it gradually rises up taa height of 15,500 feet and then for about 160 miles, as the crow flies, crosses in a north-easterly direction a series of elevated plains and ridges before it descends somewhat suddenly to the plains of Eastern Turkistan. The average height above the sea-level of the halting places on the elevated plain to the north of Noh is 16,500 feet. The vast, highly elevated plateau over which the road passes is the eastern continuation of the Lingzitang and Aksai-chin plains, which lie at a similar or in places even a higher elevation in a north-westerly direction from Noh, between the Chang Chenmo river and Kuen Lun range. To the north of Kuen Lun, there is a rapid fall into the plains of Eastern Turkistan.

This Tibetan plateau extends eastward as we shall see in the course of this narrative as far as the head-waters of the great rivers which water China for a distance, as the crow flies, of more than eight hundred miles to the Burkhan Buddha mountains, south-west of the Koko Nor lake on the road between Lhasa and Peking.

Seven miles to the east of Noh is the eastern termination of the series of lakes known to us as the Pangong but better known to the Tibetan as the Chomo Gna Laring Cho which, being literally interpreted, means "female narrow very long lake". Its extreme length from the west end at Lukung is exactly 100 miles, while its breadth nowhere exceeds six or seven miles. The depth of the Pangong lake at its west end was nowhere greater than 136 feet as found with soundings by Capt. Trotter R.E. in 1873.

A small stream, three paces broad and one and a half deep, enters the Pangong lake at its eastern extremity. Although the greater portion of this lake had been previously surveyed and described, its eastern limit was determined for the first time. It is a curious fact that the water at the eastern extremity is sweet and good to drink, while that at the west end is very brackish. It has been conclusively shown by Major Godwin Austin that this lake once upon a time drained into the Shyok, but at present it forms the most western of a numerous series of inland lakes with no outlets which we shall find stretch for a considerable distance across the elevated plateau of Central Tibet.

Noh to Thok Daurakpa

From Noh, the Pundit toiled on for many weary marches over the Tibetan plateau. The road lay eastward along a wide open grassy valley, varying in width from six to ten miles, bounded on the north and south by low grass-covered hills, through which occasional openings gave a view of extensive plains stretching away as far as the eyes could reach. Beyond the hills sometimes appeared snow-capped mountains, while an occasional shepherd's tent in the foreground and the frequent appearances of large herds of wild asses, antelopes and gigantic wild sheep (*the ovis ammon*) helped to relieve the monotony of the journey.

In almost every day's march large sheets of water were passed, generally saltish but occasionally fed by fresh water springy. At the latter, the Pundit and his companions would fill their water skins made of sheep's stomachs. Two of these would be slung across the back of a sheep as they rarely knew from day to day whether or not they would be able to obtain a fresh supply on the road. More than onee their supply of this precious fluid was exhausted and, on one occasion, the whole party were for more than twenty hours without fresh water.

For fuel, also a traveller's necessity, they were better off. The argols or dung of the numerous flocks of wild animals were a never-failing source of supply, while occasionally, but rarely, firewood was obtained in considerable quantities.

At Tachap Cho, there is a fresh-water lake and at the 27th halting place from Leh, alarge stream flowing from some snow covered hills to the north-east of the lake was found to becovered on both banks with adense forest of willow, tamarisk and other trees and shrubs termed *pena birha* and *dama* (furze).

For the first thirty marches from Noh, the heights of the camping grounds varied from 13,700 to 15,000 feet and for the rest of the journey to Nam lake, the ground was somewhat higher but there was no considerable rise or fall. The large, flat, open valleys falling by the Pundit's route, locally termed *sangs*, appear to be of much the same nature as the Pamirs between Eastern and Western Turkistan and tbe *jilgas*. *Jilga* is the Turkish word for a broad open valley of Northern Ladakh. The *sangs* of Tibet, however, would seem to have more of plain and less of precipitious mountains than either the Pamirs or the *jilgas*.

The road for the first fen marches from Noh passes through Rawang Changma or Northern Rawang district and is nearly parallel to and north of the route followed by Pundit Kalian Singh on a former occasion while on bis way from Rudok to Thok Jalung through Rawang Shoma or the Southern Rawang district. This is separated from the northern one by a low range of hills.

The Champas

The Pundit passed the salt-marshes of Khai Chaka and

Dakdong lakes from which the people of the surrounding country collected large quantities of salt and carried it for sale to Ladakh. The Pundit states that the salt forms a crust like a sheet of ice on the surface of the mud. The salt seekers sink through this crust upto their loins in mud and water and remove the salt which they subsequently wash, clean and dry in the sun.

There were two huts built of wood at Chabuk Zinga (14,400 feet) and in the neighbourhood some twenty tents of shepherds were visible. There were a few fields where barley was grown, the first signs of cultiva-tion that had been seen since leaving Noh. Nain Singh was of the opinion that, were the country more thickly populated, there would have been no difficulty in finding plenty of ground fit for cultivation. The Champa inhabitants appeared, however, to care but little for grain and lived almost entirely on meat, milk, butter and cheese, the produce of their numerous flocks and herds. One sheep load of 20 lbs. of flour afforded an ample supply for eight or ten men for a couple of months. At their permanent camps, they had large cauldrons generally made of stones. In these they used to make a very weak soup in which they threw a handful of flour. This constituted dinner for a large party. At their movable camps, they cooked in smaller vessels made of stone or copper, both of which were imported from Ladakh. All articles of copper and iron were very much valued and a small axe which the Pundit kept for the purpose of breaking ice might any time have been exchanged for two or three sheep. The only articles that these people manufactured were tents and very coarse woollen clothing. The former were black and were made from yak's hair and the latter from the fleece of sheep, which also provided material for making bags to carry salt for sale to Ladakh.

Their wealth consisted of horses, flocks and herds, and also salt which they carried for sale to Ladakhis and in return for which they obtained flour, copper, stone vessels and hardware. Most families possessed a match lock, generally manufactured in Nepal. The men of Rudok district seldom moved about without either a gun or a bow and arrow in the use of which they were expert. Like the inhabitants of other parts of Central Asia, they fired their guns while lying at full length on the ground. Each gun had a piece of white bunting attached to the barrel which was thus converted into a flag. Gunpowder was scarce and was generally preserved for special occasions.

The Pundit states that on a former journey, when he visited a large fair at Gar-tok, the young men, all expert horsemen, used to practise very successfully at a mark while going at full speed on horseback. This is amusement Capt. Trotter had often himself seen in Eastern Turkistan. There each competitor carried two guns and a bow and arrows. Having fired off his gun, he discharged his arrows.

The Champas were keen in the pursuit of game, which they killed in large quantities, partly with firearms and bows and arrows, but chiefly with a kind of trap called *redokh chum* (literally animal catcher), very similar in principle to an English rat-trap. It consisted of a ring made of rope, to the inner surface of which were attached elastic, sharp, pointed slips of wood converging towards the centre of the ring, where a space was left sufficiently large to allow the passage of an animal's foot. 'Small poles were dug in the ground near the sources of water which the wild animals were known to frequent. These traps were placed at top, hidden from view by a covering of earth and attached by a strong rope, also concealed from view, to a stout peg driven into the ground at a considerable distance. The animals, on their way to the water, passed over the holes and the weight of the body drove the foot through the ring. Once through, it was impossible for the animal to free its foot from the trap and it soon fell a victim to the swords and spears of the hunter, who lay concealed somewhere in the neighbourhood. Great number of wild horses, sheep and antelopes were killed in this manner.

The Khampa Land

From Chabuk Zinga to Hissik lake, the country was uninhabited and the road lay over a plain similar to what had already been traversed between Noh and Chabuk. The Champas at the latter place had given the travellers general instructions as to the line of the road to be followed, but it appears that the latter had diverged too much to the north and missed the encampment of Gerge Thol which, the Pundit had been previously told, lay on the route to Lhasa and which he had intended visiting, as one of his servants had a friend there through whose influence they hoped to receive assistance in prosecuting the onward journey. Nain Singh had now entered the Khampa or Kampa district and on arrival at Hissik lake on the 25th August he was greatly disturbed in mind at seeing men approaching them from a distance with yaks and ponies. Not knowing what to expect, he immediately concealed in the earth his instruments, the greater part of his clothes and a few bags of grain and remained behind while he sent two of his men to reconnoitre and make enquiries.

The strangers fortunately turned out to be residents of Gerge Thol, the place the Pundit wanted to reach and which lay about a day's march to the south-west of the Hissik lake. On the following day they went together to Gorge Thol where they found a large encampment of Khampas and had the great good fortune to encounter the man they had been looking for. It appears that in years gone by, the Pundit's servant had struck a good friendship in Ladakh with one Dingmo, a medical practitioner who was now a man of great influence among the Khampas. It was in order 'to find him that the Pundit had turned back to Gerge Thol. Dingmo did not shun his old friend but on the contrary was of the greatest assistance as he gave letters to the Pundit for Chiring Dunduk, the *Gombo* or headman of Garche Thol, another Khampa district, several marches further east. *Gombo* is the Tibetan term for headman and corresponds to Ladakhi *Gobo*. The equivalent word in Ngari Khorsum is *Godpu* or *Ganpu.*

The Khampas who inhabited these two districts of Gerge Thol and Garche Thol must not be confused with the Changpas or Champas, an entirely different race. The Khampas originally came from the country of Kham, which lies north-east and east of Lhasa. In Gerge Thol, there were 600 or 700 of them and they had about seventy tents.

The Khampas had migrated from their own country about twenty-five years prior to the Pundit's visit and they travelled via Lhasa and the Manasarowar lake and settled down in their present camping grounds which prior to that time were uninhabited. Soon after settling there, they were called upon by the *Garpon* of Gartok to pay tribute which they did annually to the extent of 5,000 *nak-tangs*.

These Khampas possessed large herds of cattle and flocks of sheep. Each tent had from ten to sixty horses and from 500 to 2,000 sheep. They despatched annually to the fair at Gyanima near Manasarowar large quantities of sheep and goat's wool, salt and gold. The Khampas were well armed with guns and swords' worn constantly even by boys. The scabbards were often handsomely ornamented with gold, turquoises and coral.

The men were fine, large, and broad-shouldered. They wore both in summer and winter *poshtin* made of sheep-skins, the hair being turned inwards. These coats were worn short, extending to the knees only and were fastened round the waist by a woollen girdle. The coats had ample space for carrying goods. They had felt hats, resembling in shape broad-brimmed English wide-awakes and leather boots with woollen tops and curved pointed toes. The hair was plaited, Chinese fashion, into pigtails. The women dressed very much like the men but their coats were longer and less roomy. They donned round leather caps and had long hair, the plaits of which were fastened with pendants, nearly reaching the ground and were profusely ornamented, chiefly with silver coins, of which the favourite was the Indian rupee. Both men and women were always in the saddle. They rode large powerful horses. Both sexes were skilful riders and were fond of sports, killing large quantities of game, chiefly wild horses, sheep and antelope. They either employed fire-arms or killed their prey with swords and spears when caught in the *redokh chum* trap as described before. The capacity for eating meat appeared to be enormous. This fondness for meat was perhaps acquired at an early age, as the food given to infants when their mothers could no longer support them consisted (in the entire absence of grain in the country) of pounded cheese mixed with butter and blood.

Between Gerge Thol and the Champa district of Shankhor on the south is a place called Gegha where a large fair was held every year in July and August.

On the 29th August, 1874, Nain Singh returned to Hissik lake, where he saw a large herd of about 200 *kiangs* (wild asses). He continued his journey over uninhabited level plains till the 1st September when at a camp called Huma lake, he met the *Gombo* of Garche Thol, a gentleman who was distinguished from his followers in that he wore a pair of golden ear-rings of such length as to rest on his shoulders. The presentation of the letter of introduction from their medical friend at Gorge Thol secured the party a civil reception.

The following night there was a heavy frost, a sign of the approach of winter.

On the 3rd September, they reached the village of Mango, the head-quarters of the *Gombo*, who had gone ahead of the travellers. The Pundit paid him a formal visit in his tent which was a large one made of yak's hair and gave him a small present of sandal-wood. He was kindly treated and on intimating to the *Gombo* that he was on his way to visit a celebrated monastery near the Nam lake, Chiring Dunduk (the *Gombo*) said that he was himself about to move his camp several days' march in that direction and proposed that they should perform the journey together. Nain Singh gratefully acquiesced. On returning to his little tent, he found it besieged by a host of curious Khampas, who were all most anxious to become possessors of the various little articles of hardware he had with him, but he resolutely refused to part with anything.

Among the visitors was an old man named Sonam Darka, about eighty years of age, a native of a country near Lhasa who had been living as a servant among the Khampas for long and had gradually accumulated a good deal of property. The Pundit, when he found that this man could speak good Tibetan, succeeded in securing his friend-ship by the present of a couple of common sewing needles and obtained from him the following information about the neighbouring countries.

The district to the north of Gerge and Garche Thol is a large un-inhabited plain called Jung Phalir Puyil, meaning literally "the desert country in which the father and son have wandered". It was so called from a tradition that the two men of the Shankhor country had, many years previously, entered this desert track for the sake of hunting but, after wandering about for many days, they both died there for want of water. Some thirty or forty years before the Pundit's visit and prior to the occupation of Garche Thol by the Khampa tribes, there used to be considerable traffic between the inhabitants of Nakchang (a district to the east of Garche Thol) and a place called Nari Tharu, some twenty days' journey to the north-east of Thok Daurakpa (the 49th march from Leh). The Nari Tharu merchants used to come fromNurla, a pmce eight or ten days' journey off in the Yarkiu. It is clear that Yarkiu stands for Yarkand and it is equally certain that Nurla is a place called Nura in Capt. Trotter's map of Turkistan, on the direct road between Khotan and Polur. According to Capt. Trotter, Sai Neuria, a place about one march to the east of Gangutagh and which is probably identical with Nura, is known for export of grains towards Tibet; the Tibetans used to barter gold for grains and cotton clothes. The traders from Nurla used to cut the throats of sheep instead of strangling them as is done in Northern Tibet. Sonam Darka also recollected a few words of their languages which the Pundit who had only recently returned from Yarkand at once recognised as Turki.

The road from Thok Daurakpa is said to traverse for twenty days' journey extensive plains and then crosses a snowy range, at the foot of which lies Nari Tharu where a considerable stream, the only one en-countered in the journey, flows from east to west. From Sonam's description of the road and the knowledge that in clear weather a snowy range is continuously visible along the road from Keriya to Charchan, it is inferred that Nari Tharu occupies a position at the foot of the northern bounding ridge of the Great

Tibetan plateau, somewhat similar to that held by Polur and Surghak and probably lies approximately in latitude 36^0 by longitude 84^0. This stream probably flows into the Great Desert and may possibly be the same that passes by Charchan. Sonam had in his youth made the journey several times but the road had now been closed for the last thirty years. The reason given was that since the discovery of borax or rather since borax had become a considerable article of trade between Tibet and Hindustan, the inhabitants of Nakchang found a good market for it in the Ngari Khorsum district, from which place they obtained their supplies of grain imlead of, as formerly, Turkistan. As may be imagined, grain was not over-plentiful. A sheep-load of flour was about equivalent in value to a large sheep.

Sonam Darka had also on one occasion, some thirty years ago, made a journey from Thok Daurakpa to Ajan, a country about two months' journey in a north-easterly direction. The road lay throughout over an extensive plain, no large mountains being seen or streams en-countered. Drinking water was obtained from a succession of small fresh-water lakes, mostly supplied by rain water. Shortly before caching Ajan country, the road traverses a bare rocky range of mountains. Ajan itself was inhabited by the Sokpo Kalmucks, a nomadic pastoral people who obtained rice and flour from the neighbourhood of Kharka which was ten or twelve days' journey beyond the southern frontier of the Ajan country. Near Kharka is a large city called Kokad, the residence of Sokpo Gyalbo, the ruler of Sokpo district, while Kharka itself contains several monasteries, one of which is the residence of Jipchun Thamba Ring-bo-che, the spiritual head of the Sokpo Kalmucks. No one would venture to travel by the road unless it was after an unusually heavy rainy season. Wood and grass were plentiful throughout.

As far as Capt. Trotter could gather from enquiries made at Yarkand and from the information collected by the Pundits, Kharka is situated about one and a half months' journey to the north-west of Nag Chu Kha, a large village on the bank of a river of the same name, and a few marches to the north-east of the Tengri Nor or Nam lake. At this village two roads diverged, one to Kharka passing in a north-westerly direction and the other to Koko Nor and Peking in the north-easterly direction. The position of Kharka thus obtained would agree approximately with an account which Capt. Trotter heard from a Kalmuck in Kashgar, which located Kharka at about a fortnight's journey to the south-east of the Lob Nor lake. It probably lies somewhere between the Lob Nor and Koko Nor lakes. It is not improbable that the country of Ajan to the south of it may be the same as the country of Anj Si which is mentioned by Uspenski in the Russian investigia as a country lying in a westerly direction from the Zaidan plain, which is to the west of Koko Nor.

On the 4th September, Nain Singh left Mango in company with Sonam Darka and Gombo Chiring Dunduk, the headman of Garche, together with their flocks and herds. There were about six tents of the nomads in all. For four days they kept company, advancing slowly at the rate of about eight miles a day. It is the habit of these people, when they have exhausted the pasturage near any one camp, to shift to fresh grounds. They were now on one of their customary moves. On the fourth day, they reached Kezing in the neighbourhood of which were very extensive pastures, sufficient for the Gombo's large locks for a couple of months.

Some idea of the wealth of these people may be inferred from the fact that Gombo Chiring was himself the fortunate possessor of about 500 horses, 400 yaks and 2,000 sheep. Other members of his tribe were even more wealthy than he was.

The Garche Khampas with about 100 tents in all had been settled in the country for some fourteen years only. They were under the jurisdiction of the *Gyalbo* of Lhasa and were very much better off than their neighbours, the Gerge Khampas, who were under Rudok. The former paid what must be to them an almost nominal tribute-gold of the value of about $ 20. This gold was obtained at Thok Daurakpa, to the east of Garche Thol, in exchange for the produce of their flocks and for borax, extensive fields of which exist at Nering lake which were passed by the Pundit on way to Kezing.

The Pundit appears to have ingratiated himself most successfully with Gombo Chiring, for that chief arranged for his onward journey with two other men, servants of a merchant from the neighbourhood of Shigatse. These men for their own sake were only too happy to travel in the company of Nain Singh and his party.

From Kezing eastward for a distance of eighty miles up to Thok Daurakpa, the country was uninhabited when the Pundit passed through it but was occupied by the Khampas of Garche at a certain period of the year. There was capital grazing and an abundant supply of water and fuel throughout. The road lies entirely in one of the broad open areas between ranges of hills running east and west. South of the Tashi Bhup lake, there are massive groups of snow-covered peaks known as the Shyalchi Kang Jang, the position of several of which was fixed by the Pundit from a distance of thirty to forty miles south of the road.

From this snowy group flows northward a very considerable stream, the Shyal river which was crossed by the Pundit in three separate branches which, although nowhere more than a foot in depth, are passable only with very great difficulty during the floods caused by the melting of snow in the summer months. The stream flows into the Tashi Bhup lake, the northern shore of which was about two miles to the north of the Pundit's road. From the eastern end of this lake issues a stream, the waters of which ultimately drain into the Chargot lake from which it then emerges under the name of the Nag Chu Kha river and flows eastward to the village of the same name lying on the northern road between Lhasa and Peking. At the point where the Pundit passed the Shyal river, his road was crossed by another track going from Manasarowar to Nag Chu Kha. The track passes south of the Tashi Bhup lake and then follows throughout the course of the stream which emerges from the east end of the lake and flows to the Chargot lake and Nag Chu Kha. This road is perfectly easy and has plenty of grass and water but the country it passes through is uninhabited throughout.

The Pundit who had been forewarned that the neighbourhood of the crossing of the two lines of the road was a notorious place for robbers took the precaution of pitching his camp two miles off the road. The custom of the robbers who infested this country was to cut the ropes supporting the tent of the traveller at night and then fall upon him and cut him down while he was attempting to escape from the folds of the tents.

While under the immediate protection of Gombo Chiring, the Pundit had felt pretty safe, but he appears, not without good reason, to have passed several sleepless nights before he again reached inhabited country.

Travelling as a Lama, he had affected great poverty and throughout the journey he kept his rupees concealed here and there in the most out-of-the-way places imaginable. His chief repository was a very old and ragged pad carried on the back of a donkey that had accompanied him from the west and which animal in consequence of the riches he bore, obtained amongst our travellers the sobriquet of *sarkari khazanchi* or Government treasurer.

The Pundit reached the gold-fields at Thok Daurakpa on the 7th September, having taken on the latter part of the journey a somewhat difficult road over the hills in order to avoid the easier one to the south, which passed round the foot of the hills, and where he thought he was more likely to meet with robbers. He had now left the Khampa country and had entered the Naktsang Pontod district in which he passed two or three abandoned gold-mines before reaching Thok Daurakpa.

Gold Mines

The Pundit found that the gold-fields in this part of Tibet were of much less importance than those he had visited at Thok

Jalung in western Tibet on a former exploration. At Thok Daurakpa, the diggers mostly dwell in caves excavated from the earth. These habitations, locally called *phukpa*, were thirty two in number, each lived in by five to twenty five persons according to the wealth of the proprietors. The caves wereas chosen as dwellings because of the proximity of the robbers whose habit of cutting down first the tents and then the owners has been already mentioned. The underground caves were naturally more secure than tents. One well armed man could defend a cave against a large number of assailants. Besides these caves, there were also seven or eight tents belonging to travelling merchants and recent arrivals. The diggers were mostly Champas from Naktsang district to the cist and south-east of the gold-fields but there were also others from Western Tibet and from Janglache, a large town on the Brahmaputra, five or six days' journey west of Shigatse.

The proprietor of each *phukpa* had also his own gold pit in which he worked in the day time only. One or twp men were generally employed in quarrying the stone in which the gold was found. The pieces of stone were carried in baskets to the mouth of the pit and were then pounded into small fragments which were deposited on a cloth fixed slantingly with some stones placed on it so as to make the surface uneven. Water poured over it carried away the lighter portion of the soil, leaving the gold in the uneven receptacles that had been formed. The largest piece of gold seen by the Pundit at Daurakpa was about one ounce in weight.

Unfortunately for the diggers, water was not found within a mile of the gold-fields and had to be brought in skins on donkeys especially kept for the purpose. These donkeys were the only animals of the kind seen by the Pundit between Ladakh and Lhasa. It appears that they did not stand the cold well, although their bodies were covered thickly with the *pashm* or wool which grows under the hair of nearly all animals in these very cold and highly elevated regions. It was always found necessary at night to allow them to take refuge in the *phukpas* inhabited by their masters.

Gold-finding does not appear to be a very lucrative

occupation and although the tax paid by the diggers to the *Sarpon* or Gold Commissioner of Lhasa, one *sarshoo* (one fifth of an ounce) per man per annum, was decidedly small, yet the profits appeared to be little more than what was necessary to keep the body and soul together. According to the Pundit, the pastoral population was far more prosperous than the gold-diggers and led a freer, pleasanter and more independent life.

The gold of Thok Daurakpa is said to be whiter and of better quality than that found further west. It was, however, more difficult to obtain both on account of the soil or rather rock in which it was found being harder to break up than the softer soil of Thok Jalung and also on account of the distance from which water had to be brought. At Jalung, a stream runs through the gold-fields. The Pundit believe that there were enormous tracts of land where gold was to be obtained by digging but where the absence of water would render the working of the mines unremunerative.

The Thok Daurakpa and Thok Jalung gold-fields wereunderthe same *Sarpon* who made a round of all the gold-fields once a year to collect taxes.

It would appear that the importance and value of the Tibetan gold-fields have been considerably overrated. The Pundit stated that besides the half-dozen places where gold-digging was then carried on in the neighbourhood of Thok Jalung, the only other gold-fields now being exploited in Northern Tibet were at Thok Daurakpa and two other centres of even less importance, Tangyung and Sarka Shyar, both about six days' journey further east. He believed that nearly all the gold collected in western Tibet found its way to Gar-tok, and ultimately through Kumaon merchants to Hindustan. He estimated the value of gold brought annually into Gar-tok at about eighty thousand rupees (about eight thousand pounds sterling).

The gold-diggers of Daurakpa disposed of their gold either to the Khampas of Garche Thol on the west or to the Champas of Naktsang Pontod on the east in exchange for the products of their herds and flocks. The rest of the gold was taken by merchants who brought tea from Lhasa or China.

A brick (*parka*) of tea weighing about five pounds was worth seven shillings or so in Lhasa and twelve shillings or more in Ladakh, accord-ing to quality and sold at Daurakpa for one *sarshoo* of gold (one-fifth of an ounce). At Thok Jalung on a former occasion the Pundit purchased one tola of gold, 72/172 of an ounce, for eleven rupees. At Thok Daurakpa the price of an equivalent amount of gold would have been about fourteen rupees.

Thok Daurakpa to Lhasa

The Pundit halted for only one day at the gold-fields and resumed his journey on the 19th September. His route lay over precisely the kind of country that he had previously traversed. It crossed several streams, all flowing to the north and ultimately finding their way into the Nag Chu Kha river. For the first three marches, the country was uninhabited but after leaving Lhung Nakdo, Champa tents were seen almost daily.

Although the plain he was now traversing was more than 16,000 feet above the sea-level, the Pundit did not appear to have suffered very much from the great elevation. The weather was mild and he spoke of the whole of the journey over the plains of Tibet as a delightful pleasure excursion when compared with his experiences over the Kara-koram and other passes on the road from Leh to Yarkand: The sheets of velvet turf covered with countless herds of antelopes must indeed have formed a pleasant contrast to the equally elevated but bleak and un-inhabited bare plains of Lingzi-tang and Despang in Northern Ladakh. The Pundit who was fond of statistics asserted that on one occasion he actually counted two thousand antelopes (*cho* and *gwa*) which re-sembled in appearance a regiment of soldiers with their horns glistening in the sun like bayonets. The horns frequently found lying on the ground served him as tent pegs.

In the Naktsang Pontod (Northern and Southern) districts, which extend for several marches east of Thok Daurakpa, there were altogether about a hundred and fifty families of nomads, all wealthy in horses, yaks, sheep and goats. Throughout Naktsang, the sheep are very large and strong and almost all black-a peculiarity of the district, those in Western Tibet and in Lhasa being nearly all white. Yaks are used almost exclusively as beasts of burden and on one occasion the Pundit met a caravan with two hundred of these animals carrying tea towards the West.

Naktsang Pontod was under Garpon Durje Puntchok, a native, whose dignity was hereditary. He collected tribute for Lhasa and remitted it to Denja Dzong (fort) further east. The tribute paid was almost entirely in ghee (clarified butter).

The Champas of Naktsang who are also mistakenly termed Horpas and Dokpas speak a language which differs but little from that of Lhasa, and the Pundit had no difficulty in carrying on a conversation with them. In the eighth march from Thok Daurakpa, the Pundit encoun-tered a lofty range of mountains which was crossed by a high but easy pass called Kilong (18,170 feet above the sea-level). This range runs southward for a length of 180 miles and culminates in some enormous peaks called Gyakharma which were fixed by the Pundit. The height of these peaks was ascertained by measurement to be 22,800 feet and Nain Singh estimates that the highest of the Targot peaks which lay too far off the road for vertical measurement with a sextant is at least 2,500 feet higher than the highest of the Gyakharma group. Targot La was visible from the Chapta pass at a distance of over one hundred miles and was believed by the Pundit to have been the highest mountain seen by him on his journey.

This range is probably not the watershed between the basin of the Brahmaputra and the lake country of Hor (the general name of the district through which the Pundit had been travelling). He was informed that to the south of the range running parallel to it, is a large river, (Dumphu or Hota Tsang-po) which ultimately changes its course and flows northwards into the Kyaring lake.

The highest peak of the Target La group is called Target Yap (father) and an enormous lake at the foot of its northern slope is called Dangra Yum (mother). These two, according to the local tradition, are the progenitors of the whole world. The group of Shyalchi Kang Jang mountains to the west is said to be one of the daughters of this union. The circuit round the mountain and lake combined is a common pilgrimage not only for the people of the Hor country but for their more distinguished co-religionists from Lhasa. Similar circuits are made round the sacred mountain of Kailas, near the Manasarowar lake.

The circuit round the lake alone takes from eight to twelve days, the distance being about 200 miles, but the complete circuit of the lake and the mountain takes up nearly a month. The country people believe that if they make the complete circuit, termed locally *kara*, once, they will be absolved of ordinary sins. To becleared of murder, two *karas* are required, but if the round is completed thrice, even the murder of a father or mother will he atoned for.

The district surrounding the Dangra lake and another smaller lake to the north of the road is called Naktsang Ombo. It is ringed on all four sides by snowy mountains and contains several villages- Naktsang, Tang-yung, Kisum, Ombo, Sasik and Chaksa. Each village contains twenty or thirty houses built of stone and surrounded by richly cultivated fields which produce a profusion of barley. The harvest was not quite gathered on the 28th of September, the date of the Pundit's arrival at Ombo, the chief village of the district.

The existence of this cultivated Ombo plain enclosed by mountains which in their turn are surrounded by endless extents of pasture land is a very curious feature.

The Pundit had not seen a single field of grain of any description since leaving Chabuk Zinga, thirty five marches to the west, nor did he again meet with cultivation until Tulung Dinga village near Lhasa, thirty nine marches beyond Ombo. The height of the plain (15,240 feet) is not less than that of the surrounding country and although somewhat protected from wind, it is not better off in this respect than the district of Naktsang Gomnak which borders it on the east. Naktsang Gomnak is also well-watered and has apparently a richer soil but is nevertheless totally devoid of cultivation.

According to the local tradition, the Ombo country was once upon a time thickly populated and covered with villages. Two thousand years ago, it is said to have been ruled by a very powerful Raja, the Limur Gyalbo, who resided in the fort called Kiung Dzong on the banks of the lake, the ruins of which were pointed out to the Pundit. The Gyalbo Limur ruled over the whole of the Hor country and his wealth was boundless. Among other riches he was the possessor of a golden saddle and a turquoise as large as a goat's liver. He was overcome in battle by Digung Chaubo, the *Gyalbo* of Lhasa, who, however, failed to possess himself of the saddle and the turquoise which were cast into the middle of the lake where they are said to remain to this day.

The Pundit is of the opinion that the Dangra Yum lake and the smaller lake of Tang-yung to the north were formerly connected together in one vast expanse of water. The Dangra lake is even now so large and the wind sometimes raises such violent waves that he compared it to the ocean. The inhabitants of Ombo or Pembo country, as it is sometimes called, although speaking the same language as the other Champas or Dokpas who live in the other parts of Hor, curiously enough have considerable differences in their religious ceremonials. Instead of the usual well-known Buddhist formula "*Om mani padmi hom*", they inscribe in the prayer wheels and on their manis the words "*Om Mate moya salendo*". They, moreover, turn their prayer wheels in the anti clock-wise direction, contrary to what all other Buddhists do and in making circuits round religious edifices, they travel from right to left instead of from left to right. Some others belonging to their pecu-liar sect are said to reside in the Kham country east of Lhasa.

The origin of this custom rose thus. When Sakya Mum came to the country, he was residing near the famous sacred mountain, Kailas. Naru Punchuk, a native of Kham, having heard of his arrival, went on a pilgrimage to see him. Arriving there, he found that the devout Sakya was constantly passing his time in circumam-bulating the sacred mount and at such a pace that his would-be disciple was unable to overtake him, although he followed him round and round for several circuits. As Sakya Muni followed the orthodox course (moving like the hands of the watch), a brilliant idea at last struck Naru Punchuk that if he were to go round in the reverse direction, he would soon meet him. This he did and secured an interview and subsequently becoming a favourite disciple he received, in commemoration of this event, permission to found the sect now known as Pembos who make their religious circuits and turn their prayer-wheels in the direction opposite to that adopted by the orthodox Buddhists.

Near the ruins previously alluded to on the banks of the lake is a large natural cavern containing the impress of the palm of Naru Punchuk's hand. It is an object of worship to the people of the country.

Thus far on his journey, the Pundit stated, a cart might be driven all the way from Noh without any repairs being made to the road. But in crossing the range which bounds the Pembo country on the east, the path was steep and difficult. There is an alternative road however, lying to the north, by which it is said a cart (supposing there is to be such a thing in this country) might easily travel from Thok Daurakpa to the Nam lake without meeting a single obstacle on the way.

The country to the east of Pembo district is of a precisely similar nature as that which Nain Singh had already passed through on the west. It was inhabited as far as the Nam lake by pastoral Champa nomads who lived mostly on the produce of their flocks and herds. No grain whatever was grown but large quantities were imported from the Slugatse and Lhasa districts to the south. The inhabitants were well-off. In addition to the produce of their flocks, they sold to the merchants of the south large quantities of salt which was obtained from numerous *chakas* or salt lakes lying from eight to twelve days' march to the north of the Pundit's road.

The country was sub-divided into districts designated successively from west to the Naktsang Gomnak, Naktsang Doha, Yakpa Ngocho, Yakpa Jagro, De Cherik, Tabaraba and Taklung Do (immediately to the north of Nam lake). Each of these as well as the district of Naktsang Ombo described before had its own ruler or *Pon*, who decided the dis-putes of his subjects and collected revenue from them. The Pons were subordinate to the, two *Jongpons (Dzongpons)* of Senja Dzong (fort), a place of considerable importance lying to the east of the Naktsang Doha district and containing from 80 to 100 houses. These *Jongpons* were officials appointed by Lhasa and were changed every two or three years. Their chief business appeared to be to collect the revenue and remit it to Lhasa and to act as a sort of court of appeal against the decision of the hereditary *Pons* who ruled over small divisions. They did not seem to have a very difficult task as their executive and administrative functions were carried out with the assistance of two or three writers only and a couple of dozen guards sent from the Gyalbo's forces m Lhasa. The revenue sent to Lhasa consisted entirely of *ghee*.

One of the most influential of the local *Pons* was the Garpon Changbo Gyalbo who resided at Katmar in Naktsang Gomnak. He appeared to exercise considerable influence in the neighbouring districts, both east and west. When the Pundit was passing through the area, he had seen a considerable force of Changpas armed with guns and bows and arrows with the object of settling a dispute with another chief who lived some distance to the east of the Nam lake. The dispute was however settled diplomatically.

The height of the plateau traversed appears to vary but little between 15,000 and 16,000 feet above the sea-level. The plain is, as a rule, con-fined between mountains which run parallel to the direction of the road. But a few traverse ridges of considerable elevation are crossed *en route*. The drainage tends to the north. The streams from the snowy range to the south find their way into numerous large lakes. These lakes are the characteristic feature of the country and the Pundit may well be proud of the discovery and survey of such a numerous and extensive system of the whole series extending from Noh to Lhasa. The only one that had hitherto been known to geographers is the Nam or Tengri Nor lake to the extreme east. Although its position with regard to Lhasa was approximately known and was marked on the old Chinese maps, yet it was only within the previous few years that its position and extent bad been determmed with some accuracy. This was done by Pundit Kishen Singh, a pupil of the veteran Nain Singh.

The largest of these newly discovered lakes, the Dangra Yum lake, is about forty five miles long, the maximum breadth being twenty five miles. Another large lake, Kyaring lake, is forty miles in length and from eight to twelve across. The waters of the former are slightly brackish but those of the Kyaring and nearly all the lakes to the east are beautifully fresh. The streams which feed them from the south contain abundance of fish and are covered with myriads of wild fowl. The Champas have a prejudice against killing and eating fish or fowl and these are well protected in this region. They get plenty of meat from their large flocks of sheep and goat.

On the occasion of a former exploration of the Nam lake by Pundit Kishen Singh, it was frozen, and although he made a complete circuit of it, he was unable to discover any stream flowing out. On the present occasion, however. Pundit Nain Singh,- having visited it in the autumn, before its waters were frozen, distinctly traced a stream issuing from its north-western extremity and flowing in a westerly direction.

It appears that the drainage from nearly all these lakes finds its way either into the Chargot, a large lake said to be twice the size of any with which we are yet acquainted in these parts or into the Nag Chu Kha, a large river which issues from the Chargot lake and flows eastward. The southern banks of this river are said to be inhabited at certain times of the year by shepherds from the De Namra district (north of Decherik). The country to the north of the Nag Chu Kha is believed to be uninhabited.

The largest river crossed by the Pundit in this section of the travels was the Dumphu or Hota Tsang-po which receives the drainage of the southern slopes of the Targot Gyakharma range of mountains and flows into the Kyaring lake, forming one of the numerous sources of the Nag Chu Kha.

One piece of collateral geography brought back by the Pundit appears to agree so well with Klaproth's map that it seems desirable to reproduce it.

Nain Singh states, " A road passes from the Nag Chu Kha village for six days' journey in a north-eastern and thirteen days' in an eastern direction through the Ho-suk country to Jakanak Samdo where it crosses the Jha Chu (Sa chu, afterwards Tsa Chu) which joins the omchu river near Chiamdo".

From Jaka, the road passes east for ten days through the Khawa country and for fourteen days through the Cheki country where it meets a river called the Di Chu (the DraChu of Klaproth'smap) and afterwards the Ma Chu, the Yalung and the Ta-tchung, one of the largest tributaries of Yang-tse. It is crossed in boats. After sixteen days in an easterly direction, another large river flowing south, called the Jhachu, is crossed; another twenty days' journey towards south-east passing by Changtang, brings the traveller to the Ambo country to a place called Chering Chitshum on the banks of the Ma Chu river which flows to China.

The Pundit took the same route along the northern shore of the Nam lake which was followed by his predecessor in 1872. From the east end ofthelake to Lhasa, the routes are identical down to the village Dam. From Dam, Pundit NainSingh followed the river of the same name in the south-west direction, instead of striking across the hills to the south-east, the direct route which was followed by the other Pundit

In the Tibetan Capital

It was not till the 12th November that the Pundit quitted the higher tableland of Tibet and after crossing the Baknak pass (18,000 feet) descended into the bed of the Tolung, an afiluent of the river of Lhasa, where for the first time for several months he found himself at a comparatively low elevation of 13,000 feet. From there a steady descent for five short marches brought him to Lhasa at an elevation of 11,400 feet. His pleasure was great on reaching theTo-lung vafley where he found cultivated fields, grain in abundance, vegetables, *chhang* (a kind of beer brewed from barley) and other luxuries to which he had long been a stranger. Ordinary cattle and donkeys now took the place of yaks as milk suppliers and as beasts of burden. Fowls and pigs were seen for the first time since leaving Ladakh. The more civilised Bodhpas replaced the Champas, and the Pundit was looking forward to a pleasant stay at Lhasa.

But unfortunately for him, the approach of civilisation brought him considerable anxiety. On nearing Lhasa, he heard a report that there were lots of rumours about him in the city. On hearing this, he halted for a day at Lang-dong and sent one of his own servants (Nendak, a native of Lhasa) ahead to engage a room in a travellers' *sarai* and to enquire whether any news had been received of the *Kahlon* of Ladakh and the caravan from Leh. The man returned and reported that nothing had been heard of the *Kahlon* and on the following day (the 18th November) the Pundit entered Lhasa.

Sodden Departure

Most unfortunately, one of the first men he met there was a merchant (an Argun of Leb) whose acquaintance the Pundit had formerly made at that place. An Argun is ahalf-bred, the issue of a Kashmiri father and a woman of Ladakh. This man, Mahmud by name, knew perfectly well who Pundit Nain Singh was and although at first he was very friendly, he subsequently changed his manner and the Pundit was alarmed lest he should be betrayed. For this reason, instead of waiting there for a couple of months, as he had wished to, until the arrival of the caravan when he would have been sullied with ample funds and been enabled to continue his explorations, he was forced to make other arrangements immediately.

He determined to send back to Leh the two men he had brought with him and accordingly gave them letters to be delivered to the *Kahlon*, whom they might expect to meet on the way. He also sent with them complete copies of all his astronomical observations and route-surveys to be delivered to the British Joint Commissioner in Ladakh, who had promised to forward all such communications to Capt. Trottet, a survey official. These papers and the accompanying letter reached the latter safely in India in January 1875 and caused him some anxiety for the Pundit's welfare

On the occasion of the Pundit's first visit to Lhasa, he remained there three months and wrote a good description of the place. The present hasty visit of two days did not add to the existing store of infor-mation. He left Lhasa on the 20th November, accompanied by his two remaining servants. Before starting, and considering that he might be betrayed, he collected the most bulky and least valuable article of his party, tied them up in an old blanket, carefully sealed the parcel and handed it over to the owner of his lodging house whom he informed that he was going on a pilgrimage to amonastery, ten days' journey to the north of Leh, whence he expected to be back in about a month to reclaim his goods. He started accordingly in the afternoon in a northerly direction but as soon as evening came, he turned round and commenced his journey towards Hindustan.

The first night he halted at Kombo Thang, only two miles out of Lhasa. The following day he reached Decheu, a flourishing town with a large monastery on the left bank of the Lhasa river. His route for the first stage was along the high road to Peking.

From Lhasa to Peking there were two roads, the one generally ased and which is believed to be open all the year round goes at first nearly eastward upto Chimado, the capital of the Kham country. It then turns southwards and passes through Pa or Ba-tang and the Chinese province of Sze-Chuen, crossing numerous snow-covered passes across ranges which divide the streams. These rise in Tibet and flow south-wards either into the sea or into the great Chinsha-Chiang, afterwards the Yang-tse. The journey from Lhasa to Peking by the route takes 136 caravan marches and the distance is about 2,500 miles.

The other or northern route which is generally preferred by travellers in the hot season is probably easier and less snow is encountered. It goes by Nag Chu Kha and crosses the head-waters of the Yang-tse from which there are two alternative roads to the Koko Nor. Thence the road passes by Sining-fu (Siling) to Peking. It was followed by the Abbe Hue in his journey to Lhasa and he took fifteen days to reach Lhasa from Nept Chu (Nag Chu Kha). Another account mentions Nag Chu Kha as sixteen days' march from Lhasa, each march averaging probably about twenty-three miles. The same itinerary by M. Uspenski, originally published in the Investigia gives thirty-four marches of similar length from Nag Chu Kha to Koko Nor; the position of the latter is now known.

At De-Cheu, the Pundit left the Peking road and turning south, crossed by the Gokhar pass (16,620 feet) the range that separates the Lhasa river from the Brahmaputra. The pass was covered with fresh snow. From it he obtained a very extensive view embracing the Yala Shimbo snowy peaks, sixty miles to the south-east and the Ninchinthang-la peaks at a still greater distance north-westwards.

On the 27th November, he reached the Samaye monastery which lies on the right bank of a small tributary of the Brahmaputra, about two miles before it falls into the greater river.

Samaye Monastery

The Samaye monastery is very ancient, famous and beautiful and is said to have been built by the great Sakya Muni himself. It is surrounded by a very high circular stone wall, one and a half miles in circumference, with gates facing the four points of the compass. On the top of this wall, the Pundit counted one thousand and thirty *churtans* made of burnt bricks. One very large *lhakang* or temple occupies the centre of the enclosed space and was surrounded by four comparatively smaller temples, built half-way between each pair of doorways.

Most of the idols and images contained in these temples were made of pure gold and richly adorned with valuable clothes and jewels. The candle sticks and other ecclesiastical utensils were nearly all made of gold and silver. The interior of the stone walls of these temples was covered with beautiful writing in enormous Sanskrit characters, which the Pundit was able to decipher although he could not understand their meaning. These writings of Sakya Muni are objects of worship to all visitors to the monastery.

The monastery also contained the Tanguir and the Kaaaguir or sacred books of Buddha. The latter are a hundred and eight in number.

Tradition says that in the reign of Tajung Dundjak, the *Gyalbo* of Lhasa, son of Gyalbo Ramba and grandson of Gyalbo Ghoja, the country was without religion and without gods. During lus reign, Sakya Muni was born in Hindustan and came to Tibet and among his early converts were Gyalbo Sumzen, the son, and Biru, the grandson of Tajung Dundjak. These two in company with Sakya Muni, commenced work on the monastery at Samaye, but whatever was rarised by day was thrown down by evil spirits at night. At last Sakya Muni thought of summoning from Hindustan one of his spiritual pupils, Labhan Padmi, who was very skilful in the management of evil spirits. He came and was presented to the *Gyalbo* to whom, however, he refused to pay respects. The *Gyalbo*, somewhat angered, remonstrated with him, whereupon fire issued from Labhan's nails and burnt the *Gyalbo's* head-dress. The wicked demons were soon overcome and the monastery was completed. On the death of the *Gyalbo*, his son abdicated and went to Hindustan as a religious mendicant, resiging his authority to Sakya Muni who is still supposed to be alive in the person of the Gewa Ring-bo-che or Grand Lama of Lhasa. The term "Dalai Lama", by which the Grand Lama is known to outsiders and mentioned by Turner, Hue and others, is never used in Tibet. Gewa Ring-bo-che, Galdan Phutong and Kuinggon Ring-bo-che are the sole names by which, according to the Pundit, the Grand Lama is known in Tibet. He is also called Da Lama in China. Similarly the great Lama of Shigatse is known to the Pundit as Panchhen (or Panjan) Ring-bo-che instead of Teshu Lamba, the name by which he is known to outsiders.

From Samaye, the Pundit travelled down the course of the Brahmaputra for two marches, passing several small tributaries. He crossed the great river, in a boat on the 30th November. In this portion of its course it is known either as Tsang-po or "The river" or by the name of Tamjan-Khamba, and its width is estimated by the Pundit to be five hundred yards. The stream was very sluggish, its current near the banks flowing at no more than two-thirds of a mile per hour. The Pundit found that a piece of wood which he threw in from the bank was carried along a distance of fifty yards in two minutes and forty seconds. Its depth was nowhere more than twenty feet. The poks used for propelling the boats were measured by the Pundit and found to be twenty feet in length. From this he found that the maximum depth was eighteen or twenty feet.

The valley through which the river flows was several miles wide. On the left bank of the stream was a stretch of sand one and a half miles wide, the whole of which is said to be under water in the months of May, June and July. During that season the river is flooded on account of the increase of water from rapidly melting snow and the rain which falls in considerable quantities from April to June. The river here is no longer used for irrigation as above Shigatse but all the small streams which issue from the mouni'ains on the north and south are thickly bordered with cultivated land.

The Pundit left the river near Tse-tang from which point he states that its general course is visible due east for a distance of thirty miles after which it encounters a range of mountains which cause it to move in a south-easterly direction. By determining the positions of some peaks on this side, he fixed the approximate course of the river for a very considerable distance. The course of the river thus made out fairly accords with that shown on Du Halden's map of Tibet. Afief leaving Gyala, according to its approximate position shown on the Pundit's map, the river is said to flow for fifteen days' journey. Brought the rice producing country of Lho-khalo, reputed to be under a ruler who was quite independent of the Lhasa authorities. Its inhabitants traded with the people of the Kombo district which lies between it and Lhasa but they had no communication with the people on their south. The Shiar Lhoba (probably the people who are known to us as the Mishmis) inhabited the country through which the great river flows to Gya (Assam). In the Lho-khalo country, the Brahmaputra is joined by two large rivers from the north.

Tse-tang is a large town on the right bank of the Yarlung Chu, a considerable affluent of the Brahmaputra. It contained two large monasteries where about 700 Lamas lived. From Tse-tang the Pundit's road lay up the Yarlung through the rich and fertile valley which contained numerous villages and monasteries scattered about on both sides of the stream. The country is very productive and contains numerous fruit trees, principally apricots and pears. Wheat, barley and many kinds of vegetables were grown. There is good grazing on the mountains which border the valley but the breed of the sheep is very small.

From Tse-tang, the Dalatang plain at the end of the valley is thirty-six miles. In addition to numerous scattered villages, each consisting of ten or twelve houses, the large towns of Netong and Chukya Phutang were passed by on the way. From the Dalatang La to the Karkang La, the road traverses for fifteen miles a grassy plateau between fifteen and sixteen thousand feet above the sea-level, through which flows a stream which rises in springs and ultimately finds its way into the Brahmaputra below Tse-tang. On the elevated region which extends from a considerable distance in the west, the Pundit again found himself amongst the Dokpas or nomad population. It is by the Karkang pass to the south of the plain that the main Himalayan watershed is crossed. On reaching it, the Pundit states, a magnificent view presented itself. The whole of the foreground was occupied by gently undulating grassy plains over which on the north-west at a distance of but a few miles rise the very conspicuous group of snowy peaks called Yala Shampa,

Other snowy peaks beyond the Brahmaputra appeared topping the plateau to the north, while in the other directions they appeared every-where at a great distance.

From this watershed which is 16,210 feet above the sea-level, the road to the Kyakyan La (a pass about seventy miles further south) traverses a high undulating plateau which is bounded on its west by a well-marked snowy ridge which runs nearly due north and south and contains numerous glaciers. The drainage of this country is most irregular. The Pundit's road for the first twenty miles from the pass followed a stream which under the name of Sikung Chu lows for forty miles nearly due east through the Chayul country and ultimately turning south-east runs nearly parallel to the upper course of the Brahmaputra which river it joins in Assam. After leaving the main stream, the road ascends a branch valley for a distance of twenty miles and then descends into a stream which flows due south for forty miles and subsequently under the name of Tawang Chu takes a westerly course and goes round the southern extremity of the snowy range which has been mentioned bounding the plateau on the west.

The portion of the plateau which contains the head-water of the Sikung river is from 13,000 to 15,000 feet above the sea-level. It is a very flourishing, well-cultivated country covered with numerous small villages containing settled inhabitants. The Chayul district is situated lower down the course of the Sikung river.

The road goes nearly due south, crossing in succession several spurs from the western range and after reaching Kyakyan pass rapidly descends into the Chukhang valley. The valley is separated from that of the Tawang by a very high ridge which is crossed by the Mila Katong La, a pass covered with fresh snow.

Between the Sikung district and Tsona Dzong, the country is uninhabited. The Pundit passed a lake about six miles long and four miles broad, entirely frozen but the water of which in the summer months helps feed the Tawang stream. South of this lake, the road followed by the Pundit is joined by another which comes from the Her country and Shigatse.

Tsona Dzong is a place of considerable importance and is a great exchange market where salt, wool and borax from the Hor country and tea, fine silks, woollen clothes, leather boots and ponies from Lhasa are exchanged for rice, spices, dyes, fruits and coarse silk called *endi* in Assam and *bhure* in Lhasa. Chinese silk is called *go-chen* in Lhasa.

This market is of considerable importance and contains three or four hundred shops. The Pundit is of the opinion that although its export and import trade is not nearly so valuable as that of Leh (the great exchange market for India and Eastern Turkistan), yet the number of traders and men employed in, carrying loads is somewhart larger. The goods imported from Hor are brought by merchants from that place. There is free trade between Hor, Lhasa and Tsona Dzong but on all goods to and from the south, a duty of 10 per cent is levied at the *chukhang* or custom-house.

The road from Tsona Dzong to Tawang *chukhang* is closed by snow from January to May or June. An alternative road lies down the Lhobra and up the Tawang rivers. The *chukhang* is not only a customs boundary but separates the Bodhpa country in the north from the Tawang valley to the south which was under British jurisdiction. The Monbas who inhabit the Tawang area differ materially in language, dress, manners and appearance from the inhabitants of Tibet and resemble, according to the Pundit, in many respects the Dokpas of the Bhutan country on the west. Instead of allowing their hair to grow behind and arranging them inplaits, as is done in Tibet, they cut them to an even length all round the head, to be arranged in the shape of an inverted slop basin. On the top they wear small skull caps made either of woollen cloth or felt. Instead of the long gown of Tibet, a short coat is worn which only reaches the knee. It is fastened by a woollen girdle in which is thrust a long straight knife.

The adjoining regions inhabited by Dafia and other Nagas, beyond the administrative frontiers, were also under British jurisdiction.

Nain Singh on his march down the valley met some Lhobas. He was much struck with the appearance of these men and especially noticed the enormous development of their arms and the calves of their legs which far exceeded in size any be had seen elsewhere. They wore cylinder-shaped hats made of bamboos. Their only garment was a long blanket folded somewhat in the fashion of a Scotch plaid and fastened round the waist by a cloth girdle which is used as a quiver for their arrows which all carry, as well as a bow slung over the left shoulder. The greater part of the arms and legs were bare. They wore no boots but ornamental rings made of rope were fastened tightly both on their wrists and legs. They had high cheek bones and Chinese-looking eyes, wore no hair on their faces but allowed that on the head to grow to a great length. The hair was drawn together behind the head and allowed to hang down.

End of the Journey

The Pundit reached Tawang on the 24th December, 1874 and Odalguri in Assam on the 1st of March 1875. The road was often deep in snow and four passes had to be crossed on the way.

Of these, the passes of Se La and Manda La were somewhat difficult on account of snow.

At Odalguri, the Pundit got in touch with the Assistant Commissioner of Darrang district who made all the arrangements for sending him to Gauhati, whence he went by steamer to Calcutta which place he reached on the 11th March, 1875.

Achievements

Before closing this account, it may be well to recapitulate the chief result of the Pundit's exploration.

In addition to the general information acquired which has been communicated in the narrative, the Pundit had made a very careful and well-executed route survey of the whole line of the country traversed, viz. 1,018 miles from Lukung (west end of Pangong lake) to Lhasa and 306 miles from Lhasa to Odalguri. Of the total distance of 1,324 miles throughout which his pakings and bearings were carefully recorded, about 1,200 miles lie through country which had never previously been explored. Numerous lakes, some of enormous size, and some rivers were discovered. The existence of a vast snowy range lying parallel to the north of Brahmaputra was clearly demonstrated and the position of several peaks laid down and their heights approximately determined.

The Pundit followed the Brahmaputra for a distance of thirty miles in a portion of its course lower than the lowest point hitherto determined and laid down its approximate course for another 100 miles. The absolutely unknown portion of that mighty river's course was thus very materially reduced. The route between Lhasa and Assam via Tawang, of which next to nothing was hitherto known, was carefully surveyed and the daily marches described.

As a frame-work for the map, no less than 276 double altitudes of the sun and stars were observed with a sextant for the determination of latitude. The close accordance of the results *inter se* and with the mapping of the route by the pacings and bearings prove incontestably the general accuracy of the work.

The temperature of boiling water was observed on nearly every pass and at nearly every camping ground (497 observations in all), adding materially to the value of the maps.

Frequent observations of the temperature of the air and the direction of the wind further added to the knowledge of the Tibetan climate.

The Pundit suffered much in health during the latter portion of the journey and his eye-sight was seriously injured from exposure and hard work in the most trying climate for long years. Having happily survived the perils and dangers of his journey through difficult countries, he hoped to receive a grant of land.

After return from the journey. Pundit Nain Singh retired from public service on a well-earned pension. In 1895 he went to Moradabad, Uttar Pradesh, to look after his estate granted by the British Government and died there of heart attack.

SECTION TWO

KISHEN SINGH

1. *Tengri Nor Lake* • 1871-72
2. *Western Tibet* • 1873-74
3. *Great Tibet and Mongolia* • 1878-82

KISHEN SINGH

In 1871, when he was just twenty one, Pundit Kishen Singh was selected for the exploration of the Tengri Nor (Nam) lake in Tibet. It was his first independent work. His party passed from Kumaon into the Tibetan province of Ngari Khorsum. Towards the end of July 1871, when in the neighbourhood of the Manasarowar lake, his progress was for some time interrupted by a band of mounted robbers who had made an incursion from the east. He evaded the robbers by taking a circuitous route through Purang. Reaching Shigatse on the 24th November, 1871, he remained there for twelve days, making enquiries as to the best route to the Tengri Nor lake and preparing for the journey. Sheep were the only animals likely to stand the journey as the roads were too stony for yaks and the country was too cold for donkeys. Kishen Singh consequently purchased fifty sheep and put all the luggage on their backs.

The explorer and the party left Shigatse on the 6th December, 1871, marching as far as the Naisang village. On the 7th, they crossed the Tsang-po by means of rafts and encamped at Peting village which had about thirty houses on the left bank. The halting point for the next day was at Cho-lo village. Here he exchanged the silver rupees he had with him for gold which he put into hollow walking sticks prepared for the purpose. On the 11th December, the party reached Dongdot-lo, a village on the right bank of the Shang, the northern tributary of the Brahmaputra. Here they found an official from Shigatse who ruled over Dongdot-lo and the numerous surrounding villages. On the 13th, they reached Chom (50 houses), with a nunnery on its west. On the 14th December, they got to Namling, (*Nam* means sky and *ling*, garden) on the right bank of the Shang river. It is a place of some importance, boasting of an iron bridge over the river and commanded by a strong fort which was the residence of the *Jongpon*, with about 100 Tibetan soldiers. Namling itself had about 200 houses surrounded by gardens, with a small *bazar* in the centre. There is a large monastery on a high hill. On the 19th, they reached Gonkiang (60 houses), with a well-built monastery on rising ground, ruled by Chu Ring-bo-Che, a high ranking lama.

On the 20th December, the explorer and the party halted at Rabdan Chuling monastery ruled by another high-ranking lama called Chaptung Ring-bo-che, said to be one hundred years of age, who was both the founder and builder of this monastery. The Lama, when Kishen Singh saw him, was very old; his body was so small and shrunk that when sitting his knee projected a great deal above his head.

From the time he left Namling on the 14th December, it was so cold that the mercury in his thermometer did not rise out of the bulb till after 9 or 10 o'clock in the morning. The streams were all hard frozen. The wind blew so hard that it tore their tent and they had consequently to make a halt of fifteen days in order to repair the damage. On the 26th, they reached Gunje. The people of this village'said that white bears called *tik-dumba* were very common from there to the Nam lake and they committed great havoc among the cattle. The next day, they reached Nai-kor (30 houses), with some cultivation. Beyond Nai-kor, there was no more cultivation and the only inhabitants were nomads called Dokpa. They kept sheeps, goats and yaks.

Hot Springs • Steaming river

On the 28th December, the party encamped at Chutang-Chaka where there were fifteen hot springs, the water of which was found to have a temperature of 166^0F, the boiling point at the place being 186^0. There were eight baths supplied by these springs. The baths were at some distance from the springs so as to allow the water to cool sufficiently for bathing. The water had a smell of sulphur. There were a number of Dokpa tents at a short distance from the springs.

From the Brahmaputra river near Shigatse upto these springs, the country was called Shang and that to the north, Lahu.

On the 29th December, the Chapting encamping ground was

reached. Here there were more Dopka tents. The road was slippery with ice and one of his men fell and broke a thermometer. On the 30th, they arrived at Pe-ting Chuja near which, on the right bank of the Lahu river, there was a large stony place about 120 paces in length, from which a dozen columns of hot water issued. These rose to a height of forty or fifty feet and produced so much steam that the sky was quite darkened with it and the noise, moreover, was so great they could not hear one another speak. The temperature of these jets of water was found to be 176^0 Fahrenheit. Similar jets were noticed issuing from the middle of the river, shooting up to a height of thirty to forty feet. They produced steam clouds and the river was free from ice for a quarter of a mile below though everywhere else, both above and below this portion, it was hard frozen.

The Jawar monastery lies about three miles to the east of these springs. The explorer went to the monastery which he found had a number of highly ornamented idols, in front of which were arranged a number of petrified stones called *naidhowas*. These were in various shapes, such as hands, shells, etc., and were also objects of worships. Jawar is the Tibetan name for Suket Mandi in Himachal Pradesh. This according to a tradition, was given in honour of a daughter of a Raja of Suket Mandi who was supposed to have married Laban, one of the big persons whose idol was there. Then the explorer passed through the encampments of Salung-Surndo and Salung, occupied by Dokpas. Beyond Salung, the only people about were thieves on the look out for plunder, against whom it was necessary to be on guard.

On the 2nd January, 1872, Kishen Singh reached Nai Sum Chuja. *Chuja* or *Chusa* means source of hot water springs. The name is given to the place from the great number of hot springs which were there on both sides of the Lahu river. The water from these springs was so-hot that the river was not frozen for about three miles below them though everywhere else it was. On the right bank of the river there were two very remarkable hot springs which threw up a jet of water about sixty feet in height. The water in falling again froze and formed pillars of ice nearly up to the full height of the jet. These pillars were about thirty feet in circumference and looked like towers with holes at the sides just as if they had been made artificially. The water was thrown up with great violence and noise. The thermometer when put inside the pillars stood at 1830 Fahrenheit while the boiling point was only 183.75^0.

On the 6th January, the party reached Dung Chuka (15,700 feet) where they found more hot springs. About ten miles to the east, there was the lofty snowy peak called Jhomoganger. On the 8th January, they crossed Khalamba pass (17,200 feet) and halted at Nagu Chuka with more hot springs around. Then they passed through Kiang pass and Dakman encampment.

On the 13th January, the party reached Ghaika camping place from where they got a view of a very large lake which was called Jang-nam-cho Chiadmo by the Tibetans and Tengri Nor in the Tartar language. A camp of several tents was seen to the east at a place called Dungche. Two of the men were sent by the explorer in disguise as beggars to enquire about the road. The camp was deserted. The only occupants were an old man and a woman, who informed the disguised beggars that the men had armed and gone out to meet the band of robbers who they had heard intended to plunder them, while they had concealed their property, women and children in the mountains. As to the road, they informed them that it went to Lhasa through Ninchin-Thang la, Jyang Hyang-pechen monastery and Tubing Dinga.

On the 16th, after crossing Gaika river which flows into Nam lake, they reached Chakri which was surrounded by a wall, ten feet high, with ruined sun-dried brick huts. The place was said to have once been the residence of a man of some rank. Two days later, the party reached Sinjim, with about seventy Dokpa tents As robbers were known to be in the vicinity, every tent was guarded by an armed man. The robbers were said to come from a northern district which was not under the Lhasa Government. These robbers consequently plundered the Lhasa district whenever they were in want created by the severe climate which killed their cattle and sheep. Sinjim, being one of the nearest places to these freebooters, was often plundered.

On the 21st January, Pundit Kishen Singh passed through Tara on the shores of the great Nama lake which was completely frozen and reached Dorkia Lugu Dong monastery on a small hill overlooking the lake. *Dor* means a rock, *lugu*, a sheep and *dong*, a face, the monastery looking something like a sheep's head. It commanded a splendid view of the lake and the surrounding snowy mountains.

The lake is a magnificent sheet of water. Near Dorkia is an island, a mile long and half a mile broad. It has a hill about 400 feet high, crowned in the centre by a temple of goddess Dorje Phamo. Kishen Singh determined to make a complete survey of the lake, and being afraid of robbers, he deposited his property in the monastery with three of his men. He started off with the remaining three men. On the 24th January, they reached Ringa Do on the margin of the lake. Here is another island called Kuhi Ne Dobo close to the shore. It is about one and a half miles long and about one mile broad.

On the 25th January, the explorer reached Jador Sumdyaling monastery which had about fifty lamas. There he saw three pyramids of sun-dried mud, each about 500 feet m circumference, rising to a considerable height. He found a great many fossil stones which were called *naidhowas* and were held in veneration. Kishen Singh saw a gigantic doorway about twenty five feet high out in the rock through which, the Lamas said, the god Ninchin-Thang La passes. Owing to heavy snow, the explorer was detained for two days at Jador. He continued his journey and passed through Nangba Do on the shore of the lake Langdang or *Chogola* where he found *shukpa* bush very abundant. Then he passed Dakmar and Thuigo Sumna shrine and reached Nai Chu Sumna on the 31st January, 1872. On the way he crossed the Nai stream, the largest in the region. It flows into the lake. It was forty paces wide and completely frozen.

On the 1st February, 1872, the explorer reached the Tas-shi Doche monastery, having thirty five lamas, situated on a low hill near the lake. To the south-east of Tas-shi Doche, there are a number of magnificent snowy peaks called Ninchin-la. To the east, there is another mass of high peaks called Nuchnin Gasa which appeared to rise higher above the Nam lake than the Kailas peak does above the Manasarowar. All these peaks were very imposing from the monastery which also commands a full view of the whole of the lake. Though the water of the lake is so saltish as to be unfit for drinking, it is nevertheless quite frozen in November. The lake is about 15,200 feet above the sea-level. When Kishen Singh saw it, the surface looked as if it was made of glass. It is said to remain in that state till the month of May when the ice breaks up with great noise. The lake contains fish, and quantities of small shell are found on the banks. It is a great resort for pilgrims.

After leaving the monastery, the party passed over open country without the tent which had been left behind at Dorkia. There was heavy fall of snow and no shelter was available. So the party had to clear off the snow and lie on the ground without any fire. They thought the cold would kill them but they managed to survive through the night. On the 6th February, they saw the sun again and were able to get some fuel and to make themselves tolerably comfortable. But whilst crossing the Sinjam chu at the side of the lake, one of the men of the party fell through the ice which was covered with fresh snow and would have been drowned had he not got hold of another man who pulled him out. This man's clothes froze hard as he got out and he was only brought round by means of a fire which they at once lighted.

On the 7th February, the party reached Dorkia monastery from which they originally started, having taken fifteen days in making the circuit of the lake. They halted at the monastery for three days and started off on the 11th, getting that day as far as Ringa Do. After two days, they reached the Jador monastery mentioned before and on the 14th, Nangba Do. Here the explorer heard there was a lake called Bul Cho (San lake) about six or seven miles to the north. He accordingly climbed a peak in that direction and saw the lake. He estimated it to be about six miles by five. A kind of borax is found by and in the lake. It is called bul and hence the name. This borax is used by the inhabitants of Lhasa and Shigatse as a spice for meat and tea and for washing clothes and for bathing. It is carried away by the traders in great quantities. They continued their journey through Langdang, Dakmar and the plain of Chang Phang Chuja where there are several hot springs.

Robbers Attack

On the 18th February, as they were about to start, some sixty armed men arrived on horseback and began plundering their property, and in-spite of their entreaties took away every thing except the instruments which they said they did not care to keep in case the authorities should find these on them and ask how they came into their possession. After a great deal of begging, the robbers gave them back apiece of cloth each with two sheep and two bags of food, a cooking vessel and awooden cup. With these they had to be content. The robbers said if they troubled them any more, they would kill them.

The explorer had intended to make his way from the Nam lake to the north as far as the city of Sining but the robbery had put him in such a situation that he had to return as fast as possible to inhabited area for food and clothing. On the way, his men fell ill due to hunger and exhaustion. On the 23rd February, the party crossed the Dam Niargan pass. Kishen Singh said that he had become so weak that he took much shorter paces than he had hitherto done. They decided to kill one of the remaining two sheep as they had exhausted their flour. At the same time seeing tents in the neighbourhood all the men went over to beg and after a long round came back with six pounds of flour and began to feel more hopeful.

From the Dam Niargan pass, there was a road to Lob Nor and to Jiling or Sining. From this pass, it is about ten days' journey to Nakchukha, a place that had a bad reputation as to the number of robbers who prey on travellers. From thence it is about forty five days' journey to Sokpohuil which is quite a barren country, infested by robbers. Beyond Sokpohuil, the inhabitants were more civilized and very kind to travellers. The Lob Nor lake is in the Sokpohuil territory and the town of Kharka is close to it. It is about fifteen days' journey from Sokpohuil to Sining city which is said to be superior to Lhasa. Good horses and sheep were procurable and shops were well-supplied with silk, woollen articles and carpets.

On the 26th, the explorer and his party halted under the

Ghana pass, The country upto this point was called Dam Niargan. On the 27th February, they reached Angichusa where they noticed six Dokpa tents. On the 28th February, they reached Lachu Sumna, the extremity of the Badam district which begins at the Chana pass. The Urirong district extends from Lacha Sumna to Dhog pass. On the 29th February, the explorer reached Siwalungi Ritu monastery.

On the 1st March, 1872, Kishen Singh and his party crossed the Dhog pass. The district of Tulung extends from the Dhog to the Cha pass. On the 2nd March, they reached Tulung monastery which had two head lamas and about a thousand monks. They found a large number of images carved on the walls and all of these were adorned with gold. The road from Lhasa to Lob Nor and Jiling (Sining) passes about a mile south of this monastery. The Sining *Kofilas* passed by this route with their beasts of burden laden with merchandise. On the 4th March, they crossed the Cha pass and encamped near the village of Langmo where they saw the first sign of cultivation that they had met with since they had left Chapting encampmg ground. Then they journeyed through Jhokar churtan and the Nehlin Dak monastery and on the 8th March, halted at Lingbu Dzong after crossing the Pen-po-go pass.

On the 9th March, 1872, Kishen Singh and the party reached Lhasa. They were exceedingly glad to get back to a civilised place where they would at any rate have no chance of being starved as they were atone time likely to be. Though the Lhasa people were hospitable enough, he found there was no chance of his being able to borrow sufficient money to enable him to march to Sining as be had intended to. With the greatest difficulty the explorer managed to borrow one hundred and fifty rupees from a trader who was going to Gar-tok, but he insisted upon the explorer accompanying him and in addition took his aneroid barometer and compass as security The aneroid which was a large one, he apparently took for a magnificent watch, and at the end of the journey, the messenger who was sent with money to redeem the instruments had some difficulty in recovering them. Not having sufficient money, the explorer decided upon returning to India, and after a long and difficult journey, he

KISHEN SINGH 83

reached the headquarters of the Great Trigonometrical Survey of India, Dehradun.

Outcome

It was Kishan Singh's first independent expedition. The route survey covered 320 miles of what had hitherto been veriable *terror incognita*. Latitude observations were taken at ten places and air pressure at twenty four. The geography of an area of about 12,000 square miles was elucidated and one northern tributary of the Upper Brahma-putra thoroughly explored, thus giving us some idea as to how far back the northern watershed of this great river lies. It will be noticed that the explorer actually went along a small portion of the Brahmaputra river below Shigatse, thus adding to our knowledge of its actual course. He was much struck with the magnificent glaciers to the south of the Nam or Tengri Nor lake and they will no doubt prove very extensive. Alto-gether he did very good work and in this first expedition showed much skill, power of observation and determination.

When a mission was leaving Yarkand for Kashgar, it was arranged for Pundit Kishen Singh to return to India via Khotan, a journey he accomplished most successfully. He obtained important geograplucal results regarding this road. The only previous account of the road is the one derived from native information supplied by Mr. R. B. Shaw. This account agrees remarkably well with that given by the Pundit.

Before leaving the region. Pundit Kishen Singh paid avisit to the Surghak gold-fields about 160 miles (by road) to the east of Khotan. Returning thence to Keriya, he found his way back to India by Polur, Noh and the Pangong lake, a route running from one and a half to two degrees to the east of the most easterly route hitherto passed, that is the one traversed in 1865 by Mr. W. H. Johnson in his journey to Khotan.

A traveller from Leh to Khotan might come by the Pangong lake, along which the Pundit travelled. But he would more probably take a short cut from Lukung to the Mangtza lake, following the ordinary Chang Chenmo route to Yarkand as far as the point where that road leaves the Chang Chenmo valley. Passing up the latter, he would make his way eastward. An easy pass is known to exist there, leading to the high table-land beyond. By adopting this road, he would save forty miles as against the more circuitous road by Noh. From Mangtza, the road lies over a series of high plateaux varying from 16,000 to 17,000 feet in height, crossed here and there by low ridges, rising somewhat irregularly from the sun face of the plain which contains numerous lakes, most of them brackish. In latitude $35°7'$ north, the Pundit crossed, at a height of a little more than 17,000 feet; the watershed of a snowy range which may perhaps be the true eastern continuation of the Kuen Lun. The Keriya stream rises from the north of this pass. The road follows down it as far as Arash or Baba Hatim (16,000 feet) but again ascends to the Ghu-bolik plain (17,000 feet) which connects the snowy range just alluded to with another somewhat lower range to the north. This large ridge is a buttress of the vast Tibetan plateau. In descending the Polur stream from the Ghubolik, from Diwan pass (17,500 feet) to Polur, a distance of 28 miles, including windings, there is a fall of about 9,000 feet. Hatim pass is called Sulphur Horse pass as it is used by the Polur people when bringing sulphur to Khatan. Sulphur is excavated in large quantities from the ground near the lake in the Ghubolik plain. Polur is a small village in the Khotan district, and from it Khotan (Ilchi) city may be reached either by the direct road (by Chihar Imam) which skirts the feet of spurs from the elevated plateau above, or the traveler may proceed down the stream to Keriya by the route followed by the Pundit.

Along the road from Khotan to Leh traversed by the Pundit, fuel was abundant everywhere and there was only one stage where there was not a good supply of grass. As far as is known from enquiry, the road was never used as a trade route on a large scale, the chief reason being fear of the Changpas or Tughliks, wandering tribes of Tibet nominally subject to the officials at Gartok and Rudok, but subject only to the extent that they would abstain from committing violent aggression on parties travelling under the protection of those autho-rities. Habibula who was elected the king of Khotan when the Chinese were turned out of the country sent messengers to try and open this route in 1861. They were seized by the Changpas and compelled to return to Khotan with the threat that any subsequent explorers would be put to death.

The inhabitants of Keriya and Polur went as far as Ghubolik to procure sulphur. They also went west towards the head of the Yurung-kash (Ilchi) river where they searched for gold and jade but it would appear that although the Khotanese claimed the country up to Yeshil lake, the head of the Keriya river, as their boundary, yet from fear of the Changpas, they almost never went quite so far to the south. Changpa in Tibetan means northerner while the Turkish name for the same people is Taghlik, i.e., mountaineers. The Champas probably had equal reason to fear the Turks from the plains and appeared not to wander further north than Rikong Churnik, the ridge to the north of which separated their grazing grounds from the plains on the north. A considerable stream flows through the plains and the Pundit's guide asserted it was the head of the Yurung-kash river. It would thus appear that, owing to the mutual hostility of the two races, there was a large tract of neutral ground extending from Rikong Chumik to Ghubolik which was never occupied by one or the other.

Here the Pundit saw large herds of yak, antelope and jungle sheep A (*oves ammon*) which had apparently never been scared by the sight of man. Near Rikong Chumik were the remains "of numerous huts and others were frequently seen along the road. But fortunately for the Pundit, he did not meet or see a single human being between Ghubolik and Noh, a distance of 244 miles, a circumstance which enabled him to complete his route survey upto Noh without interruption.

From Noh, he tried to get to Rudok but was not permitted to do so. In fact, the inhabitants tried to compel him to return by the way he had come and it was with great difficulty that ht at last got permission to go to Leh direct. Anticipating a search by the first people he should encounter, he had, when nearing the village of Noh, concealed his instruments and papers in a bush. He was duly searched but, of course, nothing was found, and he afterwards succeeded in again getting possession of his valuables. In Tibet, the great difficulty encountered by persons entering in disguise was always on the frontier where the examination was very strict. When once allowed to pass into the interior of the country, there was little to fear.

In 1878, Pundit Kishen Singh set out on a long journey to Great Tibet and Mongolia which lasted four years and brought out the very best in the young adventurer and explorer. Starting from Darjeeling on the 24th April, 1878, accompanied by his faithful companion, Chhumbel, and another servant, Ganga Ram, engaged for the exploration, he reached the right bank of the Tista river at night fall. The next day he arrived at Kalimpong, a small market with fifteen or twenty shops. The market was held every Sunday and they halted for three days in order to collect supplies for the journey. On the 29th, they arrived at Pedong village; on the 30th at Rinag and on the 1st May, at Chujanchen village. A heavy fall of rain detained them there for a day. On the 3rd May, they reached Lingdam. on the 4th, Pangdam and on the 5th, Gani, all these being customary halting places. On the 6th, they crossed the Jelep mountain and arrived at Nathang, also a halting place. Snow now began to fall and detained them for three days. On the 10th May, they arrived at Kabug where grass was abundant. The villagers of Rinchen Gang migrated there for the months of October, November and December to pasture their flocks and yaks. On the 12th May, crossing the Kubung La or Bodh La (pass) which was covered with snow to a depth of three feet, they arrived at Langia, a halting place. Here fire-wood and grass were plentiful. The 13th May brought them to Rinchen Gang (invaluable rock), a village of thirty houses and a gompa (monastery) with ten or twelve Dabas and a Lama. This village lay in the Domo *patti* (group of villages). All the villages of this *patti* were situated on the banks of the Ammo river which flows from the north to Lho or Bhutan. They were sparsely inhabited as the soul is poor and yields but little corn; only one crop was raised annually. *Ne, Dau,* turnip and potato were grown.

On the 16th, after travelling three miles, the party reached Chumbi on the Ammo river, the residence during the summer season of the Gyalbo (Raja) of Dainjung or Sikkim. It was a large solid square, three-storeyed palace, surrounded by a stone wall, having two large gates, one to the north and the other to the south. There were some forty houses close to the south of the pace. Following the bank of the stream, they reached Galing Kha village containing forty houses. Gong Kar Gom-pa is situated on the other side of the stream. On the 17th, the party arrived at Dag Karpo, a halting place. The route from Kubung to this place was very narrow and rugged.

On the 18th, they reached Phari, a fort on the top of a small soli-tary hill, about 1,200 paces in circumference at the base. The fort, some 200 feet above the surrounding plain, had steps leading up to it on the east. It had no tower or enclosing wall. The country round it was level for about four miles, but not cultivated. There were some 200 houses to the south-east of the fort. The Jemo-Lha Ri (female god peak) is visible from the surrounding plain. About twelve miles to the west are twelve *chuchans* (hot springs) the waters of wlach are reputed to possess different healing properties, so that they'are said to cure twelve different diseases. The people of this neighbourhood very seldom sought medical treatment but when taken ill, they were content to bathe for a week or so in the springs.

Two *Jongpons* ruled here for periods of three years. duty was to guard the road and levy taxes, equal to one-tenth the value of any merchandise which passed and to decide cases of a civil and criminal nature. Servant Ganga Ram, having fallen ill, detained the explorer there.

Leaving Phari on the 16th August, the group halted at Chu Gid Thence crossing a small mountain, they passed the night of the 17th at Tu-na, a village with ten houses, and on the 18th, reached Ka-la-shar, a village of sixty houses. Here they saw some cultivation. Some eighteen miles from Tu-na and to the right of the road lies Ram or Bam lake, the water of which begins to freeze about the middle of October and a month later it is so hard frozen that none flows out. A thaw usually sets in about the beginning of February. Near Ka-la-shar and to the west is another lake called

Ka-la. The villagers of Ka-la-shar spend a good deal of time fishing and catch many a large fish in nets. On the 19th, the explorer halted at Sa-ma-da and on the 20th, arrived at Trang-go, having passed a small hot spring on the road.

The 21st August saw them at Gyantse, a small town on the right bank of the Pen-nang Chu (Nyang river). The town is situated by the side of two small hills which lie east and west and are united by a saddle. The western hill is further connected, with the chain of mountains to the north. On the eastern hill there is a large fort similar' construction to that of Phari and on the western hill a. gompa inhabited by about 500 Dabas. In the gompa there is a *churtan* called Pangon churtan which is considered by the Tibetans a most holy place. *Churtan* or *chiorton* is a coloured building of varying height, rising in rectangular blocks each diminishing in size. In the centre of the topmost block, there is a carved wooden tapered piece on the summit of whicil is a golden crescent and ball. The central portion is hollow and images, religious books and other objects of veneration are placed within it. Besides the fort and the temple, there were about 1,000 dwelling houses on the sides of the double hill. Woollen cloth called *nhambu* was manufactured at Gyantse. There was a large market and traders from Nepal and China resided there. The explorer remained therefor six days to exchange his merchandise. The road from Sa-ma-da to Gyantse was rugged and stony.

On the 28th, Upsi village was reached where there was a large *giakhang* or stage house, and on the 29th the party halted at Ra-lung village. The road from Gyantse to this place was smooth, wide and level. Crossing the Ra-lung La or Ka-ropass by an easy ascent, they reached Dza-ra on the 30th. To the north of the last named pass lies a very high peak near the base of .which is a small glacier. On the 31st, the explorer reached Nang-kar-tse stage-house close to the Yam-droktso or Palti lake. This lake was the largest he had seen. It was like a horse-shoe in form and almost encircled a small hill on which was a large temple dedicated to Dorje Phamo. A number of villages were situated on the hill. The lake had a great number of fish, not longer than a

...hasa. They were caught by boring holes

...er, travelling along the northern shore of
...rty reached Pe-de (fort) stage-house and
... Kam-pa pass, it arrived at Kam-pa-par-
...s is on the boundary of the Tsang and U
... province. On the 3rd, a mile from the
...t to the right bank of the Tsang-po
...h was crossed at Chak-sam (iron bridge at
...ridge and arrived at Chu-shul (fort) stage-
...e bridge is about 100 paces. On the 4th,
...nk of the Kyi Chu, was reached. The river

...ember, 1878, the explorer with his party
...he replenished his stock of merchandise.

...sa from the west along the Dre-phung road,
...to the left (north) and Chiakporito the right
...nost prominent objects, raised especially in
...above the foliage of moderate-sized walnut,
...ther trees.

...the Kyi Chu river flanks the city, running past
...a deep and moderately rapid stream, some
...banks gradually sloping down to the water's
...s situated in the Kyi Chu valley, rising some
...Dre-phung road. Chiakpori, with its three
...nedical school for young Dabas who evinced
predilection for drugs, imported or otherwise, and prepared
according to the recipes obtained from Hindustan. The Po-ta-la
presented an enormous pile of lofty buildings, covering a rectangle
about 400 yards in length and some 200 yards in width,
surmounted at intervals by five gilded gebis.

Gebis are erected on the roof of buildings which contain
images for worship and outwardly serve to indicate the presence
of the latter. A gebi is shaped like a square tent with a single pole,
its sloping sides first curve gracefully inwards and then widen

towards the base) which varies in length upto some thirty feet; the corners of the square are ornamented, each with the figure of a tiger. The frame for a gabi is made of wood which is covered with metal plates and these- all coated with gold; each structure is surmounted by a golden *kalas* which, aparkling in the sunlight, presents a dazzling and gorgeous spectacle, visible for miles around.

The celebrated po-ta-la was not only the residence of the great Lamas (Da Lamas) or Chief Priests of the Buddhists spread over Great Tibet and Mongolia but it contained the remains of all the former Da Lamas. These were buried in coffins within the buildings of Po-ta-la and the sites were marked by structures called *kulungs*. The buildings formed one solid block, rising to various heighis at different places, representing sometimes as many as seven storeys or floors. They con-tained various images which need not bealluded to here, excepting the monster image of god Jamba. This image was of prodigious dimensions; the figure is internally of clay and is well gilded externally. It is seated on a platform on the ground floor and its body, passing successively through the second and third floors, terminates in a jewelled and capped monster-head. In all, the figure and the platform are seventy or eighty feet high.

Buddhism is the religion of the countfy. Now the essential feature in Tibetan worship is the performance of circuits around an image. Not peculiar to Tibet only, such circumambulation is also required in parts of India. This is also recognised in the use of the prayer-wheel (or khorlo or mani or thuge Chomo) by which the transcribed prayers are made to circumgyrate but the circuit may obviously be made in two directions, i.e., clock-wise which is a rule with the majority who are known as Nangbas, or anti-clock-w)se which is the practice of a small sect of Tibetans called Baimbus (Pembos). The Nangbas have sub-divisions named Ningma, Sakia, Cuba and Gilukpa. Applying the required process to the case of the monster image of Jamba, it will be seen that the pilgrim has to perform three different series of circumambulations on as many floors, the first around the god's legs, next round his chest and lastly around his head.

were uncommonly sociable and jovial. They drank a fermented liquor. In fact, from childhood one and all drank but they were rarely drunk. The priests were no exceptions except that they were not to drink within a gompa, at leaste not openly. Social gatherings were enlivened by musical performances on the flute and a kind of guitar with bell accompaniment. Men and women danced together to the tune of music, standing in rows on planks which actes as sounding boards, and stamping them in unison, now in quick, now in slow measure. On great occasions, the *ache lhamo* were called in and the audience entertained to a theatrical performance. Finally in the summer months, when the air was mellow and the evenings lengthened, the people picnicked undertrees the whole day long.

Notwithstanding their social tendencies, the citizens managed to pick up a comfortable living, chiefly by trade, and observed the require-ments which residence in the holy city imposed, :Lhasa was circled by a broad and well-made road which defined the limits within which all those who wished to make sure of a happy state resided. This road was called the: Ling Khor. Within its limits, no blood was shedand so the butchers and slaughter houses were placed without it. The day was recognised begun when a loud report, as if from: a cannon, issued from the vicinity of the *Amban's* residence. This happened about 4 a.m. and again at 9 or 10 p.m. After the morning report, the people were to be seen in dense crowds on the Ling Khor, all moving in oine and the same clock-wise direction as laid down by their religion. A similar round was made by the devout in the eveing, to say nothing of smaller circuits around Jhio (called Bar Khor) and other shrines. This was imperative at least for the common people. As to the great and wealthy, they urged that their presence would only interfere with the piety of the people. So they engaged substitutes who were, however, rigorously required to circumambulate for their masters. But whether done in person or by proxy, a careful reckoning was kept ofthe number of rounds performed and the excessively devoted persons made the circuit by the method of successive prostrations full length on the road, each prostration beginning where the preceding one ended, called *kiang khor*.

The Government of Tibet consisted of Dalai Lama, one *gyalbo* wo was also a Lama, four secretaries and five counsellors. The Dalai Lama was the chief ruler in Tibet and was consulted in cases of emergency. He was the last resort of appeal and his decision was invariably unquestioned. The *gyalbo* was his Prime Minister and next to him in rank. His soul is also supposed to transmigrate into another body. There were two *ambans*, who were representatives of the Chinese Government. These *ambans* were originally established in Lhasa with the professed object of protecting the Da Lama who however found their presence embarassing and of a nature that he could dispense with. Besides these dignitaries, there was an officer or captain from Nepal. His importance however was evidently only secondary in degree, and in fact the distinction of riding in a *palki* (palanquin) was an honour enjoyed only by the Da Lama, his *Gyalbo* and the two *Ambans* who were not permitted to travel by any other means whatever.

During his stay at Lhasa, the explorer employed himself in learning the Mongolian language. Morever, during June and July of 1879, he took a series of air thermometer observations.

Lhasa • Mongolia

After spending some time in Lhasa, waiting for a caravan to start for Mongolia, the explorer heard that one was about to leave. He went at once to the *Gorpon* or *sardar* of the caravan and enquired about the date of departure but could obtain no definite answer beyond that the caravan might start about the month of February. He pressed the leader to fix the date but failed. "My long experience has taught me", he said, "that when the date is fixed, the robbers" spies who are here communicate it to their masters and then the caravans never arrive safely at their destinations." In November, the caravan leader sent for the other traders and the explorer and begged them to excuse him from going to Mongolia on account of his being under a heavy debt of 50 *tamimas* or *kurs* (one *kurs*=156 rupees in Indian coin) which he must liquidate before leaving the city. This was very discouraging, as they had no other experienced man to lead them. As last the traders and the explorer agreed to subscribe and pay off his debt. After four months' further delay, he gave up the idea of conducting the caravan and the explorer had no alternative but to wait for another.

In August, one arrived from Mongolia and half of it was to return Immediately. Pundit Kishen Singh approached the leader and, with his party of six, left Lhasa on the 17th September, 1879 in the company of a *kafila* which consisted of 105 souls, sixty of whom were Mongols who in a few instances were accompanied by their wives. The remainder were Tibetans (or Bodpas). The Mongolians were all mounted without exception and besides that, each person led a horse laden with his property. In fact Mongolians of either sex, with the command of numerous horses in their own country, are so accustomed to riding that they wonder and laugh at pedestrians. Even their shepherds ride round their flocks, In a word, no Mongolian will walk on any occasion when he can contrive to ride. The Tibetan members of the *kafila* mostly walked, leading their laden horses. All were armed with spears, matchlocks and swords, a custom so universal in Tibet as well as Mongolia that even the monasteries had adopted it recently. In the present case the necessity of weapons was all the greater for *kafilas* were special objects of plunder for the bands of mounted robbers who roamed over large tracts of the country and appeared suddenly when least expected. Hence the dominant thought which governed all procedure in a *kafila* was how to escape being plundered. To this end, the present assemblage of travellers proceeded cautiously, being proceeded and followed some two or three miles by a couple of horsemen from their party to give warning of approaching danger. Otherwise, they exactly followed the advice of their Mongolian guides to whom experience had brought much wariness as well as considerable skill in detection and recognition of foot-prints on the ground.

Ordinarily, camp was struck about sunrise and the travellers proceeded on their journey, keeping close order. A helpless individual who may not be able to keep up with the party on account of illness was left to his fate, with some food and water placed near him. Generally he was never heard of again. A brief halt was made for tea at 10 a.m. after which the much was continued up to between 2 and 4 p.m, when camp was formed for the night. The Mongolians and the Tibetam occupied either flank with the horses between them. The forelegs of the horses were also generally hobbled with iron-hinged fetters, rendering locomotion for the time being impossible. Grass was always abundant and the horses fed within the limits of their tether. While some set up tents, others collected the dung of beasts, generally plentiful ind, the sole fuel procurable. A pair of bellows is an essential article in every Tibetan family, whether resident or travelling, for without its help the dung could not be ignited.

For food, they mixed a hasty dish of sattu as a preliminary to the chief meal of the day. *Sattu* was consumed in the form of a paste made :with water or tea. Tea was prepared by thoroughly boiling powdered brick tea and adding to the strained decoction, butter and salt. It was served in small cups, chiefly wooden, one of which every individual carried day and night on his person. There is no occasion to convert butter into *ghee* in a country so cold. Butter is sold sewn up in leather balls of various weights upto some 30 *seers*. The principal item of food at dinner consisted of meat boiled in water and eaten by itself without bread. Infact, flour was scarce and bread was, therefore, regarded as a luxury. The soup was thickned with a few pinches of flour and plenty of *chura* which was abundant all over the country and was in daily use by rich and poor alike. *Chura* is the most valuable article of common consumption in all Tibet and Mongplia and one of the largest products of these countries where milk is plentiful. It is made by boiling down butter milk to thick paste and drying the latter. In value, *chura* is about twice as expensive as corn flour. Excepting a few wild roots, no vegetable was procurable. After closing the business of the day, tobacco was smoked in pipes, the bowls and mouthpieces of which were made of metal and the stems of wood. Singing or music or other needless noise was objected to, as it might attract undesirable attention. After sending out a guard of two Tibetans and as many Mongols, the travellers fell into well-earned sleep.

On the route to Mongolia

Three quarters of a mile from Ramoche Jhio temple in Lhasa is a garden named Dab-chilinga and the same distance further and to the east of the road is a parade ground named Dabchi where the Tibetan troops displayed their military skill twice a year. A mile eastward from Dabchi is Chiangro village (10 houses). At a distance of one mite from the parade ground is Sera Gompa, containing about 5,500 monks for whom food was provided by the Lhasa Government. Two mites and fifty paces east is Parisiga, a hamlet of five houses, and on a spur of the Pen-po-go mountain, about 500 paces to the west, is Keclrang Gomapa. Then they passed Hungusiga village (4 houses), a *romkang* or cemetery where the Mohammedans of Lhasa bury their dead, Khutho Gompa which is situated on a spur of the Pen-po-go mountain and Gakenska Chenkang, a temple dedicated to one of the passionate and vindictive gods. Continuing their journey for about 1-1/2 miles, the *kafila* reached Lingba Dzong, a ruined fort, when they stopped for the night. The road was very good for four miles. The remaining part of it was stony and rugged but having an easy gradient. Forage was abundant.

The next day, after a difficult ascent of about two miles by a rough and stony road, they reached the Pen-po-go pass (16,320 feet). No trees were visible but a small kind of grass covered the whole range. From the pass, the descent is precipitous for about 2-1/2 miles. Further down, they reached Baya, a small village. On the way, they found two monasteries, namely Langta Gompa and Nalenda Gompa. Then the road crossed the Pembu Chu (Pen-yu-ne) stream, one and a half feet deep fifteen paces broad. The kafila halted at Debungsiga or Nalmar village of twenty houses. It lay in the Pen-po patti (sub division). This locality was well-cultivated. The fields were watered by irrigation cuts led down from the Pembu Chu and other streams.

About 3-1/4 miles from Debungsiaga was a fort called Lundub Dzong with fifty houses around it. Two *Jongpons* who resided in the fort had charge of the Pen-po *patti*, extending from Pen-po-go to the Cha pass. The caravan crossed the Cha pass. About

4-3/4 miles from the pass was a camping gorund where they halted for the night of the 19th September. Near this place is a large gompa called Talung Gompa or Jang Talung where the well known Lama named Ma Ring-bo-che resided with about 300 Dabas. Grass and fuel were abundant. The road was stony.

On the 20th September, after crossing the Talung Chu, three feet deep and thirty five paces wide, which joined the Kyi Chu, the caravan reached Phondu fort, having fifty houses, at the confluence of the Rongi, Migi and the Talung Chu. Further up, they reached Chamchunang, a deserted village on the right bank of the Migi river. The Talung district extended from the Cha pass to Phondu fort. The tract of land, which lay to the left of the Migi river in the south-east of the road and between the Pondu fort and Chamchunang was called the Phondu district.

On the 21st September, the caravan arrived at Chiomo Lhakang (50 houses) with a small tample on the bank of the Migi river. Further still is Monio pass (14,960 feet). This pass has an easy ascent and very gentle descent. It formed the northern boundary of the Reting district which extended to Chiomo Lhakang southwards. About half a mile further, they passed the night at Lani *ta-sam,* a halting place. At this place, there were fifty tents occupied by members of a nomadic tribe. At the time of the arrival of the caravan, there was fall of snow abnout a foot deep.

Upto Chiomo Lhakang, it was a succession of ascents and descents between precipitous hills. The passage was so narrow at places as to admit only a single line of horses. The people lived in houses.

From Chiomo Lhakang a change of aspect commences and is fufly established at Lani pass in the Dam district. The traveller has now mounted the Chang-tang (Chang-thang), a tract so peculiar as to deserve some special notice.

The Chang-tang area

The Chang-tang is a vast and marvellous expanse of high undulating land of which, for various reasons, very little was known. But Kishen Singh gained considerable valuable information. This high land, it will be seen, is only some 100 miles broad to the west near Skardo. It is widest on the meridian of 86^0 where it is some 500 miles across and to the east it ends in an inclined width of some 350 miles from where it slopes further eastwards, rapidly losing its characteristics and merging into the cultivated lands of China. Its length is about 1,500 miles, and in area it is some 4,80,000 square miles. The western and southern edges are fairly well known from Skardo to Niamcho, not so the region eastwards upto Namohon and its northern edge. The strip of Changtang falling in the explorer's present travels lay between Lani pass and Niamcho on the south and was bounded on the north by the Kuen Lun range (Angir-takhchia to Namohon) so named by Prejevalsky, Russian explorer and also independently recognised by the Pundit as probably the Kuen Lun he crossed when going to Yarkand. This, however, is by no means AK's first introduction to the Chang-tang.

This enormous tract of high tableland is believed to be generally some 15 or 16 thousand feet above the sea level, rising to its maximum somewhere in the vicinity of the Manasarowar lake. In a word, it stands above the perpetual snow line in Europe and hence this expanse of land, which otehrwise would be invaluable, is utterly unifit for cultivation. It is similar in character throughout and presents a succession of easy undulations, wellcovered with earth and almost free from stone. The knolls in places from ridges which sometimes carry high and snowclad heads but invariably the inclines are gentle and there are no precipices; water is plentful and in places there are even large and handsome lakes, as the Manasarowar, Tengri Nor, etc. Further, the whole Chang-tang is coated by a short succulent grass which from May to August covers the undulations with the softest of green carpets, expanding far away and visible for even fifty or sixty miles in the clear crisp atmosphere. But besides grass nothing else will grow on this high land. There is no wood or shrub of any kind for fuel. The produce of the Chang-tang is solely suited for graminivorous animals, such as wild yaks, goats, sheep and deer which roamed about in wild state. The weaker of these animals provide food for the wolf, jackals and *yi* (a large wild cat). The grass bears seed and is probably propagated chiefly by that means, but other seeds as of wheat and barley, though they germinate and produce fodder for cattle, yield only seedless ears and hence no food for man.

The northern portion of the Chang-tang is wholly unoccupied by man, being far too distant from lands where corn or other products necessary for human life are produced in sufficient quantities to supper its wants. It is however overrun by enormous herds of wild animals, chiefly graminivorous. This uninhabited belt borders other-belts on both north and south which are dotted more or less by nomadic camps. The belt to the south is the continuation of the Chang-tang and is peeled by Tibetans who live invariably in rectangular shaped tents, black in colour, made from the hair of the yak. The northern tract is beyond and below the Chang-tang and consists of sandy wastes, not frequently diversified by areas, which are peopled by Mongolians living in round white tents made of felt. Thus the inhabited belt of Chang-tang lies between the white-tented Mongolian nomads to the north on the sandy lands and the black-tented Tibetan nomads to the south on the continuation of the Chang-tang.

The Dokpa Tribe

Beyond the common fact of residence in tents and similarity in features and religion, there are wide differences between the white and black-tent nomads. The Mongolian is peaceable and generous, little desirous of change and anxious only to be left to his own devices. His land produces both corn and a variety of animals and with these he is content and happy. Not so the Tibetan nomads whose necessities alone tend to acquisitiveness. Unable to grow corn on their high land, they have to barter it with other articles from their southern neighbours. These black-tent nomads are called Dokpas. Throughout the considerable length of their country, they resemble one another closely. They all dress and aim alike and have similar occupation and habits. And in fact clans now in the vicinity of the Manasarowar lake, where they are less lawless than elsewhere, claim that their ancestors migrated from Chiamo-Golok, some 1,000 miles away to the east. Apart from the unavoidable association with others, they keep chiefly to their own clans. Most probably these highlanders have maintained their semi-isolation, the primitive manners and customs of their progenitors for many centuries past. To them might is always right but they accept the right of a fellow clansman to his property and his right to pursue his own business in a manner lawful to him. They roam in mounted bands far and wide in search of plunder.

Notwithstanding their predatory habits, it must be said that they all acknowledge the Da Lama as their spiritual head and perform periodical pilgrimage to Lhasa in order to present themselves with due reverence before their high priest. But on these, as on all other occasions, they invariably keep an eye open to business proper, and the devotional nature of an errand is not permitted to interfere with convenient opportunities for plundering their neighbours. So the Dokpas come to be trusted by none, unless perhaps by their own clansmen.

At least a few words of special notice are also due to the vast number of wild animals abounding mostly in the large uninhabited tract of the Chang-tang. They suffer diminution from only one cause and that is the occasional extreme severity of winter, when, deprived of grass, they die inthousands as their skeletons testify. But apart from tlis, tliy lead the most peaceful of lives, multiplying without hinderance, for enemies in the shape of sportsmen were practically absent. These wild animals, otherwise useless, meet one essential need. There dung (specially of the yak) provides excellent and abundant fuel without which no traveller could cook lus food consisting entirely of flesh and live to cross the Chang-tang. As a rule, Tibetans never warm themselves by fire.

Tibetans trust to warm clothing and feeding with flesh for conservation of their body heat. In spite of the absence of all vegetables and even the smallest pretence of ablution, scurvy, leprosy and in fact all skin diseases were unknown. While ailments of any kind whatever were exceedingly rare, a bath would be about the most disagreeable infliction that could possibly be imposed on a Dokpa. Babies upto the age of two or three months were occasionally washed before being coated with butter. As for Dokpa women, nobody without risking pretensions to good manners and even respectability could commit the indiscretion of washing her face and in fact any offence of the kind would certainly justify even her friends considering her as an exceedingly fast and probably not quite a proper person. Though very healthy, the Dokpa ages young, losing his teeth and even eye-sight when perhaps only forty years old, nor does he live to a great age. It maybe due to the hard and-strenuous life and extremely cold climate of the table-land.

The vast numbers as well as the perfect unconcern of wild beasts soJmetimes proved very embarrassing to Kishen Singh on his return journey between Nomohon and Niamcho, the portion which travellers pass very rarely. Wild yaks were seen in such considerable herds that some three or four thousand beasts were visible at a short distance. At the same time, these handsome black brutes, without a single speck ofwhiteand with long hair trailing so low as to conceal their legs, looked impressive. Occasionally a solitary monster bull with wicked eyes and questionable intentions deliberately walked upto within only ten to twelve paces and inspected the explorers inquisitively, as if with a view to further proceedings, friendly or inimical. It was impossibfe not to regard these attentions with awe. The considerable physical power of the handsome, solid looking brute, with longhair nearly touching the ground, gave him the appearance of enormous girth with solid mass from hump to hoof. His jet black coat glistened in the sunshine and as his small reddish eyes seemed to dance with mischief, which the solid horns above were fully capable of accomplishing, he cocked his tail, whisking about its bushy, hairy pendents and pawing the ground vigorously and stood in doubt whether he should consider the travellers friends' foes or only curiosities. Thus situated, the explorers prudently steered their course as far from their visitor as circumstances permitted. A wild bull-yak, adds Kishen Singh, will probably weigh one and a half to two tons and his head and borns are full load for a strong man.

Returning now to the *kafila*. On the 22nd September, it reached Lani pass (15,750 feet) by an easy ascent of 2-1/4 miles. The Lani range comes from the east and far off in that direction are some high peaks covered with perpetual snow. A mile further is a Dam *chuchan* (a hot spring of the Dam district) in which inhabitants of the neighbourhood bathed at least twice a year. There were three square tanks, twenty one feet long and two feet deep, which were always full of water. The temperature of the water of these tanks was roughly estimated to be 120^0. In these tanks, the bathers remained immersed upto their necks until perspiration came from their foreheads. Then they left the tank and lay down wrapped up warmly for some minutes. After this, they drank some beer and ate food. About 1-1/4 miles from the hot springs was a halting place called Yar Khorchen, where there were three small houses, two for the shelter of travellers and one for *khorchen* (a large *khor* or *khorlo*).

A *khorlo* is a revolving drum-like cylinder made of paper covered with red parchment on which is written the sacred formula in large golden or red characters. The paper also has the same formula many times repeated and printed on it by characters engraved on wood. *Khorlos* are of various sizes. The smaller ones are covered with silver, copper or brass plates and are constantly held in the hand. The paper, is folded round a reel through which passes an iron pin. A thong is fastened to the lower end of the pin of large *khorlos* and is used for revolving them. It is believed by the people that constantly keeping the *khorlo* in motion purifies them from sin.

The Dam Velley

The Dam velley is about fifteen miles long and five miles broad and is watered by the Dam river, a tributary of the Rong. Three miles west of the halting place is a permanent house which belonged to Chigeb, the ruler or *lumbardar* of the Dam valley. There were some 200 tents of nomads whose occupation is the grazing of cattle consisting of ponies, yaks, goats, and sheep. Some of them are traders who bring *bul* (a kind of soda) and salt from the Tengri Nor lake and exchange them for corn and cloth from Lhasa. In addition, their own valley furnished several other commodities for exchange, for instance, yaks, goats, sheep, ponies and butter.

This country is too cold for asses and hence neighter asses nor mules are generally found in thise parts, although in the immediate neighbourhood of Lhasa they are both in abundance. Some of the mules are very tall (about 14 hands) and are valued at 700 or 800 rupees. These nomads are Tibetans and they are very stout and warlike. The valley is noted for its pasturage.

The head Lama had about 300 mares, stabled under the chaiie of a *Chi Pon* (master of the stable). They are milked everyday in summer and a kind of fermented liquor is prepared after the Tibetan process of distillation for the use of the head Lama. It is the only liquor which he is allowed to take. About two days' journey from the valley is the Nam or Tengri Nor lake. Wild people were found scattered over the hifly regions and it was some ten days' journey to the north of the lake. The caravan halted two days at Yar Khorchen (14,460 feet).

On the 25th September, 1879, the caravan reached the Chiokche pass. The pass has a gentle ascent and similar descent on the other side. It forms the northern boundary of the Dam district. Four and three quarter miles further, they crossed the Lhai Chu, two feet deep and thirty paces wide. It issues from the Ninchin-thang-la range and falls, into the Migi river. Potamolam, one of the high peaks covered with per-petual snow is about twenty three miles south-east. They stopped for the night on the left bank of the Lhai Chu

On the 26th, the explorer and the caravan passed along a good road wtach was connected by an easy pass catted Shangshung. During the march, they passed some nomad tents at intervals and spent the mght at a grassy level piece of ground.

On the 27th, the party met the Yu stream which flows from the east and issues from a small lake. The united stream flows northwards and is called Nag Chu.

On the 28th, after an easy ascent, the caravan crossed the Khorchen pass over a spur from the range to the east. The pass forms the northern limit of the Shangshung district which is said to contain about 500 tents of nomad tribes. Then they crossed to the left bank of the Nag Chu and reached Mane Khorchen where they passed the mght. From this place, a direct road branches to Sining-fu or Siling, a large city of the Chinese Empire, situated about sixty miles to the east of the Koko Nor lake. They chose the circuitous road by Shiabden Gompa where they hoped to replenish their stock of provisions which was running short.

On the 29th, after marching 5-3/4 Illiles, the caravan reached Shiabden Gompa with about 100 Dabas. It was surrounded by some 150 houses and tents. There was a large house for the Jongpon. One and one quarter miles to the south was a group of hot spring within a circumference of about half a mile. The thermometer gave a temperature of $140°$ for one of the springs. Shiabden Gompa (14,930 feet) is in the Nag chu Kha district. Grass is abundant. The district contained some 3,000 tents of nomads. Some of the tribes were much addicted to robbery which they committed far off to the west. The climate is cold. Supplies were procurable.

Currency

Tibetan silver coins were current in all these districts. There were no gold or copper coins. The silver coins were of two kinds, one known as *chanja paulung* was an old coin, had no alloy in it and weighed a quarter of a tola (weight of an Indian rupee). The other coins were distinguished by the names of the rulers who issued them, had alloy in them and weighed half a *tola*. Both kinds of coins had the same value which was equivalent to six Indian *annas*. They bore the common name of *tanka*. For smaller change, coins were cut into pieces. The Indian rupee was also current. They spent three nights at Shiabden Gompa.

On the 2nd October, after marching 86 miles, they reached Thaigar La (pass) by an easy ascent. Two miles off the pass is a lake named Mora, two miles long and 1-1/2 broad and around it were a number of nomad encampments. Eastward of the lake, a road ran to Ta-chien-lu, a great tea market. The party camped for the night at a short distance beyond the pass.

On the 3rd, after marching 31 miles, Kishen Singh and party reached the direct road from Mane Khorchen. Here they heard that a gang of mounted robbers from the Jama district, about 300 in number, was returning by the road laden with the booty obtained from the Tengri Nor district. It consisted of about 100 hill ponies, 300 yaks and 5,000 goats and sheep. To escape an attack, they diverged again towards the north-west and after marching about two miles reached the place where the ponies belonging to the Mongolian caravan, with which the exploit was travelling, had been left behind for pasturage when going down to Lhasa and the caravan waited there till the gang passed. At 4 p.m., they started and proceeded north-east for about 2-1/2 miles, again struck the direct road and halted at the base of a mountain. About forty miles to the north is Sutodamparabga, a snowy peak.

On the 4th, the explorer and the caravan reached the Tatsang pass by an easy ascent. This pass is on the boundary between the districts of Nag Chu Kha and Jama. The latter contained about 1,500 tents. This district was governed by two *Ambans* who resided at Sining Fu. After crossing two small streams, they reached Khamlung encamping ground (15,050 feet) where there were about fifty tents and here they remained for the night.

On the 5th, after an easy ascent for a mile, the explorer and the caravan crossed the Khamiung range. To the north of the range lies the Ata district, containing about 500 tents. They left the direct road, as it was not safe owing to its being much infested by robbers. They kept the same northern route which was seldom used by travellers. Two miles to the east is a lake about eight miles in circumference. They remained for the night at the camping ground named Giaro (14,540 feet) on the left bank of the Saung Chu in Yagra district.

On the 6th, after travelling about eight miles, the party arrived at the bank of the Yagra Chu (Tang) river, which issues from the Tangla range and flowing to the south falls into the Saung Chu.

The road from the Dam district to this place was good and

wide but further up it was rugged and stony and passed through a narrow valley between two long spurs of the Tangla range. Three and a half miles further, they reached Yagratodh encamping ground (14,950 feet), with some eighty tents occupied by the nomads, where they stopped for the night.

On the 7th, crossing the Yagra Chu to the left bank, the Pundit saw three snowy peaks to the north-west. The caravan re-crossed the same stream. Further, they passed a snowy peak to their right. More snowy peaks were visible in the north-east. They stopped at a camping ground. Snow fell during the night.

Tang pass (16,380 feet) was covered with two feet of snow which fell on the preceding night. Tangla is a long range of mountains running from the west, possessing several snow peaks and spurs. It is the northern boundary of the Yagla district which contained about 1,000 teats. About a hundred 'miles to the west of the pass is the Amdo district which is sparsely inhabited by nomads. Beyond it to the north and west, the only inhabitants were of a backward race. They clothed themselves inskins of animals and dwelt in small tents also made of skins. Some of them possessed guns obtained from Tibetans by bartering hides, they could manufacture their own ammunition. They used these gam for killing wild animals whose flesh they roasted and ate. They declined to eat vegetable food, even when offered, as they said it made then ill.

The inhabitants of the country between the Dam and Yagra districts live chiefly on meat and *sattu*. No tree grows in these districts. Dry dung of both the wild and domesticated yaks is used for fuel. Grass is abundant. The country to the north of the pass was uninhabited even by nomads.

Proceeding for 3-3/4 miles by awide and level road along the left bank of the river, the explorer and the caravan reached Kentinsiring, a halting place.

There wild animals were numerous, for instance *dong* (yak), cho (deer), goa (a species of antelope resembling the chamois), *na* (goat), *nhen* (mountain sheep), *chianku* (wolf), *haze* (a kind of fox), *yi* (cat), *kiang* (ass), *chipi* (marmot), *rigong* (rabbit), *abra* (rat without a tail) and *domo* (brown bear). During winter, the chipi does not come out of its den and is believed by the Tibetans to sleep. It yields a large quantity of fat which is used as an ointment for gout. One species of *domo* called *mide* has feet resembling those of a man and is very savage. It often walks erect and attacks any human being it sees.

During the night, three feet of snow fell. The members of the caravan had much reason to fear robbers and they, therefore, formed themselves into groups, each consisting often men to be on guard at night.

On the 9th, proceeding for six miles, the caravan met five mounted robbers. On being questioned, they said that they were residents of the Yagra district. They followed the caravan for two marches, intending to carry off their beasts of burden, but were unsuccessful as they were given no opportunity.

About twenty-five miles from the last halting place, the explorer saw a large lake about seven miles in circumference. Five and a half miles further away, they crossed a pass by an easy ascent and descending from there at an easy gradient for 2-1/2 miles, they reached Yakinhap chiga, a halting place where they rested for the night.

On the 10th October, 1879, on the way, they saw two snowy peaks to the north-west; two more snowy peaks were visible in the north-east. They passed the night at a halting place called Ataghapchiga (15,080 feet).

On the 11th, after marching seven miles, they crossed a pass with a slight ascent. Seventeen miles beyond the pass, there is a camping ground called Marusen Khua on the bank of the Maurus (Di Chu or Thoktho) river (14,230 feet), close to a small freshwater lake. They halted there at night. There was no trace of road beyond Ataghapchiga and they were guided by some Mongolians in their caravan who recognised the route with the aid of certain hill peaks.

On the 12th, they arrived at the right bank of the Maurus river. It is supposed to issue from the Tengri Nor lake and to water Chinese territory. It flows here in seven channels, each about forty paces wide, the entire breadth of the river including the islands being 800 paces and the maximum depth three feet. The banks of the channels are boggy. One of the horses sank upto its belly but they succeeded in extricating it.

A stream running from the north-west joins the Maurus two mites to the south-west of the route. Small bushes called by the Tibetans taru. about a foot high, were found growing along the banks of the river. These bushes were thorny and bore a small yellowish round fruit which had an acidic taste and was pickled. The height of the bank of the river is 14,660 feet at this place. Four and three quarter miles further is a pass having a slight ascent. About thirteen miles from the pass is a halting place, called Bukhmangna, a little below the top of another pass with less height. From the left bank of the river to Bukhmangna, they had no fresh water. Wherever water was found, it was brackish, and that of a small stream which crossed the road had also the same taste. The caravan stopped at the pass for the night. The general character of the pass and the neighbouring plains is that they are bare of trees, although covered with grass and verdure.

On the 13th, after proceeding ten miles; Kishen Singh and the caravan crossed a larger river called Ulangmiris (Namchu-thai Ulangmiri or Chu Mar). Five miles from that place is Kangchinar camping ground. Here they found several pools of fresh sweet water. The road was good and lay along the wide plain between two ranges of mountains, some ten miles distant on either side.

On the 14th, 10-1/4 miles from the camping ground the caravan came to cha cku (salt water stream) coming from the north-west and flowing to the south-east. Then they crossed another cha chu, one foot deep and twenty paces wide flowing from the left, which issues from the Dungbura range. From these, the snowy peak was visible at a distance of seventeen miles to the south-east. Recrossing the same stream 4-1/2 miles further on, they reached Dung-bura encamping ground. Dung means shell and bura, blowing. This place is so called as it is said that when one of the Grand Lamas went to see the Emperor of China, he came down to welcome him here and below the shell. One foot of snow fell here. The road was good as on the last stage.

On the 15th October, 1879, after crossing Dungbura Kuthul (pass), the caravan halted for two nights at Dungbura Namado encamping ground on account of a fall of snow. Namado in the Mongolian language means the other side and Chamado, this side.

On the 17th, the day's march was almost entirely over snow. They stopped near pools of fresh water. Next day they regained the right route which they had missed owing to its being hidden beneath snow. The water of most of the streams crossed on the way was brackish. They halted at the base of Koko-shili range.

On the 19th, after crossing Koko-shili Kuthul (pass), the caravan reached the Koko-shili encamping ground (13,430 feet). They were obliged to remain there for two nights due to snowfall. The beasts of burden of the explorer suffered badly from the snow and were unfit to proceed with the caravan in the morning. Out of the three ponies winch had fallen ill, one died but the other two recovered. As there was no fear of being molested by robbers, the explorer and his party of six were left behind to follow when they could.

On the 21st, Kishen Singh reached a small half-frozen lake of fresh water where he passed the night. He easily tracked the caravan by the marks of the horses' hoofs on the snow.

On the 22nd, the Pundit and his party came to a small lake where they met a Mongolian caravan going to Lhasa. It was composed of about 150 men and women, 80 camels and 100 ponies. When asked if they had seen their caravan, they at first answered in the negative but afterwards acknowledged having observed far off along the opposite bank of the Ma Chu river, a long line of what they supposed to be wild animals which they now agreed must have been the caravan. As a rule, the members of caravans are very considerate towards each other. They never fail to aid any person or persons whom they find separated from or deserted by their caravan. They treated the explorer very kindly and, unsolicited, offered them a large quantity of provisions from which he took five seers of sattu. At noon they reached the right bank of the Ma Chu or Chu Mar river. They searched for a ferry but in vain. They had to cut a way through the ice from one bank to another because the half frozen river was not hard enough to bear either baggage animal or man. They however lost a pony and a mule which stuck in the bog and which they could not extricate. His companion, Chhumbel, lost his toe while crossing the river. This made their progress very slow. fn the darkness, they could not find any fuel and passed the night without food. To recoup themselves, they halted on the following day. The height of the right bank is 14,040 feet and that of the left 14,050 feet. The entire breadth of the river is 700 paces. It is two feet deep and is divided, into five channels. It is said to flow into the Chinese Empire.

On the 24th October, 1879, after crossing the Angirtakchia stream which joins the Ma Chu river, the explorer halted at Mugzisolma. Here he saw tracks of their caravan. On the 25th, he reached Angirtakchia camping ground. From the Dam district to this place, grass and dry yak-dung which are so necessary for the travellers were abundant. Wild animals were numerous. The route, generally speaking, was good.

On the 26th, he crossed the Angirtakchia Kuthul pass. Angirtakchia is probably the same range as is called Kuen Lun, and here and there had peaks covered with snow. The explorer halted near the turn of a stream. Snow fell in the afternoon. Scarcity of grass, which was covered with snow, caused the death of two of his animals. That day they had a rugged, stony and narrow road.

On the 27th, he crossed the steep Naichi Kuthul pass. Naichi is a small range which shoots off from the long range of Angirtakchia. At Arnthun camping ground at the base of the pass there was a camp of Mongolian nomads. They encamp here for a portion of the year to pasture their flocks and herds. The explorer returned with his poor animals to bring the baggage which had been left at the last stage due to loss of their beasts of burden and fortunately found the same Mongolian caravan which they had met on its way to Lhasa. It appeared that the caravan had returned from the Koko-shili camping ground as it could not proceed to Lhasa on account of snow. The explorer stopped at Amthun for a night. This was the first stage where they found firewood obtained from thorny trees, about six feet high. Grass was abundant. From Lhasa upto this place, their direction had in general been northerly but henceforth they proceeded eastward.

The Mongols

On the 28th October, 1879, the explorer reached Naichi, a nomad camp often tents. From Yagra to Naichi, the country is quite inhabited. Mongolian tents are made in a curious manner. When the tent is pitched, it bears a resemblance to a dome; it is round at the base. The wooden framework, when set up, presents a lattice-like appearance. For the sake of convenience in packing and carriage, it is divided into five, seven or nine pieces, according to the size of the tent. Each piece when rolled up looks like a bundle of sticks. The top piece has an opening of a coarse woollen cloth called *chhingba* or *phingba* bound round with a long rope which keeps it tight. They do not divide the tent into compartments. It has only one opening for ingress and egress which is closed by a kind of rough door made of planks fastened together by wooden pins. They cook inside. A tent about twelve yards in circumferance can be made for twelve rupees.

The general direction of the Naichi valley, which is a subdivision of the Taichinar district, is from west to east. The level portion is about fifty miles long and with an average breadth of three miles. It is bounded on every side by low mountains, on which no snow was visible, and even when snow falls, it quickly melts away. The valley is intersected length-ways by the Naichi Gol (river) which receives only a few tributaries from the mountains but is mostly fed by numerous springs of fresh water along its banks. The ground is generally smooth, being furrowed here and there by the beds of dry mountain torrents. The valley is covered with rich pasturage which affords sustenance to large herds of ponies, *dumba* sheep with thick tails, camels (Bactrian) and goats. At the eastern end of the valley, the river widens to thrice its previous breadth.

The valley was occupied by nomads who dwelt in tents, ten in number, each containing about six souls. They shifted their camp from place to place along the whole valley for convenience of pasturage. Their diet chiefly consisted of milk and boiled flesh.

Grain formed only an in-considerable portion of their food and was imported,from the Korluk district about one hundred miles to the north. The people like the rest of the Mongolians were hospitable. They milked their mares. This, when rendered acidic by the addition of sour milk, is called *cheka* and a kind of spirit distilled from it is called *arki*. Yaks are rare.

The Mongolians are well-built and stout and are peace-loving. Their marriage customs are very simple. A man courts his intended bride for two years after which the parents construct a new tent for them and provide a feast for their community. After feasting and dancing, the marriage ceremony is considered to be complete.

The explorer stopped at Naichi for five days. There he overtook his own caravan but it started before he was ready to accompany it. The Mongolian caravans intended to remain there till the snow cleared off. The height of the camp was 12,010 feet.

Kishen Singh replenished his stock of provisions, purchased more beasts of burden and on the 3rd November, 1879, resumed the Journey. On the 4th, he crossed to the left bank of the Naichi Gol (river) which is forty paces wide and two feet deep and has a fast current. Two and a half miles further on, he reached Thaglaga, an encamping ground of the nomads, with a wide level plain, where he halted for the night. These encamping places are distinguished by circular raised platforms over which the tents are pitched and on which fires are lighted in iron grates. Fuel and grass are in abundance. On the 6th, he reached Shiarthoge (10,370 feet), an encamping place.

On the 7th, after crossing the steep ascent of Khokhotham, he encamped at Saikhanthoke, a nomad camp. On the 8th, after crossing streams, he halted at Gile, an encamping ground. Firewood was found but no grass. On the 9th, his route lay through a valley but further on he passed a sandy plain. He encamped for the night on the right bank of the Naichi Gol (river) where there was no grass and his beasts of burden fared worse than in the previous stage.

On the 10th November, 1879, after travelling 6-1/2 miles,

he entered a tract where grass and fuel were abundant. Five miles from there was a nomad camp, called Goimo, situated in a densely wooded forest, six miles broad and about 100 miles long. The forest trees, named by the Mongolians as *humbu, harmo* and *chhak,* are about six or seven feet high. The *harmo* bears a kind of black or red fruit, in flavour like the raisin, which is gathered in November for future use and for merchandise. Tall grass occupied nearly the whole forest. Some fifty tents were scattered here and there. Nomads, generally speaking are very stout and their lips have a yellowish colour. Their wealth consists of live stock, such as sheep (the species which has a thick tail), goats, camels (Bactrian), ponies and Mongolian kine. The last are like the hill cows of Hindustan but are covered with somewhat longer hair, generally of a greyish colour. The principal articles of diet are boiled flesh, milk, butter and *sattu;* the last was brought from Korluk. Brick tea is in general use in Mongolia. The climate is mild and very salubrious. During the rainy season, the soil is moist and a kind of white saline incrustation spreads over the trunks of trees from which after a time they die. In that season, insects such as gnats are very troublesome.

From the point from where Pundit Kishen Singh entered the grassy tract, his route changed to an easterly direction. The Naichi Gol (river) flowed into a lake, called Hara Nor (Daolastan lake) which is about sixty miles in circumference and has no outlet. The water of the lake is brackish. About 100 miles to the north-west is Hazir, the residence of the *Jhasa* (Chief) of the Taichinar district. Hazir contained about 500 tents and some of the residents were very wealthy, having as many as 500 ponies and 5000 goats and sheep. Naqmads of the Taichinar district are met with up to about 150 miles to the west of Golmo but from there is a dreary uninhabited plain which extends about 150 miles. The Tanthus (men with white turbans), probably the inhabitants of the east of Khotan are said to live on the other side of the plain. They sometimes cross it in their hunting excursions and take shelter in the tents of the nomads. Some six years ago, seven mounted Tanthus are said to have taken shelter in the tents. After some days, when they had obtained full information respecting the movable property, they butchered the occupants one night and absconded with their wealth. Since then, the Mongol nomads stopped living on the border of the uniinhabited plain.

Mongolian women, generally speaking, wear no ornaments. Their dress is a kind of long loose garment which hangs to the ankles. The clothes of men and women are made of woollen skin of wild animals, Women generally occupy themselves in making clothes for their husbands and children. The men trade with Lhasa and China.

Their manner of salutation is peculiar. They repeat the words *amurbhaino* (safe and sound) and stretch out their open hands when they salute an equal or a stranger. When they salute a man of rank or a king, they first put their right hand on their forehead and then repeat *amur bhaino* and stretch their hands as before.

Kishen Singh found the nomads very hospitable. No sooner does a caravan approach them, than they crowd around it and civilly ask the questions: "Is your health good ?,, and (LIS your journey safe ?" Further, they invite the members of the caravan to lodge with them. They present their guests with tea, butter, milk, meat and a kind of fresh cake fried in oil which is brought all the way from China.

The explorer stopped at Goimo (8,790 feet) for ten days. A glass of his sextant had become loose and caused him much anxiety.

Let us now describe the natural features, climate and nature of the route followed from the Lani pass to the Golmo Camp. The caravan continued its course across that high land observing every precaution against robbers. The country up to the Tangla range, being occupied more or less by nomads, was easy to travel as the track was sufficiently worn at intervals and was readily recognisable. But north of the range, no track whatever was apparent and the Mongolian guides, frequently at a loss in which direction to proceed, mounted neighbouring heights in the hope of recognising some familiar landmarks, and otherwise shaped their course from one prominence to another. At times, travellers strayed considerably and, in some instances, starting from the Lob Nor, as they imagined, straight for Lhasa, have been known to arrive at the Manasarowar lake. It may be noted that at the Saung Chu, the direct road via Di Chu Rab Dun was rejected and a more westerly course adopted as less likely to be infested by robbers. Hence on crossing the Kuen Lun (Angirtakchia) range, the party descended on the northern side into Mongolia at Naichi. Here a complete change of aspect presented itself. The travellers now passed along an undulating valley, from one to three miles wide, bounded by hills described as sandy and conglomerating information, a description which applies generally to all the hills seen in Mongolia.

The most striking feature, however, now prevailing was that the surface of the land had a whitish coat, called bacha, decidedly saltish in taste and this was seen all over Mongolia. This saline powder was more-over easily raised and driven about in clouds by the wind which blows persistently and with considerable force. The travellers painfully realized the presence of salt in the dry air by cracks in their skin where it was not protected by clothing. In a word, the grassy carpet and clear crisp atmosphere of the Changtang was now replaced by an arid whitish waste while the air, generally laden with haze, sometimes become so dense in high wind that the view around hardly extended beyond a hundred paces. The salt even affects the scrub and trees which are now met with and in a peculiar manner it adheres to the bark. A white coat is formed around the roots and it gradually spreads upwards; eventually theplant is killed. But wherever water appears on the surface, vegetation abounds luxuri-antly. The grass in particular grows green and strong, rising to two or three feet in height. It is to this bountiful provision that the Mongolian owes his ability to rear large numbers of horses, camels, sheep, goats, and other animals for which the country is celebrated. The Mongolian camel is a valuable beast of burden in the winter months when it has a very bushy coat of long hair but the whole coat is shed in summer when the beast not only becomes quite slack but also loses its strength. and energy and is practically useless. Still the country as a whole (referring of course only to the area traversed) consists mostly of sandy wastes and is one where salt predominates and permeates so generally that the Mongolian finds it unnecessary to take any in his tea and hardly even with soup and meat while to cattle and sheep none whatever is given.

Passing onwards from Naichi, the *kafila* proceeded along the narrow valley already mentioned, until on arrival about Golmo they debouched into the verdant and wider valley in Taichinar. This valley has been traced from Shang Tsaidom (east) by Tengelik or Golmo from where it passes westwards, south of Hazir. Several rills of water run in its bed which is moreover green with grass and foliage and presents a valuable tract for pasturage. But between it and the northern hilly ranges, there runs a dry barren belt of earthy sand which contrasts the more prominently with its proximity to the green valley below.

Dispersion of the kafila began at Golmo. After suitable farewells and mutual offers of hospitality which occasion might hereafter permit, the company exchanged hearty congratulations on their cunningness and sagacity by which they had evaded their enemies, the robbers, and had escaped being plundered. Unfortunately, as will be seen hereafter, these congratulations proved premature to at least several of the travellers, including the explorer, who proceeded eastward to Tengelik.

Along the route followed in Mongolia, the population are all nomads, except in the town of Sachu where the people live in permanent houses. These nomads resemble the nomads of Northern Tibet in several respects, including general appearance. They are, however, more amiable and certainly more honest and in fact the Mongolian (Mongolu as he calls himself) ascribes his immunity to lightning to his own truthfulness and respect for his neighbour's property and points with an air of superiority to the robbers of Chiamo-Golok and Banakasum from whom he suffers grievously and who, he says, therefore suffer frequently from thunderbolts. As a matter of fact, the country of robbers is one of mist, cloud and lightning. The Mongolian is normally very friendly. An individual of either sex pairs with but one mate and even the Daba (or priest) who is also a nomad is socially permitted to adopt a consort, although the law forbids him a wife. He lives largely on flesh, tea and butter and is also not without corn of kinds. His fondness for milk is as conspicuous as in a calf and in order to indulge in this taste, he levies contributions on all animals alike, including sheep, camels and even mares. The mares are said to yield only a little milk each time it is drawn; the secretion, however, is rapidly restored. So the Mongolian repeats the milking process at short intervals. It must also be added that he is exceedingly partial to intoxicating liquors in which every one indulges, regardless of sex or age. But though he may get drunk, he seldom quarrels and even if his legs are no longer reliable, he can still sit on his horse and travel in safety, as he has done from the time when he was but a baby. He can read and write in characters of his own which differ from the Tibetan.

Like his southern brethren, the Mongolian owns spear, matchlock and sword but these are meant for defence only. As a true Buddhist he observes non-violence. He argues, says the explorer, "If I fight, I may be killed", and so at the first burst of the robbers' war cry, he vacates his tent almost with alacrity and betakes himself to safer localities, until his enemy has stolen his horses and departed. A Mongolian's riches consist mostly of horses, besides various other animals. It is not costly to keep them and there is no more trouble after gelding them. They are sturdy and docile and are much attached to their master who is fond of them in turn. When attacked by robbers, he conceals such articles of property as he may possess in odd places and thus, running away, he has at least the satisfaction of knowing that the tent he necessarily leaves behind is quite empty. The robber knows this too and so confines his attention to the horses solely. No Mongolian is so poor as not to own half a dozen horses. In a few instances, there are herds of even 500 beasts. One stallion to every twenty or thirty mares is reckoned the proper pro-portion.

The following was the common scale of barter in Mongolia:

2 goats = 1 sheep

12 sheep = 1 colt (over a year old)

2 colts = 1 pony

Now going back to Kishen Singh. From Golmo, he reached

Hurtholhale, a nomad camp, on the 21st November, 1879. Here he visited a ruined enclosure of mud walls of an ancient date. It is said that it was erected by nomads as a safeguard against the incursions of the marauders from the east. Their route had lain through the heavy jungle mentioned before. Grass and fuel were abundant.

On the 22nd, they came across a stream coming from the south which, flowing for some miles to the north, loses itself in the desert. There was a nomad camp of fifty tents, called Thugthe, on the bank of the stream. From Thugthe, a route branched off northward to Sondshu (Chonju). At the Thugthe camp, water was obtained from wells as there was no spring or stream within several miles of it. In these wells, water is found very near the surface of the ground. They were detained here for two days as two of their ponies had got astray.

On the 25th, the Pundit reached Dala, a nomad camp where there was a spring of fresh water. Continuing, he arrived at Chugu on the bank of a stream which, flowing to the north, loses itself in the desert. A spring of fresh water was found on the way.

Next day the party reached Dhanahotho. He saw no glass of water along this portion of the journey, but from nomad encampments visible here and there at a distance from the road he concluded there must have been water in the vicinity.

On the 27th, he noticed on his route several springs of fresh water. Then he crossed a low sandy ridge. Five and a three-quarter miles from there is a brackish stream which flows to the north-east. Saft is found incrusted on the banks of the stream. This kind of salt is in general use in the country. The explorer heard of no rock or mineral salt being found anywhere. Three and a quarter miles further, he arrived at Tengelik (7,720 feet) near the junction of a stream coming from the south-east with the Bai Gol (River). There were one hundred tents, ten houses and a few fields. One crop of barley was raised annually. The Bai Gol running from the east after watering the Tengelik plain flows to the north where it is lost in the desert. The explorer here overtook his old caravan which had left him at Naichi. The members of the caravan who were Mongolians and residents of the adjacent places took leave of the remaining members, and went to their homes. Only the Tibetans who were to accompany the explorer remained. They decided to stop there for a few days in order to rest their animals and to replenish the stock of *sattu* which had run short. They did not observe any water mill in Mongolia but noticed small hand mills made of light red sand-stone brought from Hoiduthara in the Korluk district. Two days after their arrival, some of their *kafila* friends and they went out shooting as they had heard that the wild animals in the mountain to the south, half a day's journey, were unequalled in fatness and flavour and that their skins were valuable. They huntedfor four days and succeeded in shoot-ing some animals (wild yaks and wild asses). On the fifth day, they returned from their trip and intended to start next morning, the 5th December, 1879.

In fact the morning of their intended departure had arrived when, as the dawn was yet breaking, the robbers' war cry of Ullul-lulhil-lu-lu-u suddenly burst on the peaceful encampment. The robbers, some 200 in number, had effected a complete surprise. The Mongolians, according to the precedent, at once scattered far and wide without making even a pretence of resistance and the robbers, having seized the horses they coveted, next attacked the small party of Kishen Singh and the Tibetans. There was some firing on both sides but numbers prevailed. Eventually when the owners returned to their tents, now practically empty, they found a single dead robber shot in the conflict, whose dress and arms enabled them to recognise that the marauders belonged to the dreaded band of the Chiamo-Golok whom the unfortunate travellers had hitherto successfully evaded. The robbers succeeded in carrying away about 300 ponies belonging to the caravan and the residents. The victims were robbed of most of their property, barring only two loads containing petty articles of merchandise. After the robbers had departed, the nomads from the adjoining encampments having collected together for a chase, the travellers joined them and followed in pursuit of the robbers till the evening. Although they did not succeed in coming up to them, they returned the next day with whatever the robbers could not carry in their flight and had left on the road. This consisted of fifty ponies, mostly lame or otherwise unfit to keep with them, andsome property which they found too heavy and unprofitable.

The caravan now dispersed. The Mongols had already taken leave and as for the Tibetans some of them, feeling they were unable to continue their journey, returned to Naichi to join the caravan going to Lhasa, and some remained at Tengelik, waiting for some other opportunity to return.

Tengelik Onwards

The losses the explorer incurred here crippled him and his two com-panions most deplorably; still he collected the remnants of his effects and, bravely refusing to turn homeward, set his face towards Sachu and resolved on further exploration. He was obliged to discharge his Tibetan servants as their services were no longer required. The general direction of their route from Goimo to Tengelik was from west to east. Having hired three bullocks on which to load what remained of his property, he left Tengelik for Korluk on the 13th December, 1879. Some of their Tenge-lik friends accompanied him to barter flesh and leather and stopped at Harori, anomad camp. They halted there next day also on account of the owner of the bullocks not having arrived as promised.

On the 15th December, they crossed to the right bank of the Bai Gol river. The horizon towards the north ws generally hazy. Thirteen miles further on, they reached Dabasutha, a nomad camp of four tents where they stopped for the night. They day's route was level and sandy.

On the 16th, proceeding about eight miles further, they reached Hara-husun, an encamping ground on the right bank of a branch of the Bai Gol which, flowing north-west, loses itself in the desert. The forest which commenced near Golmo ends here. There were a variety of small birds in it and a bird like the golden pheasant which the explorer had noticed nowhere else was found inlarge numbers. They stopped there for two nights to allow their bullocks to graze as they were informed that there was no grass throughout the next stage.

On the 18th, they forded three brackish streams, the beds and banks of which were incrusted with salt. There was no fresh water for miles. In winter, travellers obtained it from the upper layer of ice but in other seasons they had to bring the supply from Hara-husun. After flowing north-westward for some miles, these streams lose themselves in the desert. After crossing a pass with an easy ascent, they halted two miles beyond it. They found no grass and no water, but firewood was abundant. The chain of mountains they crossed that day runs north of the Taichinar district from east to west and is of a sandy formation. It looked higher in the middle than atits eastern and western extremities. It separates Taichinar and Korluk districts.

On the 19th, they crossed a low ridge. Then they reached Chakangnamaga, an encamping ground at the northern corner of the lake called Thosu Nor (Tossun), about twelve miles long and eight miles across where it is broadest. Its water is brackish and impregnated with sulphur. Close to the camp is a hot spring the water of which flows into the lake. Water for drinking and cooking purposes is obtained from the upper layer of ice on the surface of the lake. This camp is at the junction of the roads from the Taichinar and Jun districts. The roads proceed by the western and eastern shores of the lake respectively to Hoiduthara and Gobi in the Korluk district. The latter district is a granary of the nomads of Taichinar and Jun. The encamping ground abounded in firewood and dwarfed trees but grass was scarce. They halted there for the night. From Hara-husun to this place, the path was good but during the rainy season it became muddy and difficult near the salt-water streams mentioned before.

On the 20th December, 1879, traversing the western shore of the lake for twelve miles, they arrived on the right bank of Korluk Gol (river) which, emanating from the Korluk Nor (Kurlik) lake, empties itself into the Tossun lake. The latter is said to have no outlet and is surrounded by a low sandy ridge. Then they arrived at Sukhai, the residence of he Hoiduthara men where about a hundred tents were dotted about. The nomads remained there for three or four months in winter, pasturing their camels on the leaves of the dwarfed trees with which the plain which is about twelve miles broad and fifty miles long abounds, while they sent their ponies, goats and sheep to pasture on the rich grass and verdure of the mountains to the north of the Hoiduthara. About four miles to the east is the Korluk Nor lake ten miles long and nine miles broad, which is fed by a stream and a river. The stream, coming from the north-west, waters the barley fields at Horga andlidcte-thara which produced large quantities of grain. Gobi is situated on the right bank of the river and close to the lake.

Gobi had a large nomad camp of about one hundred tents and had some ten subterraneous store houses for grain. Fields, after being once cultivated, were allowed to lie fallow for the next three or four years so that the soil, which is not manured, may recover its fertility. Before sowing the seeds, the soil is turned up with a plough drawn by oxen or with a kind of small pick-axe. Only one crop of barley or *ne* was raised in a year. Other grains did not thrive there, the climate being rigorous. Gobi is about seventeen miles from Sukhai which is on the opposite side of side of the lake. It was the seat of the Besi (Chief). All deputes, civil or criminal which arose within the Beli's jurisdiction, were referred to him for decision.

Korluk Nor lake is said to contain a great number of fish but these are never disturbed by the Mongolians. The surface of the lake freezes in winter and after snow has fallen on it, it becomes the high road for travellers both on foot and horse-back.

At Sukhai, their Tengelik friends who had come for corn setted their business and departed. As the sale of their merchandise consisting of glass beads or such other valueless articles as the robbers had left was very slow, Kishen Singh had no means of proceeding further and was obliged to wait at Sukhai for an opportunity.

Happening one day to go to Gobi, Kishen Singh fortunately met a T'ibetan of Gyantse, finding him helpless, treated him very kindly. This Tibetan had some twenty years ago migrated to Sirthang in Korluk where he married and settled and had now become a man of influence and position. He advised the Pundit to stay till the warm weather returned when he promised to take him to his home and arrange for his onward journey. He engaged him and his two servants, Chhumbel and Ganga Ram, to look after his camels in return for food. The Tibetan had come to Gobi to attend to a case which was pending in the *Besi's* court. A K and his servants remained in his service at Sukhai (8,T70feet) and Hoiduthara (9,200 feet) for two months and twentynine days. Five peaks, with patches of snow on them, were observed from Sukhai about twenty miles north east. These peaks are on a long range of mountains having a direction east by south and west by north.

About twenty miles to the east-south-east of Gobi and at the eastern extremity of Korlung district, there was the named Golmo, containing about forty tents and ten store-houses like those at Gobi. The names Khuhu and Koko are derived from the Russian explorer. Colonel Prejevalsky's map. The explorer says the names are identical and should be'Khokho' which like 'Onbo' signifies blue. It was the seat of a *Beli* who ranked higher than a *Besi*. Tulang (Dula-kitt), the seat of the *Whang*, is said to lie forty miles to the east-south-east of Khukhu. The *Whang* is the chief officer in the Koko Nor province which consisted of the Tulang, Khukhu, Korluk, Taichinar, Jun, Baron, Shang and Banakasum districts. The nomads of the last district were addicted to robbery. They were of Tibetan descent and were distinguished from the nomads of the other districts in that they live in black tents made of yak's hair, while the Mongolians occupied tents made of coarse woolen fabrics. The Mongolians are honest, hospitable and peaceful people.

From Dulan-kitt, a road, proceeding south-east for about twenty-five miles and thence north-east for about forty miles, leads to the western side of the Koko Nor lake or Tso Onbo (blue lake). The lake is about 280 miles in circumference and contains a small island, called Tso Ning (heart of lake), on which is a gompa inhabited by about twenty Dabas. There is no spring of fresh water. The Dabas of the island gathered their supplies of food during the four months of winter. The water of the lake is then frozen and affords a convenient means of communication with the shore. A considerable number of fish was taken from the lake for sale at neighbouring settlements. Salt, found encrusted on the bank of the lake, was also an article of merchandise. The Arnbons of Sining-fu, when on tour, halted at the lake for the sake of fishing. At the south-eastern extremity of the lake was a large gompa called Kumbum consisting of about 3,000 Dabas, whicil was a great seat of religious instruction for the Mongolians. The lake is considered sacred~aitd Buddhists circumanibulate it as a meritorious performance. It was a dangerous pilgrimage as the southern shore was infest by robbers. Donkyr (Tankar), a well known place of commerce, lies about 100 miles to the east. Some eighty miles further is Sining-fu where two Ambans resided. Further east is Alasha under the rule of a Whang. The ruler was the son-in-law of the Emperor of China, Woollen carpets of every description are woven there.

Mongolians are Buddhists and hold Lhasa to be a sacred city and chief seat of learning. It was in Lhasa only that the degree of *Gisi* (learned), which was conferred by the learned members of the three gompas of Se-ra, Dre-phung and Gaden, could be competed for. The examination was difficult and entailed more than twelve years of continuous study, principally of religious books. Afterwards also, certain preliminaries had to be gone through. The candidate provided a feast for the Lamas and Dabas of the gompa to which he belonged, at which he expressed his intention to compete. Information was then sent to the other two gompas and a committee of examiners was constituted from among the possessors of the *gisi* degree in the three gompas. A *Gisi* ranked higher than a Daba, but lower than a Lama, and was held in high respect by men of all classes. He was not allowed to marry or to cohabit with women. Mongolian Dabas were not under the same rule of celibacy as those of Tibet and they could marry. They must, however, wear the special garments when they worshipped or perfomed any religious ceremony.

Mongolians of the Koko Nor province pride themselves that among them was born a hero, named Tenjen Gombo who, having conquered Siling and Alasha, finally became Emperor of China and in whose family the empire still continued.

On the 28th February, 1880, the settlers at Sukhai moved to Hoiduthara, five miles away, to commence ploughing their fields. The sowing took place in April and the harvest was reaped in September. At Hoiduthara, they spent nineteen days herding camels, after which the explorer and his two servants were permitted to go to Sirthang and three camels were lent to them for their baggage. FromTengelikto Hoidu-thara, the route had almost a northerly direction but thence it turned west.

Leaving Hoiduthara on the 19th March, carrying a supply of water, as there was no water on the road for some distance, they halted on the dry bed of a stream for the night. Firewood was abundant but no grass. Further, their route lay within a narrow valley with some springs of fresh water. After crossing a low pass, they entered somewhat open country with pasturage for the camels. A deep hollow between two large boulders' full of snow, supplied water to travellers during four months of winter. The route from Hoiduthara to this place was somewhat stony and was narrow in part. From the road, two snowy peaks were visible about 30 miles north-west. Then they reached Soiidabu (Chonfu) where they halted for two nights.

On the 24th March, 1880, after travelling thirteen miles, they saw the Baga Nor lake about three miles south-west. It is about six miles long and four miles broad and contains somewhat brackish water. Then the route brought them to Baga Tsaidam with fifty scattered tents. There was no cultivation. Grass and water were abundant. *Tsaidam* signifies a trading place or market. Baga used to be the market visited by the Chinese for borax which was found encrusted on the margins of the Baga Nor and Ikhe Nor lakes. They remained there for two nights.

On the 26th, they arrived at a large spring of fresh water from which the route continued along the base of the mountain on the right, crossed a low pass and struck the direct route to Ikhe Tsaidam and halted there. On the 27th, they arrived at Ikhe Tsaidam (10,480 feet) where there were about one hundred tents. This place previously exported borax to China. Ikhe Nor lake, close by, is about sixteen miles long and eight miles broad and is fed by springs only, several of which were visible from the road along its margin. Supplies were procurable although at high cost. Grass and firewood were abundant. On the 29th, Kishen Singh halted at Ijia, close to a range of hills, where there was a large spring of fresh water said by the inhabitants of Korluk district to be very wholesome. Ijia was covered with rich pasturage and was frequented by nomads of Ikhe Tsaidom during March. On the 30th they encamped at Urel with three tents. On the 31st March, having filled their leather bags with water, they crossed a low pass, encamped in an uninhabited place two miles beyond. Next day after journeying across a large plain, they reached Chaga, also called Ulan Guzar an encamping ground, close to a spring of fresh water. From this place, a road leads to Mukhai to the south from where the Mongolians of the neighbourhood obtained the material for the wooden framework for their tents. On the 2nd April, they came to an *obo* (a place of worship) where there were a number of flags on an artificial mound and some fifteen scattered tents. Thirteen and a half miles further is Yembi in Sirthang.

Sirthang is an extensive grassy plain surrounded on all sides by a sandy waste called Shialla. The plain is about twenty miles long with an average breadth of seventeen miles and is irrigated by several springs of fresh water. A few small pools of salt-water supply the inhabitants with salt. There are two lakes of which the water is drinkable, about nine miles apart and which are joined by a small stream. They are nearly equal in size, about four miles by two and a half miles and are full of fish on which a kind of otter preys. There were some 300 tents scattered about Sirthang but this number was reduced to about fifty m winter when the cattle, especially the young ones, were driven for protection from severe cold into the small narrow valleys on either side of the northern range which is thirty miles away. Good pasturage abounds in these valleys.

Wild people existed in some of the valleys of the northern range. They had a thick and dark skin, were well-built and apparently well-fed. They wore no clothes except skins, nor did they dwell in tents or huts but lived in caves and glens and under shelter of overhanging rocks. They were ignorant of the use of arms in the chase and lay in wait for prey near springs of water or where salt encrusted. They ate even rats, lizards and other small animals. They were remarkable for their swiftness of foot and when pursued, even a horseman could not easily catch them.

Whenever they saw a civilized man, they ran away in great terror. They knew how to kindle a fire with the aid of flint. They flayed the animals they killed with sharp-edged stones. Sometimes, but very seldom, they stole goats and sheep grazing in the valleys.

In the area, wild ass, chamois, yak, wolf, rabbit, brown bear, beaver, etc., were met with. The Bactrian camel and the horse were also found in a wild state.

It is believed that at a very remote period a Mongolian army from Thorkoth invaded Tibet to assist the Lhasa Government against its petty neighbours, then ruling in the Ngari Khorsum and Ladakh. Their animals, now existing in a wild state, are supposed to have sprung from the stray animals of the army. The Mongolians of the vicinity believe themselves to be descendants of the followers of the same army and say that the country before that invasion was uninhabited. All these animals excepting the wild horse are hunted, some for their flesh, some for their hides and others for both. Neither the flesh nor the hide of the wild horse are useful.

It does not rain more than three times during the whole season, thunder and lighting are rare too; snow falls very seldom. From February to June, dust-storms which occur almost daily are very troublesome, one sometimes lasting for a week continuously. From the middle of June to the middle of September, the springs remain frozen.

The Mongolians had built a walled enclosure at Yembi for their Lama, looked up to by all as their spiritual guide. They were tolerably well-off, though there was no cultivation, for they obtained what was needed from Saitu, five days' journey. There they have exchanged camesl, goats, sheep, horses, wool and butter for corn. Corn was also brought from Naichi and Nahuli. Cooking and other utensils were obtained from China. The dress of both sexes was very similar. It consisted of a long garment, shaped like a large cloak. It was made of either cured skins, felt, coarse woollen cloth or broad cloth of bright colours. The first was worn in winter, the second during spring, the third in summer and the fourth on festive occasions.

Thorkoth, an extensive and rich tract of Mongolian territory, lies about a month's journey on the north-west of Sirhang. It was governed by a *Whang*. For several generations past, these *Whangs* died at an early age, leaving the management of the territory to their wives. The mother of the present young ruler, fearing the same fate for her son, sent for several distinguished Lamas to perform some religious ceremony to ensure a long life for him. A famous Tibetan Lama of Tsang in Tibet had now come to Sirthang to perform a sacrifice with the object of warding off an incursion of the Banakasum robbers, about 1,000 in number, who had resolved to make a raid on that territory.

To Saitu (Sachu)

After spending some three months at Yembi (9,690 feet) in seeling the merchandise left by the robbers at Tengelik and waiting for any traders proceeding to the Lob Nor, the explorer eventually resolved to go to Saitu. The merchandise he disposed of here consisted of small beads of red clay and myrobalans. The latter found a ready sale at the rate of 2-1/2 rupees a *seer* but as the former were not much in demand, being only worn by women in necklaces, their disposal took time. He also his woollen *chogas* (long cloaks). All these articles fetched about Rs. 200 in silver, three horses and four colts.

As the explorer's servant, Ganga Ram had heard that the Hu Hu (Mohammedans of China) were at war with the Emperor of China, he was afraid to accompany him further and desired to remain in the Koko Nor provinace for some years. Ganga Ram tried to instigate the other servant, Chhumbel, to desert Kishen Singh and indirectly tried to persuade even the explorer to give up his design. Finding him determined to go to Saitu, Ganga Ram one day, during the explorer's temporary absence, despatched Chhumbel to a distant place to fetch some goats due to the explorer in exchange for some articles of merchandise and availed of this opportunity to desert him, carrying away with him 150 rupees worth of silver, two horses and three colts, together with a small telescope. This happened in July 1880. Next day, when the explorer returned, he found no one in his tent but Chhumbel's explanation on his return with the goats soon after and the remembrance of the other's previous attempts to dissuade them from proceeding further left no doubt about his desrtion. The position of the explorer now was very desperate and he had sacrecely fifty rupees worth of things left.A friend who heard of the case sympathised with him and was ready to send men to seize Ganga Ram. But some travellers arriving at that time to visit the Lama informed him that they had met Ganga Ram at Urel and that he had told them to let the explorer know that he would return after three months after selling the ponies. Kishen Singh had no hope of seeing him again. Thus he and his remainig faithful servant, Chhumbel, had become practically paupers.

Under these circumstances, no one could have reproached the explorer, had he now endeavoured to retrace his steps. But he once more rose above adversity, gallantly making his way onward to Sachu. Being reduced to such straits, he was obliged to again take up service and he and Chhumbel tended herds of ponies and goats for about five months but then, getting tired of that work, they determined to move on with the limited funds he possessed and, when those should fail, to beg their way.

On the 3rd January 1881, as some men were going to Saitu to exchange goats and sheep for corn, the explorer obtained his employer's permissino to go with them. The employer was a thorough gentleman and on their departuer, he gave Kishen Singh a horse worth Rs. 40 and warm clothes together with provisions. He arrived at Harasiring, ana encamping ground at the other extremity of the Sirthang plain, where he halted for the night.

Proceeding northward from Tengelik, there is little of note of discuss, until he reached Yembi in the Sirthang district. He found an extensive plain, well-watered, covered with grass and affording excellent pasturage for large herds of animals. Horses in particular were most numerous and might be counted in thousands. Yet, the climate was by no means genial and this was not so much in consquence of unusual cold, as owing to the prevalence of strong biting winds which blew persistently and almost continually, excepting in November and December. There was little snow or rain but distant clouds, without mist, were frequent. Water froze readily in the open air, exceptmg in July and August, and in winter months successive cakes of ice were formed at the' spring. Sometimes mounting up curiously one above another in piles over six feet high. It was, however, chiefly the piercing wind which made the climate of Sirthang exceedingly severe in January and February, when all young and tender animals were removed for protection to various enclosed valleys in:the hills to the north.

About thirty miles away towards north-west of Yembi is a high snowy peak called Amandapara which the inhabitants of Sirthang supposed to be the abode of Shib-dag (the protecting god of Sirthang). At several places in Sirthang, obos (poles to which strips of cloth were attached) were erected where incense was burnt to propitiate that deity.

On the 4th, traversing the sandy tract, about 13-3/4 miles broad, forming the northern border of Sirthang, and then walking up hills and down streams, the Pundit found a Mongolian tent on the right bank of the stream which flows for 7-3/4 miles in such a narrow ravine that travllers had to walk over its frozen surface or wade through it, according to the season. The valley then opens into a sandy plain and near its northern extremity is an encamping gound where he stopped for two nights. Grass and firewood were abundant. The party had a snowfall about two feet in depth.

The explorer had heard at Sirthang that about three miles to the west of this encamping ground was a tent occupied by a woman who and her husband had in their youth been carried away by Tanthus (men of the white turban) of the Lob Nor district, formerly occupied by Mongolians, and went to see her. She told him that the Lob Nor lake, around which was a population of Tanthus, Mohammedan by religion, was about 250 miles away to the west, that the route leading to it was uninhabited and water and grass could only be procured at certain places known to those who frequented it. She advised them to return to their tent before evening because a demo (brown bear) had lately committed great ravages in the neighbourhood. The explorer met no bear but the old woman's son, who accompanied him for some distance pointed out to him a wild man on an opposite spur two miles off, coming towards them but who, on seeing them, turned back. As he was at a large distance, Kishen Singh could not see him well enough to verify or add to the description already given.

On the 6th, the explorer and his servant arrived at a small spur from, a sandy ridge running east to west. From here, a road branched off to Naichi city, about fifty five miles to the "east The city contained a market surrounded by houses (built of sunburnt bricks), about 1,000 innumber, and was well known as a market for the sale of corn, the produce of the surrounding fields. Proceeding further, they stopped for a night at the base of a sandy ridge where they found neither 'grass nor water nor firewood. Of the last, they had however, draught a supply and having found some snow in a sheltered place, the party melted it.

On the 7th, after crossing a sandy ridge and traversing a sandy plain, the explorer arrived at Changja, an encamping ground on the left bank of a river. Here he found grass, firewood and a few dwarfed trees. A cart-road went up the left bank of the river to the south-east whence firewood and a sort of long grass were brought to the cities of Saitu and Nahuli. The carts were like those common in Hindustan but were drawn by horses.

Arrival Sachu : the northernmost point

On the 8th, they reached the suburbs of Saitu, where they

saw some cultivated fields and houses here and there. Passing through these, they crossed the river by a bridge 250 paces long and five paces broad, with railing on both sides of it. The river abounded in fish which was caught by angling.

The most northern place visited by the explorer was the town of Saitu or Sachu (Russian explorer Colonel Prejevalsky's Ssatschu). It was surrounded by small villages in the midst of an extensive and very fertile plain watered abundantly by a river which here flowing nearly north and south, ran close to and west of the town, where it was crossed by a strong bridge with two flat openings Seen from the south, the town. and the surrounding villages were concealed amidst high trees, backed by low hills, visible in the distance to the extent the hazy atmos-phere of Mongolia permitted. The most attractive feature on which the eye rested was, however, the extensive and green expanse of cultivation in which Sachu stood. This pleasant verdure, contrasting with the generally arid surface of Mongolia, extended .fully to Nahuli on the north-west and probably twenty miles in all direction. The land was highly fertile and, enjoying as it did anample water supply, the harvests were large and varied in kind. On them the prosperity of the place mainly depended.

The city was in the shape of a quadrangle, about 1-1/2 miles along the east-west line and some seven or eight miles the other way. It was surrounded by a parapet pierced with embrasures at intervals. Accommodation for the garrison was provided in the four corners of the surrounding wall. There were four gateways, one on each side of the quadrangle and the two roads joining the opposite gateways were the main thoroughfares of the town. The shops and dwelling houses were built mostly along these roads, covered with straw spread over rough wooden frames. The north-west angle at the junction of these main roads was enclosed by a branch road and north of which stood the residence of the *Daloi* (governor), the jail, etc. The four entrances were gated but the structures were mostly out of repair and the wall enclosing the city had several gaps in it.

The population of Sachu and the surrounding villages was almost exclusively Chinese. The people were commonly polygamists and in certain respects fared unfavourably with the Mongolians. The latter were honest, hospitable and generous while the former were not merely thrifty, but exacting. *Sakhangs* (restaurants) were common and popular and food including vegetables and fruits was abundant and cheap. Notwithstanding the fertility of the Sachu plain, the climate, as all over Mongolia, permitted of only one harvest in the year. Sugar was imported. Intoxicating liquors were plentiful and drunk by one and all witout exception. Opium was also consumed, chiefly by smoking, and could be raised in the neighbourhood though not to the extent required. It was sold by weight againswt an equal quantity of silver. But notwithstanding alcohol and opium, the Chinaman was peaceful and law abiding. For slight offences, punishment could be so severe as to cause painful deaths. Capital punishment could not be ordered by the Daloi wither sanction from China but fatal results were however attained with actual decapitation, which was the recognised form of legal execution As to houses, they were all one storeyed and consisted of small rooms There was no window glass. The walls were built of blocks of clay or sun-dried bricks and the roofs of scantlings laid close together with plenty of earth beaten flat above them. Fuel and straw were plentiful. The rainfall did not make the place cold, notwithstanding its high altitude.

On the whole, Sachu could not be compared with Lhasa in point of interest, wealth or population. Its people were nearly all of a single nationality, the Chinese, and its trade was mostly with the north and west, the traffic being carried in carts drawn by two or three horses.

The explorer mentions the singular Chinese coin *temiman* (or *doje* or nabchuma), a mass of silver not unlike a cocked hat in general outline and euivalent to 156 Indian rupees. Hence the coin must weigh about four pounds. The kurs (an ingot of silver equal to about 156 Indian rupees) was the current corn. There were two smaller silver coins of the same shape, one weighing five and the ten *lens*, equal to fifteen rupees ten annas and thirty one rupees and four annas of Indian currency respectively. Ordinary lumps of silver were used for small change, which necessitated weighing and testing and for still smaller change brass coins were used, 500 of which were equal to one rupee. The following was the scale of weight used in Mongolia and Saitu :—

    10 *chens*   —   1 *len*

    16 *lens*   —   1 *jing* (5 toals of Indian weight)

    25 *jings*   —   1 *dug*

    10 *dugs*   —   1 *ten*

In exchange for a sheep, worth four *chens* of silver (1-1/2 rupees of Indian currency), 3-1/2 *dugs* of wheat were given. *Ne* and millet were also sold at the same rate. Besides these, other grains, *viz. kauli* (a kind of corn found in Saitu and used for distilling liquor), Indian corn, *masur* (a kind of pulse) and pea were cultivated. Rice was dear as it was imported from Yarkand. There were no water mills for grinding corn, but mills worked by horse-power were employed instead.

Saitu surpassed Tibet and Mongolia in the excellence and abundance of its fruits and vegetables. These were however inferior in flavour to those of Yarkand. Among the fruits and vegetables were apple, pear, plum, cucumber, melon, water-melon, mulberry, walnut, guava, radish, carrot, turnip, mustard, etc. Sugarcane was unknown but a kind of honey-cake was brought from the north. Cotton was cultivated and manufactured into a kind of coarse cloth. Cho Gombo, the Governor of Laindu Chondu one of the provinces of the Chinese Empire to which Saitu is subordinate) came here on tour of inspection and established a manufactory for weaving silk cloth and also posted ten good workmen for teaching the art of silk-weaving at Saitu. The Chief articles of diet were bread, cooked vegetables, meat and milk, pigs and fowls were reared, because their flesh, when boiled, was much relished.

The climate of Saitu was generally healthy and bore a great resemblance to that of Yarkand. The inhabitants of Saitu were asstout or well built as the Mongolians. The colour of their dress was generally black or blue, white being employed for mourning. In winter, they wore clothes padded with cotton. They kept locks of hair on the top of their heads, which were plaited and hung down behind. The women wore a cap of the Chinese pattern and several coats of various colours put on in such order that the sleeves of the inner-most extended to the wrist, whilst those 'of others decreased in succession. Over these was worn a short coat which came down a little below the hips, with sleeves a little short of the elbows. A loose pair of trousers in place of petticoat completed the costume. Their feet were small, being not more than six inches in length. When a girl was three years of age, an iron chain, more than a seer in weight was hung round her neck and when she attained her fifth year, this chain was removed and her toes were bound with strips of cloth so as to cause them to turn inwards. This unnnatural twist of the toes sometime produced sores. Women never exposed their feet before men.

To Kishen Singh, the Chinese people of Sachu proved inhospitable and ungenerous and like others, who were poor and feriendless, he was regarded with distrust, so that further progress northwards which he contemplated was prohibited. Nor was he able to retrace his steps towards Hindustan and had to prolong his stay at Sachu. After selling his horses, as it was very expensive to keep them in the city and not knowing what length of time he might be detained, he and chhumbel set up as fruit-sellers to obtain their livelihood.

Here he suffered from a peculiar disease called by the natives *bam* in which red blotches appear on the legs making it difficult to walk or even stand up. It is accompanied by fever and loss of appetite and & some cases looseness of the teeth also. This complaint, he was told is brought on by walking bare foot on a particular land of soil, and, il not properly attended to, disables a man for life from using his Iowa limbs. Various heating and intoxicating drugs were administered and in ome plasters were applied but what he found efficacious was radish juice rubbed over the afflicted limb, which was then wrapped round tightly with cloth and kept warm. This brought on perspiration and gradual relief.

Reverse Journey

After Kishen Singh had been there for seven months, the head Lami of Thuden Gompa in the Derge district in Tibet, with whom he wa acquainted, happened to visit Sachu. Recognising the explorer, the Lama obtained leave to taba him back with his party. Seven days later they left Sachu and returned to Yembi which they reached on the 15th August, 1881.

They remained in Yembi for ten days. As a direct return to Tibet was impossible in view of the limited means at his disposal, and oi consideration of safety, the explorer and his servant, Chhumbel, took service with the head Lama-of Thuden Gompa and started on the 3rd September with some Mongolian traders. Retracing their steps via Chaga (Ultan Guzar), Urel, Ijia, Ikhe Tsaidam, Baga Tsaidam, Shonshu (Chonju) and Sukhai, they arrived at Chakangnamaga on the 17th September.

Marching over sandy plain via Mchiangsi encamping round and fording a branch of the Bai Gol (river), they reached Jun Tsaidam where there was the house of the *Jhasa* of Jun. Near this house there were some fifty tents. The road from Lhasa to Siningfu passed by this place. They spent the night of the 20th September on the left bank of the river. Grass and firewood were found in plenty.

On the 21st, they forded the Bai Gol (river) three feet deep and five paces wide which, flowing to the west, intersected the explorer's previous route near Tengelik. The river issues from Alak or Alang and Thosu Nor (Tossun) lakes and the two branches, after flowing through the shang district and uniting in the vicinity of Shang Tsaidam, divide into two streams some miles east of the *Jhasa's* residence. Nine miles from the Bai Gol (river), they entered

Baron district. The Jun district, which extended from the salt-water stream to the Baron boundary, contained some 500 tents and was similar to the Taichinar district in its cultivation, forest, etc. Four and a half miles from the baron boundary, they arrived at Chakcharnamaga, a Mongolian nomad camp containing about thirty tents.

At a distance from the encampment towards south-east is Baron Tsaidam, containing some houses and tents. It was the residence of the Jhasa of Baron and had some cultivated land in the vicinity. Kishen Singh heard that his servant, Ganga Ram, was at Bana-kasum where the black tent nomads resided. He sent a man to persuade him to rejoin them. On the man's return he learnt that Ganga Ram had feigned illness and was afraid to return to him. Ganga Ram had purchased herds .of goats, sheep and mares with the intention of settling in the district of. Shang and sent word to the explorer to give up the journey for the present and join him.

About twenty miles to the east of Shang Tsaidam is the Shang district, containing about fifty houses, some tents and a little cultivation. It was reported that this district was given to the Lama of Tra-shi-lhun-pa Gompa by the Emperor of China for performing a number of miracles before him. This tract of the country which included the districts of Taichinar, Korluk, Jun, Baron and Shang, is called Thabu Tsaidam on account of the five *tsaidams* of Ikhe, Baga, Jun, Shang and Baron being situated in it.

To the east of Shang was Bana-kasum, a district full of robbers, and south-east of the latter was Chiamo-Golok district, the inhabitants of which were also addicted to robbery. To the east of Chiamo-Golok was the large district of Amdo. The inhabitants of these three districts bore strong resemblance in language, manners and customs to Tibetans.

In the company of the head Lama of Thuden, Pundit Kishen Singh was obliged to ride a horse down to Chakangnamaga from whence the track which bifurcates eastwards (new to the explorer) was followed. Here he became a bullock driver to the party and walking by these beasts was able to reckon his own pace as usual to Baron Tsaidam. For the remaining distance to Thuden Gompa, the track ran in the vicinity of the Chiamo-Golok and Bana-kasum robber clans. To provide for an escape from marauders, if necessary, every individual of the party was required ro ride. Hence for this portion, the explorer with commendable ingenuity reckoned the paces taken by the right foreleg of his steed and the result showed that a horse steps as equally as a man.

On the 7th October, after replenishing their stock of provision and collecting such other articles as were needed, their party left chakchang namaga under the guidance of two Mongolians and stopped for the night at Hadho where there was cultivation On the 8th, they entered a narrow valley. A foot of snow fell there. There were no habitations but duirng winter the nomads of the Baron district brought their cattle here for pasture.

The party saw a novel spectacle here. A demo (brown bear) was found taking out *chipis* (marmots) from their den. As soon as he had got one out, he put it under his hind quarters and thinking that he had thus secured his prey commenced his search for another. This necessitated his inclining forward which gave the poor captive opportunity to get up and escape. The bear continued his labour till they were all taken out, but at last found that all those he had captured before had escaped and the one he had got hold of last was his only prey.

The next day, the party, crossed the steep Namohan pass aross Angirtakehia range. An open valley lay before them and they learnt that there was a lake called Dungar, about twenty miles in circumference situated at a distance of some fifty miles to the east, at the northern base of the Amnimanchenporna range. They forded the branch of the Bai Gol (river). The robbers adopted the route along this valley in their plundering excursions against the Mongols. Four miles further they crossed one of the streams which fall into the lake on the banks of which the inhabitants of Niamcho district sometimes washed for gold. They stopped for the night on the bank of this stream. Water and grass were in abundance but there was scarcity of fuel.

Marching up hills and down streams, they crossed the Ma Chu river. Tins river is distinct from those bearing the same previously mentioned. A snow storm caused them to miss the direct road and they arrived at a pass over the Lamathologa range (round like Lama's head) which contains several round peaks. Then on the 14th October, 1881, they crossed the Dugbulag stream. They saw a large number of wild yaks grazing along the banks of this stream. These animals came so seldom in contact with any human beings that they did not even notice their presence but the explorer was informed that sometimes, when excited, they would attack passsers-by. The Dugbulag stream forms the northern boundary of the Niamcho district. Five and a half miles further, they met two men of the Niamcho district who informed them that some fifty mounted robbers from the Chiamo Colok district had lately gone up the Dabulag valley to the west to plunder the travellers *en route* from Lhasa to Sining-fu. The party stoped for the night near the northernmost winter encamping place of the Niamcho nomads.

Marching further, they saw several springs of fresh wate and a hot spring. They also saw a snow peak, believed to be sacred and named Garlojhio, about four miles towards north-west. They passed by the village of Niamcho, where there were about a hundred tents and fifty houses and which was the residence of the ruler of the district. this district has a population represented by about 1,000 tents and he fields in the vicnity of Niamcho village were cultivated to some extent. Niamcho lies a litle to the west of the junction of the Di Chu with another stream.

Proceeding ahead, they crossed a steep pass, which was covered with three feet of snow, and after a difficult descent, arrived at Dhingo village, containing ten houses and having some cultivation. This was the first village the explorer met with on their route since they left Baron Tsaidam, and marching further they entered the Tindhu village, containing ten houses, where they halted on the 17th October, 1881.

Niamcho district extended to the last mentioned pass. To the east of Niamcho, there wefe three more districts named Mogonzen, Garoche and Jachukha. Below the pass lay the Gabaand Rablu sub-division of the Derge district.

On the 20th, they passed through Kanzo Gompa which contained a cetebrated image of Jhio (a Buddhist god). This is believed to be a holy place and was inhabited by about 150 Dabas. Then they passed by Chioti Gompa inhabited by about 300 Dabas and having some 100 houses about it. The Lama of this gompa was one of the wealthiest persons in the Gaba sub-division. Sometime age he visited China and brought back a cuckoo clock which was an object of much curiousity among his neighbourers. Proceeding a mile down the stream, they arrived at Thiso village, containing thirty houses, where they stopped for the night. Supplies were procurable at all these villages and cultivation was seen in their vicinity. One crop of *ne* and wheat was raised annually.

On the 21st, they reached Thuden via the villages of Khutho and Laso. Thuden Gompa (11,990 feet) is a small monastery and had only fifty Dabas. This was the first opportunity the explorer had of observing stars since leaving Yembe in September 1880. He and his servant, Chhumbel, remained here for about two months waiting for their employer, the head Lama to pay them. The head Lama on arrival gave them some money and a letter for a friend of his at Kegu Gompa, asking the latter to help them on thier way to Lhasa.

The Chang-tang, commencing at Namohan, was left behind at Niamcho and nothing further need be said of the country up to the place as it has already been described. Kishen Singh continued his journey towards Ta-chien-lu Kishen Singh entered the tea-track at Kegudo. This track later strikes the line from Siling to Lhasa at the Mora lake. In general appearance, the whole tract of the country along the route via Ta-chien-lu, Ba-tang and Gartok, distinct from the place of the same name in Ngari Khorsum, to Lao village (north of Jio Gompa) is pretty nearly alike. It is rocky and of course all mountainous. Although caps of snow are visible occasionally, the hills are neighter lofty nor severely precipitous and the track runs along moderate inclines. The districts of Jokchen and Yulung are two most famous yak breeding districts on this line. Other equally favourable localities were to be found in the Hor country.

Over grassy undulations, generally the road or passage was ample in width but in a few instances, as along the left bank of the Di Chu, beasts of burden could pass only in a single file. There were patches of cultivation at intervals. Grass and water were plentiful and even wood (in addition to yak-dung) could be obtained occasionally for fuel. Moreover the track was not liable to attacks from robbers except occasionally in Jokchen and Yulung near which the Chang-tang borders on the north east.

Herds of yak and *jophos* carrying tea were met several times, for as stated, the explorer was now on Jang-lam or northern tea routes between Ta-chien-lu and Lhasa. Occasionally, traders returning from Kegudo were also seen, carrying deer-horns, woollen fabrics, skins of wild beasts, pods of musk and the like which they had obtained in barter for tea.

Bidding grateful farewells to the head Laina of Thuden Gompa who had befriended the explorer, Pundit Kishen Singh continued his journey towards Ta-chien-lu and left this Gompa on thei 26th December, 1881. He and his servant now had to travel on foot, Goini along the bank of a stream, they passed Laindha village and reached-Churtan Karpo (11,440 feet), one of the sacred shrines in the Derge district. The shrine is situated near the junction of the stream with the Di Chu. the Churtan. there was the village of Thandha, containig forty houses. Then he passed by the villages of Rangna, Dwinda, Dhokor, Jindha, Bari and Dends and Bhonchi Gompa and stopped at Thombudha village for the night. About a mile to the west of this village is Rankna Gompa. That day's road was stony and through valleys and all the villages they passed by had some cultivation about them.

On the 27th, after marching along streams and crossing streams and small passes, they passed Kegu Gompa a little to their left, inhabited by about 300 Dabas. A quarter of a mile further they reached Kegudo village (11,860 feet) containing about 200 houses, where they halted. That day's road was rough. They passes *en route* several nomad camps. Kegudo was a large village and had about forty shops kept by the Chinese and Tibetans. It was a place of trade. The chief articles exported to China were stag's horns, musk pods and coarse woollen cloth, in exchange for which tea and silk cloth were imported. The stage is hunted during the springs as in that season its horns are young and soft. These horns were highly valued in China on account of their medicinal properties, and a pair of antlers was sold there for Rs. 150 to Rs. 200. The latter which his former employer gave him for his friend at Kegu Gompa was delivered and the latter recommended him to a trader going to Ta-chien-lu. He stonned there for sixteen days.

Leaving Kegudo on the 12th January, 1882 in the service of the trader, Kishen Singh and Chhumbel started for Ta-chien-lu along the route which, branching off from the Mora lake, passed that village. They passed opposite Tangu Gompa. The general direction of the route from Baron Tsaidam to this place was southwards but now turned to the south-east. Further they arrived at Benchin Gompa. There heyo stopped for the night. On the 13th, after crossing rivers and a small pass, they halted at Khansar village. From Hadho in the Baron district to the pass just mentioned, no trees and bushes were seen, but onward, the *padam* (a kind of fir), *changma* (a kind of willow), *shan* (a tree not recognised) and wild rose-bushes were met with.

Then they passed by the Shiongo Gompa and came near the Di Chu, now flowing from the north-west. The river flowed there is a narrow valley and was frozen here and there so that it could be crossed. Further, they passed by Siti village, Donthok Gompa and Dugung village where they stopped for a night. Supplies, firewood and grass were procurable there. The path passed the hamlets of Shau and Dondi and brought the explorer and his servant to Dwinthang Gompa which continued about 100 Dabas and was surrounded by about 100 houses. Continuing along the left bank of the river, they arrived at *dukha* (ferry) where the river was crossed by boats during the summer. Then came Sila village (10,390 feet) where they halted for a night. Next day they passed Rarang village opposite which was the Dhingo Gompa and then onwards Chiti Gompa. Journeying through scattered hamlets, they came opposite to Chingo Gompa surrounded by about fifty houses.

They arrived next at the well-known temple Dolma Lhakang (10,930 feet) where they put up for the night. About one quarter of a mile to the north of this temple was Losino village. Various kinds of corn and vegetables were cultivated along the banks of the Di Chu and these included wheat, *ne*, pea, *masur*, *sarson*, turnip and radish. About fifty miles to the south-east and on the right bank of the Di Chu is the town of Derge Gonchen. It had a large gompa and was the place of the Derge Gyalbo. Some fifteen years earlier, the inhabitants of the Nia-rong district who are the most warlike of the Tibetans invade ar conquered the town and pulled down several of the palaces. The Gyalbo had a large printing establishment, the printing being executed by means of engraved wooden blocks and this establishment contained blocks for almost all the books existing in the Tibetan language. To economize space and material, the blocks were engraved on both sides

On the 17th, having proceeded along the left bank of the Di

Chu after a steep ascent, they came to Kaphu Gompa, and passing by the hamlets of Baga and Rara, they came to Ngali Gompa. Proceeding further, they stopped at Chiri village (15 houses) for the night. Continuing and crossing a spur and passing Gainjo and Jongo Gompas, they arrived at Dojam, a nomad camp. There they learnt that they were likely to meet mounted robbers of the Chiamo Golok district during the next day's march.

On the 19th, they crossed a pass on the boundary of the Jokechen sub-division of the Derge district. They passed several nomal encampements and marclang further they got to Jokechen Gompa which had about 200 houses and 100 tents in its vicinity and here they halted. The streams drain generally level and open valley covered with rich pasturage which affords subsistence to large herds of yaks, sheep and goats belonging to nomads who were numerous in the valley. On the 20th, they gained a pass by a steep ascent which formed the boundary between Jokchen and Yulung sub-divisions of the Derge district. Proceeding further, the explorer and Chhumbel arrived at Yulung, a nomad camp. They stopped there for the night. That day they encountered ten mounted robbers near the Miri pass but fortunately the sudden approach of a Tibetan officer dispersed them. On the 21st, marching along the left bank of the Yulung Chu they passed by the residence of the Yulung *Pon* (ruler) situated in a small plain at the south extremity of which was a thick forest containing a species of stunted oak, *deodar*, birch, rhododendrons and several kinds of plants and bushes.

On the 22nd January, 1882, they reached the top of a spur, the boundary between Derge, Rongbacha and Horko district. The spur is well clad with forests and sawyers from Ta-chien-lu were engaged in turning out timber for the use of the inhabitants of the swurrounding places. From the village, the Yulung Chu stream turns to the north-east and after some miles joins the Ja Chu. Marching further, they passed by Riphung temple, Lagarkhando and Durkug villages, and Daje Gompa, considered to be one of the principal gompas of Tibet and reached Ringo village (10,550 feet) where they stopped for two days. The village was surrounded by extensive cultivation. Houses were well built, as timber was easily procurable. The road from Kegudo village to this place was generally good though along the Di Chu it was raher stony and rugged. On the 25th, they crossed the Ja Chu over ice. The river rises in the Jachukha district to which it gives the name. It was crossed by boats in summer. Marching along this river through fields and habitations, he passed by Bhiar, Nona and Kanzebo gompas. The last is so big, old and sacred that people of the neighbouring districts swear by its name. Rongbacha and the districts to the east of it were governed by two officers who had their headquarters at Kanzego. From here, the Ja Chu takes a south-easterly course. Some miles further on, it cuts through the southern snowy range and waters Niarong district, tbe inhabitants of which are very brave and were said to have conquered the neighbouring districts. They baffled the Chinese robbers sent against them some fifteen years ago. At last the Lhasa Government won over their chiefs by bribery and thus subdued them.

On the 27th January, 1882, they crossed a pass, the boundary between Rongbacha and Dau districts and passing trough some small gompas and hamlets reached the village of Dwinda. That day's path was stony and rugged. Travelling through hamlets and cultivation, he passed Gori village and crossed a low pass which formed the boundary between the Dau and Dange districts and arrived at the gompa of Dango, inhabited by about 2,000 Dabas and surrounded by a thousand houses. his gompa was also far famed and was adorned with golden cupolas. Then they arrived at Bathog village. Next day they came to a top of the spur forming the boundary between the Dango and Tan districts. Then going up and down and passing various hamlets, they reached Yathok village. All the villages along that day's route were situated on the left bank of the stream, the opposite bank being covered with forest trees. Travelling through several hamlets, they passed Nichong Gompa. The stream which the explorer had followed from the Dan sub-division, is here known as Tau Chu. It joins the Ja Chu and the united stream lower down is named the Nag Chu. Then they reached Giaro village beyond which the hill sides were covered with thick forest.

On the 1st February, 1882, they reached the foot of the steep Minia pass which formed the boundary between Tau and Minia districts. Marching further through an uninhabited part of the Minia district, they reached the village of Khansan. The route from Giaro to Khansan passed through heavy forest and the robbers from the Niarong district generally plundered travellers in the neighbourhood of the pass. Next day, they reached the village of Shao where they stopped for the night, Supplies, firewood and grass were procurable. Cultivation was scanty in the vicnity of the villages of this side of the Minia pass. Each hamlet had near it one or more old, stone-built square towers which were necessary in former times as safeguards agaisnt bands of plunderers who infested the country. After crossing streams and two low passes, they arrived at Tombadu. Their path was over undulating ground and they passed several nomad tents and a breeding establishment for horses belonging to a Tibetan official.

On the 4th, they crossed the Sama La and the Gi pass. The latter pass also crosses over the snowy range which divides into two ranges running to the right and the left and from it a path branched off to Lhasa by way of Li-tang. Continuing their progress, they arrived at Chithong Giachug.

A *giachug* is a posting stage where a relay of horses is kept. Here at Chithong Giachug, there were also twenty-five houses where travellers coule lodge and obtain food on payment. These rest houses were very comfortable and well furnished and their managers were ready to supply anything on demand but as all articles had to be. brought from Ta-chien-lu, they were dear. That day, mow fell and the path from the Gi pass was rugged and stony and lay through a narrow valley. They saw some nomad tents here and there but met no village between Tombadu and Sama La.

Ta-chien-lu

Leaving Chithong on the 5th February, 1882, they arrived at the gate of Ta-chien-lu city (8,310 feet). It is a small city situated in a very narrow valley resembling the English letter T in form enclosed on all sides by the snowy mountains which rise in precipices of stupendous height. It contains two streets extending north and south, about 3/4th of a mile along the banks of the stream, each of which consisted of a row of shops on either side of the ppaved roadway about fifteen feet wide. At the end of these two streets, a large stream from the west jointed the one flowing through the city and the joint stream then flowed to the east. There were four gates, one at each end of the two streets, with doors made of thick boards, and the stream was bridged over at a number of places with timber to facilitate communication between the streets. The houses were built of stone and timber and were generally high and double storeyed. There were four gompas at the four corners of the city. The city was governed by an officer titled *Thain* (literally "sky" and therefore means highest officer) assisted by several junior officers. Another officer called *Chiakla* also resided there and he had jurisdiction over the original inhabitants of Ta-chien-lu.

Ta-chien-lu was well known as the emporium of all the Chinese tea which was brought by porters from a distance of some twenty days' journey and was hence carried by beasts of burden to various places in Tibet and even to Kashmir itself. When moist, it was shaped into bricks, each weighing about five'lbs. and costing from six annas to three rupees, per brick according to the quality of the tea; these bricks of tea were known in Western Tibet and Kashmir by the name of *damu*. The price of a *damu* of tea in Leh varied some twenty years ago from five to eight rupees. During the journey from Kegudo to Ta-chien-lu, Kishen Singh met several traders returning to their homes with ea estimated to aggregate not less than 300,000 lbs.

The climate of the Ta-chien-lu valley in winter is very severe owing to a continuous fall of snow for weeks, while in hot weather it was comparatively warm from the circumstance of its being surrounded by high mountains. The Chinese and Tibetan traders were numerous, being about equal in number. The language and religion of the native inhabitants of the city resembled those of the Tibetans. With the exception of small gardens for raising ordinary vegetables, no cultivation was carried on in the Ta-chien-lu valley. Corn and different kinds of vegetables and fruits were brought from some distance eastwards, where the soil is better suited for cultivation. Some small bushes alone grow on the hill sides and a few stunted trees had been planted here and there in the vicinity of the houses. Timber and firewood were brought down the large stream from the south, which joins the main stream about 4-1/2 miles before reaching the city. The streams abound in fish which are caught by angling. The same currency and weights as used at Saitu were obtained here but the Indian rupee was also current.

At Ta-chien-lu, Kishen Singh was once more in a town and amidst comparative civilisation, circumstances which however rather aggravated the consequences of his property.

Having heard that two Jesuit Fathers lived outside the city, close to the northern and southern gates, the explorer determined to visit them in order to enquire about the safest and surest route to India, and also to try to obtain through them means to prosecute his journey. One day he met one of them who received him very kindly but as in the course of the conversation the missionary did not raise the question of the explorer's means, the latter did not think it fit and advisable to trouble him. He however presented the Pundit with six rupees and gave him an introductory letter to his brethren at Ba-tang and Darjeeling and avised him to return by way of Tibet it fit and advisable to trouble him. He however presented the Pundit with six ruppes and gave him an introductory letter to his brethren at Ba-tang and Darjeeling and advised him to return by way of Tibet in preference to that by China, as the former, he said, would take only 40 days to reach India and moreover required no passport which would be necessary for the latter. Returning to his quarters, Kishen Singh glanced at the missionary's letter and found that the missionary and he disagreed in their dates, for what the missiionary had put down as the 11th, he made out to be the 12th February, 1882. Unfortunately he had no opportunity of seeing him again. The explorer and his servant remained at Ta-chien-lu for eleven days during which he was unable to take observations for latitude owing to cloudy weather and continuous fall of snow. It is from this place that the two tea-routes to Lhasa diverge, one folowing the *Janglam* or northern route and the other *Junglam* or southern and official road as stated elsewhere. It may be added here that the whole tract of country passed through from Thuden Gompa to Lao yielded but one harvest annually. It will be seen that from Ta-chien-lu, the explorer trvaelled along the official road. He however had occasion to leave this road to Gar-tok, proceeding south-west to Sama as well as presently explained, so that it was not until his arrival at Lho Dzong that he aain joined the *Junglam*.

The explorer reached Chithong Giachug on the 16th February, 1882. The next day he crossed the Gi pass (14,690 feet) and thence took the Ba-tang route along a stream which runs to the west. Passing by Chachukha Giachung, Thicho (Ti-su) and Anya Giachug, they reched Thondo Churtan, also called Hache, on the 18th and halted near the *churtan*. The following morning was the New Year's Day of the Tibetean calendar and in keeping with custom of the country they gave themselves a holiday. After resuming their journey along the stream they reached Golokthok Giachug. On the way they passsed many hamlets, with cultivation around them, and found the inhabitants contnuing the festivities of the New Year's Day. The path was good.

On the 21st, after passing Kashi Gompa and after steep ascent they gained Kashi La pass (14,710 feet). Proceeding further, they passed Urong Dongu Giachug and halted at the hamlet of Zi-ra (3 houses). That day's road passed through a forest.

Following the stream, they passed the hamlets of Urongshi in the Urongshi district which extends from the Kashi La (pass) in the east to the Nagechukha village in the west. They arrived at Kharingbo Giachug and after crossing some streams by wooden bridges reached Nagechukha village.

Nagechukha village (8,410 feet) was situated on the bank of the Nag Chur river and consisted of some forty shops scattered her and there and surrounded by high mountains covered with grass and thick forest trees. The forest was full of wild animals among which a species of stage with a thick, flat, long tail was remarkable. The inhabitants were very fond of breeding hogs and hunting dogs. The former are of two kinds, the Chinese or broad-ered breed and the common kind found in India. Two crops were annually raised, one of bareley and wheat and the other of millet, *dau*, turnip and other edible roots.

To cross the river, the previous sanction of the headman of the village was required. The explorer and his servant, therefore, went to him to obtain permission but as soon as the headman heard their request, he suspected them to be thieves, as he said that every one in the country was celebrating the new year festival and that no one but thieves travlled at that time. The headman ordered them to stay there for four days during which time he would get information from the ruler of the city of Ta-chien-lu whether any theft had lately been committed in the city. After four days, they were set at liberty and having paid two annas to the keepper of the bridge, they crossed the 100 pace wide river. This river, as mentiioned before, is former by the junction of the Ja Chu and Ta Chu and flowing to the south, falls into the Di Chu which flows through the Chinese Empire. Marching further, they passed by Margen Dongu Giachug. Then travelling up two passes and down the streams, they passed the gompa of Golak and reached Golomthok Giachug where they passed the night of the 1st March, 1882. That day's road was rugged, stony and undulating and from the pass last mentioned, it lay in the Litang district. Cultivation was found here. Grass, firewood and supplies were abundant.

Smallpox was prevalent in this vicinity and to prevent its spread a kind of snuff was administrered by the Chinese physicians. This snuff had the same effect as vaccination and its use brought out a few pimples here and there over the body, accompanied by a slight fever. These pimples dried in time and the dried up matter which fell from them was used for preparing the antidote.

Crossing a few streams they passed the *giachugs* of Tamarathong and Hapchukha (Ho-chu-ka) and reached a small *giachug* of one house. From Hapchukha to this place, they passed about 100 tents of nomads and were that a little to the north of this junction. Washing for gold was carried on and that the gtold found there was very fine in colour and quality. After marching along undulating ground, they arrived at Li-tang, a small city containing about 2,500 houses.

Li-tang

Li-tang (13,400 feet), one of the richest towns in Tibet, is situated to the north of a plain and at the end of a spur from the northern range. This plain is watered by a stream named Li-Chu (Li-tang river) flowing to the south-east. The plain is covered with grass and contained several springs of fresh water. Its greatest length is about fifteen miles and the greatest breadth eight miles and it was peopled by a large number of nomads. There was no cultivation and corn was brought from a distance of about three days' journey to the south, while rice and *gur* (a coarse kind of sugar) were brought from Yuna (Yunan), a large tract of country belonging to China and some 300 miles away to the south-east.

Here, as in Lhasa, the popular festival of Chiango chiopa was celebrated during the first month of the year. Thyis month is called *Molam Chemo* or the month of asking blessings, owing to the brief that favours asked for it it. are sooner granted by the gods than those sought at any other time. A large earthen figure, triangular in shape, called *chiopa* was made and painted with various colours. The figure with a number of smaller ones similar in construction and arranged around it, was placed in the verandah of the gompa. This gompa was inhabited by about 2,500 Dabas. A fair commenced on the 16th day of the new year, i.e. the day of full moon (in March) and lasted two days, during which a large gathering of the inhabitants of the neighbourhood took place. The town had a long *bazar* (market) which contained about 100 shops kept by Chinese and Tibetans. A road branched off from here to Derge Gonchen.

On the 7th March, 1882 3-1/4 miles from Li-tang, they crossed a stream to the south. On its right bank is a hot spring which has a kind of saline incrustation about it. Half a mile to the north of the spring is a *rito* (a place of retirement for religious contemplation) with some out-houses for attendants, where the Lama of LI-tang resided. Then they reached Jiambothok Giachug. Here they halted. Marching further they passed Garalarch Giachug and Mane Ringbo, a long wall cextending a mile and faced with thin rectangular smooth stone slabs, on which sacred formalue and religious precepts were engraved. Further on they arrived at Nyenda Giachug, where they stopped on the 9th March. As a distance of three miles towards north-west is Gombone, a place of pilgrimage at the foot of a mountain.

On the 10th, after crossing streams, they arrived at Rathi Giachug. The path passed through a forest of *padam* tree and there were many nomad tents scattered along the route. On the 11th, they reached Rathi pass (15,340 feet), the boundary btween the Li-tang and Ba-tang districts. Then they passed the *giachugs* of Tashu and Pang-tha-mo situated in the midst of a thick forest. The path was rugged, stony and undulating. On the 13th, they passed a hot spring where five tanks with high curtain and partition walls were built and around which were a number of tents belonging to persons who had come to bathe. The batching was continued for at least a week. Then they reached Chioti Gompa in Ba-tang, where they rested for three nights.

This gompa, which is protected by strong, high curtain walls, is about half a mile in circumference and was inhabited by about 1,000 Dabas. The inhabitants of the Saingan sub-division in the Ba-tang district, who lived along the banks of the Di Chu, about a day's journey above the village of Ba-tang, were very turbulent, having on several occasions robbed travellers. Ba-tang (8,150 feet) is a considerable village or rather a small town in a valley enclosed by hills and is situated for the most part on a level strip of gorund on the right bank of the stream near its junction with the main stream. There were about 2,000 houses including fifty shops. On the left bank of the stream was a house belonging to a Jesuit Father. Two cropps were generally raised here as a Nagechukha. The general direction of their route from Tachien-lu to Ba-tang, was westerly.

On the 16th, passing a gompa and three villages, they reached the ferry and the village of Dabana (7,700 feet) and crossed the Di Chu by ferry boats. Travelling through a populated country, they crossed a pass by a slight ascent and reached Konzukha Giachug situated near the boundary between Ba-tang and Makham districts. On the 19th, they passed Lhamdun Giachug. Near this place was a temple dedicated to Namba Nacho. A route branches off from here to Chiakla Chakra where salt was found. To the south of Chiakla Chaka is a snowy range named Khahrpo, culminating in some peaks held sacred, which pilgrims circummambulated. They stopped at the village for two nights on account of fall of snow.

On the 21st, they reached Gartok or Makham (11,920 feet) which is quite distinct from the place of the same name in Nagri Khorsum. This was a large village under the Government of Lhasa, containing about 700 houses with a large gompa and a building for the residence of the two *Jongpons* and had some cultivation near it.

The explorer and his servant here left the Lhasa route which proceeds north-west for about 180 miles via Dayag till it reaches Chiamdo on the left bank of Chiamdo Chu. Thence it turns south-west for about 110 miles, crossing *en route* the Giama Nu Chu, and joins the route they eventually adopted nver Lho Dzong. They followed a footpath towards Zayual, a district about 100 miles north-east of Sadiya in Assam. On the 24th, they reached the village of Lao.

On the 25th, marching down the narrow valley which was well cultivated and had a number of houses scattered about it, they arrived at the ferry of Sambo Dukha (9,450 feet). The arrangement for crossing consisted of a thick leather rope stretched very tight from an elevated point on one bank to a lower level on the opposite bank. The rope was secured round stout poles half buried in the ground and was strong enough to bear the weight of men and animals. The method of crossing was very simple. A semi circular piece of wood would slide along the rope. Another rope was wrapped round the object to be transported and its ends were tied to the two ends of the wood. For recrossing the river, another rope was similarly stretched in a suitable locality close by. The length of the rope-bridge was estimated to be about 130 paces. Crossing the bridge, they reached Jio village where they stoped for the night. The path was narrow, rugged and stony.

On the 26th March, 1882, they crossed Jio pass and then arrived at Cha Churtan (10,640 feet). This *churtan* which is one of the sacred places in Tibet was surrounded by about thirty houses. They found here two species of crow; the one common in Tibet has red beak and legs and black feather and the other has spotted or piebald feathers but black beak and claws. Both of these were numerous here and the cultivators had to keep a watch over their fields to prevent the seed which had lately been sown from being eaten up by them. They stopped for three days on accont of snow. On the 31st a stiff ascent brought them to the Ghotu pass, then covered with snow. A difficult descent took them to a small frozen lake. They passed two nights in a forest under a *deodar* tree as they were suffering badly from ophthalmia brought on by the glare of snow. The explore had no mountaineering equipment, windproof clothing, sun-glass, etc. and had to learn about frostibite and snow-blindness in the hard and painful way.

On the 2nd April, they arrived at the village of Dayul (15 houses) on the right bank of the stream along their route. After crossing a wooden bridge half a mile away, they reached the gompa of Dayul (11,450 feet) which was surrounded by about 100 houses, including a large one, the residence of the *Jongpon*. Dayul is situated in a narrow valley in the midst of a thick jungle abounding in wild sheep and musk deer. The price or musk as sold in the pod was two rupees per *tola*. Large quantities of this article were carried from these points to China. Patches of cultivation were found here. They were informed that no person was allowed to go beyond the district of Dayul which extended from the Jio pass to the Koli pass on account of Smallpox which was then raging in the district. But the *Jongpon* of Dayul was going to Sanga Chu Dzong, sixty-five miles due west by direct route. Kishen Singh and Chhumbel requested the *Jongpon* for permission to accompany his party but the latter refused.

The *Chyam* or the lady of the *Jongpon*, taking AK and his servant as holy pilgrims, asked them to wait and take alms. What Kishen Singh could not get by asking a blunt officer, he wanted to accomplish with the help of the fair sex which had helped him so many times during his extensive journey in Tibet. He was fully aware of the independence enjoyed by the Tibetan women and the respect and honour she receives in her society.

While receiving alms, A K and Chhumbel pretended to weep and requested her to intervene to get the *Jongpon's* permission to accompany his party. They told her that they belonged to Kha-tse-thang near Lhasa, which was her parental homeland. They lady's heart was affected by the weeping and by the reminiscence of her parental home and shee left pity for them. She promised that she would plead with the *Jongpon* on their behalf and assured them that the request would be granted She ordered them to get ready to accompany the party on the 4th April. They returned after expressing their gratitude.

As promised, the *Chyam* sent word through her servant on the 4th April asking them to proceed. AK and Chhumbel joined the party with gratitude. After crossing the Koli pass, they passed by Koli village, Jior Gompa and vilage Joir where they stopped on the 5th April. They had a heavy fall of snow that day. Next day, they reached Thangshu Dukha (7,160 feet) and crossed the Diama Nu Chu, also called Nu Chu, which is deep and rapid. They crossed here on planks which were propelled by oars and kept from being carried down the current by some of the boatmen holding on to a rope stretched across the Nu Chu. The river issues from the range in the north of Zayul district and finally passes by Rin Chiako, a noted place of pilgrimage in Burma. Then they passed by the villages of Yu, Hakha and Ji where they stopped for eight nights. Towards the south is the snowy range of Riraphasi which is regarded by Tibetans from all parts of the country as an object of deep veneration and which they circumabulate in great numbers as a religious exercise.

Having heard that Tila pass would soon be practicable, as the snow was melting, they left the village on the 17th April and went through Niakho village, and on the 20th ascended the Tila pass (16,110 feet). The district of Nu Chu Giu lies between the two passes, Koli to the north-east and Tila to the south-west. They passed through thick forest and reached the hamlet of Rika. On the 22nd, they reached the gompa of Drawon (8,300 feet) on the bank of the Zayul Chu. From there a route branches off to the fort of Sanga Chu Dzong, about fifty miles to the north, where two *Jongpons* resided. Then they reached the hamlet of Chikung opposite which and on the right bank of the river is Gowa village. On the 23rd, after crossing a wooden bridge, they reached the hamlet of Dabla. On the 25th, they crossed the Zayul Chu by a wooden bridge about 100 paces long and reached the junction of the Rong-thod Chu and the Zayul Chu rivers and then reached Shikha in the district of Zayul.

It will be seen that from Ta-chien-lu, the explorer travelled along the official road. He however had occasion to leave this road at Gurtok, proceeding south-west to Sama (as will be presently explained) so that it was not until his arrival at Lho Dzong that he again joined the *Junglam*. From Lao village southwards, the country changes in various ways. The hills are very rocky, rugged and precipitous and with exceedingly narrow valleys. Cultivation was plentiful to the extent of the ground available and not only were the crops abundant but the climate admitted of two harvests in the year. The country is called Rong. It is understood that the Rong lay south of the explorer's route by only some twenty or thirty miles. The province of Po-to lies just north of Po-me in the

Rong. Thus far, the route followed from Lao to Ata Gang pass via Sama lay throughout in the Rong. It is in this portion of his journey that the explorer saw the heaviest snow-clad and presumably the highest mountains.

Proceeding south from Lao village, the lofty peaks of Khaharpo, perhaps about 20,000 feet high, attracted his attention, A distinction may be noticed between the snow hills of the Chang-tang and those of Rong. In the Chang-tang, the snow cap is a round bluff and is immediately followed below by the coat of grass which covers the undulating ground and extends continuously down to the ordinary levels of the high land. In the Rong, the peaks are precipitous and pointed, the snow line is followed by a belt of a mile or so of grass, succeeded by brushwood which grows stronger and higher and ends in lofty and large timber trees.

From the Koli pass, the Rirapphasi peaks, estimated to be some 20,000 feet high, became visible. They are plainly connected with the Neching Gangra range which which was crossed at Tila pass (16,100 feet). The explorer was now in the horse-shoe shaped basin of the Zayul Chu, one of the feeders of the Brahmaputra, and travelled down the bed of that river to Sama, with the lofty Neching Gangra range on the north and its lower continuation on the south, both ranges being visible at intervals. He had no doubt that the peaks of the Neching Gangra were the loftiest he had seen and by estimation placed their hight at some 25,000 feet.

Zayul district

Shikha was the winter residence of the officer of Zayul district. The buildings, about twenty-five in number, constructed by the land owners for these officials, lay in the lands of the village of Rime. They were made of timber and some of them were two-storeyed. The officers who resided here were: a *Jongpon*, a *Shian-u* (the civil and magisterial officer of the district), a *Jam Pon* (custodian of the bridges of the district), and a number of subordinates and attendants. This place was also the resort in winter of traders from all parts of Tibet. The district of Zayul, which extends from the Tila pass to the Ata Gang pass, is bounded on all sides by lofty ranges. The range to the north is known as the Neching Gangra. The spurs which shoot off from them are thickly covered with large trees and long grass, the latter affording good nourishment to wild and domestic animals. The explorer was surprised to hear that though the forest was full of game, no venomous serpents or carnivorous beasts were to be found. The domestic animals bred by the inhabitants were oxen, *jobos* and *jomos* (male and female animals obtained by crossing a bull and a female yak or vice versa), horses, hogs and fowls. Cows were never milked because it was supposed to render the calves weak but the milk of the *jomo* was in general use. The climate of the district is mild. Goitre was a common disease from which very few escaped.

The inhabitants of the district were very simple in their habits. The dress of both sexes was made from a kind of striped cloth woven from a mixture of hemp and wool. The men shaved their heads like Dabas and Lamas but the women dressed their hair in two long plaits wound round the head and tied together in front. The hair, thus arranged, looked like a cap from a distance. They used no umbrellas but hats of straw or reed to protect their heads against sun or rain. The language differed very much from the Tibetan which however they understand very well and their mode of expressing themselves was amusing as they spoke in a very loud tone and with much gesticulation. They professed Buddhism but rarely visited gompas or other sacred places and had full belief in the sacrifice of pigs and fowls which they offered to propitiate gods during times of distress. They burnt their dead like the Hindus of India.

The chief articles of diet were rice, unleavened bread, meat, a kind of paste made by boiling flour of various grains and some vegetables, mostly found growing wild. They mixed a large quantity of chillies with their food. They raised two crops. The one reaped in October and November, comprised paddy, *kodo* (a small grain called *mandwa* in India), Indian corn, millet, *dau* and varieties of pulse grains such as *kulath*, *masur*, *matar* and *urad*. The other crop which was harvested in April and May consisted of barley, *ne*, wheat and *sarson*. Of fruits, the lemon, plantain, walnut and peach only were found in the district.

The district was much frequented by traders from the Mishmi or Nahong tribe, who lived in the forests of the British area bordering it. The articles of merchandise which they brought for exchange were *shugshina* (the bark of a plant used for making paper), *ram* (a kind of grass which yields blue colour), *choi* (a kind of grass which yields yellow colour), *shingcha* (a root of a plant exported to China for colouring silk and which according to some is also used there as medicine), deer-skins and various kinds of cloth from Assam, and exchanged them for salt and horned animals.

The district is considered by Tibetans as the warmest place in their country and therefore any person who was guilty of a crime requiring transportation for life was sent to Zayul by the Government of Lhasa to undergo that sentence. These culprits were branded over their foreheads.

No sooner had they entered Sikha (4, 650 feet), than the explorer and his servant were made to pay a rupee to the *Jam Pon* (the custodian of bridges) as a ferry-toll and were soon afterwards seized by the Shi-u, who ordered them to remain in quarantine for twenty-two days owing to their coming from the district where small-pox was raging. The road from Gartok to this place was narrow, undulating, stony and rugged and its general direction was south-west only. The mercury in the explorer's instruments had leaked away near the Koli pass because Chhumbel fell on the slippery road. On the 23rd May, 1882, they reached the hamlet of Singhu (7 houses) and then Sama village (7 houses) situated near the border of the autonomous tribal area under British jurisdiction which was inhabited by Mishmi (Nahong), Lhoyuli and other head-hunting Nagas.

From Sama he took a cricuitous route around the Tasng-po.

KISHEN SINGH

Tsang-po merely means a large river and the word is equally applicable to all large river. The proper name of the river, south of Lhasa, is Tsang Chuor Nari Chu.

With the Rong left behind, the explorer was once more in a country similar to that already described, such as he had passed through before reaching Lao village, and yielding only one harvest annually. These features with but little variation continued along the remainder of the exploration. At Lho Dzong he rejoined *Junglam* (southern road) and again met bands of traders between Lhasa and Ta-chien-lu. Leaving the road at Chomorawa Giachug, he turned south to Tse-tang.

Onward to India

Hearing that the Ata Gang pass on the latter route was at that season impracticable on account of snow, and as the small amount of money then in their possession was not sufficient to cover the expenses of that long journey, they employed themselves in going about from house to house in the villages of Singu, Sama, Rima and Duning, reciting from Tibetan sacred books, and thus succeeded in collecting some twenty rupees.

On the 9th July, 1882, they resumed their journey along the Rongthod Chu and passed the hamlet of Dungtang where they halted. The headman of this hamlet had a slave about thirty years of age, purchased from a Mishmi, who had kidnapped him from Assam some sixteen years ago. On the 10th, continuing up the right bank of the river, they reached Bona-thang village. Afterwards they passed opposite Thaling hamlet and then the hamlets of Timi and Di and Chiangs gompa and reached Thoyu hamlet on the 14th. Here they remained for two nights. They saw a lad from Assam, seven years of age, who had been sold as a slave by a Mishmi the previous year. On the 16th, they arrived at the hamlet of Tithong which contained a large house built for the Shian-u of the Zayul district who occupied it for three months in the rainy season. Then they passed the gompas of Jungu and Murgu.

On the 19th, they reached the village of Sonling (6,200 feet). The inhabitants of this village were esteemed the wealthiest in the Zayul district. About forty five miles to the north-west is the sacred peak called Pemakaun, which was rarely visited by pilgrims as they had to pass through the country of the Lhobas who were much addicted to robbery. The Lhobas inhabit the Lhoyul district to the north-west of the Mishmi country. Their manners and customs were similar to those of the Mishmis though their language is somewhat different. They brought the same articles of merchandise as the Mishmis and exchanged them for salt at Sonling. The explorer stopped there for three nights.

On the 22nd, they resumed their journey in company of some travellers who were going to the district of Nagong. They passed the hamlet of Isamedh and reached Lsatodh. Rice-fields were numerous between Dabla and this place. On the 28th, after crossing some streams, they passed Sugu and reached the village of Ata (7,950 feet) where they remained for six nights. Elegant wooden cups were made there. This was the most northern village in the Zayul district where cultivation was found. Grain was cheap and the inhabitants of the Nagong district went there for purchases. It is said that from the spurs of the mountains of the west, the snowy speaks of the Neching Gangra range on the east are visible. These peaks are objects of religious veneration to Tibetans.

On the 3rd August, they crossed a stream, which issues from a glacier. The path winds along the south-eastern side of the glacier which stretches from the north-west, and by a stiff ascent comes to the encamping ground of Chutong where they halted. From Sikha to this place, with the exception of cleared and cultivated spots in the vicinity of the villages, the hill sides are covered with forest trees. On the 4th, after crossing a steep pass and passing by the southern edge of the continuation of the glacier mentioned before and following up the western edge for a mile, they came to the pass of Ata Gang over the Neching Gangra snowy range. Proceeding over the glacier, they arrived at a small unoccupied house (height 14,690 feet) probably built for the accommodation of travellers. They stopped there for five nights owing to a continuous fall of rain. Some five tents belonging to nomads were seen in the vicinity.

On the 9th, they reached Lhagu village where little cultivation was visible. The road was level. Grass and firewood were abundant. On the 10th, after skirting a glacier, they passed Khansar and the Ngongjhio temple. Then crossing a stream by a wooden bridge, they arrived at Shuiden Gompa (13,650 feet) situated in a lonely spot on high level ground overlooking the river. This gompa had about 100 Dabas and was surrounded by about 150 houses. Having arrived there from Zayul the explorer and his servant were suspected by the official of being escaped convicts, but some days after their arrival a rich man from Rima happening to visit the gompa obtained permission for them to proceed. A route branched off from this place to Sanga Chu Dzong. On the 20th August, 1882, they passed the villages of Ranya and Rahu and rested at the temple of Nan-khazed. Grass and firewood were abundant. A shorter route to Lhasa, practicable for foot passengers only, passed through po-me and Kongbo but on account of the prevalence of smallpox, it was closed that year.

On the 21st, they crossed a low pass. The district of Nagong extends from the Ata Gang pass to this pass. Then they passed Gonkha and Dongsar village containing about forty houses and a gompa. This village (15,850 feet) is situated on an extensive and well cultivated valley. They remained here for four nights and took service with a rice merchant who had brought that article from Zayul and was taking it to Shiobado (Shobando) district about 100 miles on the same route that the explorer was following. The rice was carried on mules. Continuing, they passed Dongo gompa and Diu village. From Ata Gang pass to this village, the road was generally speaking good.

Marching, they passed Bungyu and crossed the Bungyu pass

covered with snow. This pass is on the boundary between the districts of Damsi and Pashu. Then crossing another pass, they reached Tapsing. Then they gained a pass after a gradual ascent and crossed a large stream by a bridge called Giok Jam, fotry five paces long. Near this bridge (Height 11,040 feet) and on either bank of the stream are several hamlets, Cultivation was carried on there and peaches and apricots were found in abundance. A toll of four annas was levied from each passenger for passing across the bridge. On the 4th September, they passed Baimbu gompa, Rango village and reached the gompa of Niopha. That day they passed through an inhabited part of the country.

On the 5th, they crossed a pass where the district of Pashu ends and that of Lho Dzong begins. Travelling through a narrow valley, they gained another pass. Descending, they passed Ong gompa and the village of Chukpodesa. Two miles to the north of this village on the left bank of a stream, there is the fort of Lho Dzong (13,140 feet) where two *Jong-pons* resided. Near the fort is a large gompa, a *giachug* and about 150 houses. They stopped there for the night of the 6th. They struck there the high road from Ta-chien-lu to Lhasa.

The following is the list of the *giachugs* (travelling stages) from Gartok to Lho Dzong fort. Against each stage is given its approximate distance from the preceding one is *Lis* (a *Lis* is roughly eaual to a mile) :

	Lis		*Lis*
Gartok			
Risi	.. 60	Chiamdo (on the left	80
Nimago	.. 70	bank of Chiamdo	
Dayagi Sachain	.. 60	Chu)	
Rasi	.. 60	Lungdha	90

Asi	60	Lagang	90
Dayag	60	Nulda	80
Jiamdo	60	Mari	90
Gham	50	Shang-ye Jam (on the	80
Wangka	50	left bank of the	
Bagang	50	Giama Nu Chu)	
Pangdha	60	Lho Dzong	120
Mongpho	70		

On the 7th September, 1882, they left the fort, and retracing their steps of Chukpodesa village, crossed a pass. Their route now entered the district of Jithong (Jithog). On the 8th, passing by several villages and two gompas, they arrivead at Shobando (12,470 feet) which possessed about 200houses and some shops, a gompa and a stagehouse. Some officials resided there. As the rice merchant's journey ended at Shobando, the explorer and his servant tok service with a trader from Charong who was going to Lhasa. Marching, they gained a pass by a steep; ascent and entered the district of Pembo. On the way further, they found some tents of nomads who remained there during the rainy season. On the 10th, after crossing a pass, they came to the *giachug* of Bari. Then they arrived at a pass and, descending, reached Lache giachug. The nomads of Poto, on the tract across the snowy range to the south of the route, sometimes robbed the travellers. On the 12th, after crossing a stream and a pass they arrived at the large gompa of Pemba. Then they passed Chiakra, Bargo and Urgeritamdha *glachugs*. The path from Lache Gompa to this place is level and lies through an inhabited part of the country.

On the 14th, proceeding further, they gained the Shiar Gang pass by a steep ascent. Their route now lay through the district of

Arig. Then they passed the *giachugs* of Namgialgon and Nuldokar and Arig Gompa and reached Ji village where they replenished their stock of provisions. Then they passed by Alado, Alagak, Alachiago and Aladochug *giachugs*. On the 20th, marching up a steep ascent, they gained the pass of Nub Kong (17,940 feet). Here they entered the district of Lharugo. Then they passed two lakes and arrived at Chachukha Giachug where they stoped for the night. Grass and firewood were procurable.

On the 21st, proceeding up and down, they arrived at Lharugo Giachug (13,690 feet) where there were about sixty houses, a stage-house and a gompa. From this *giachug*, a road branches off to Lhasa. There was scarcity of firewood and grass. The general direction of their routh from Lho Dzong to this place was westwards. On the 23rd, they reached a pass named Archa by a steep ascent. Continuing, they reached the eastern extremity of a lake, about four miles long and 1-1/2 miles broad. The country aound afforded rich pasturage to herds of cattle belonging to the nomads of the neighbourhood. Proceeding along the southern margin of the lake, they passed Gole Giachug. Then they crossed th pass of To (17,350 feet) and reached Donthog Giachug. The country between Alagak and Donthog was uncultivated. Continuing, they passed by Laru Giachug and on the 27th, reached the small town of Giamdo (10,900 feet), situated above the confluence of two streams. The town consisted of about 100 small houses with a main street lined by about 200 shops, running through it. The shops were kept by the Tibetans, Chinese and Nepalese. At Giamdo, there was a mint where Tibetan money was coined. Cultivation was carried on in the vicnity and wheat, barley and other coarser grains were raised. They stopped there for two nights. Continuing, they trvelled through Sangsur gompa and Cam Giachug, passed opposite Nimaring Giachug and reached the Gia La (pass) by a steep ascent. This pass in on the south-eastern boundary of the Rongbo district which commences from the To pass.

On the 2nd October, 1882, they arrived at Chomorawa Giachug. Here they left the road to Lhasa. There are four giachugs, viz., Whezarsang (Euzer), Riu-cheu-ling. Medu kongkar and De-chen on this road between Chomorawa and Lhasa. Then they took a path named Uri Bar-khor, which was trodden only by pilgrims from Lhasa when going round the range of mountains to the south of the city. Parting company with the trader, they gained a pass by a slight ascent. Descending, they found some nomads and remained with them for two nights.

Killer Insect

The nomads were engaged in burying animals which had died from a certain disease named *sango,* supposed to be caused by an insect half an inch long. The head of this insect is black and its body is of a dull yellowish colour. These insects are common all over Tibet. They swarm under the grass and any animal that grazes onit is at once attacked by fever which almost always proved fatal. The fever afterwards becomes contagious and attacks other animals and even the men who herd them or eat their flesh. The explorer was told that all animals which die of this disease are found with their head towards the north and their tails crooked. Persons who suffer from it are first attacked by fever followed by boils which appear under the arm-pits and on the elbow and knee-points. Very few animals or persons recover from it. The only measure adopted by the inhabitants is one of precautionary nature.They eat scorched insects to fortify their system against the poisonous effects of the living ones. These insects are not easily discovered as they remain hiden under the grass and the only time for unearthing them is summer when the place where they exist is free from snow. People put on the spot a large copper vesel turned downwards and kindle fire over and around it. After a time, the vessel is removed when a number of these insects are found scorched underneath. One scorched insect is given to a man as a prophylactic. They are also given to animals, mixed with salt.

On the 4th, they passed the gompa of Jingcho, Kanadeya village, the fort of Hoko (Horga) and Yachu village and on the 5th, they reached the hamlet of Khatha (11,260 feet), containing five houses and situated on the left bank of the Tsang-po, where they stopped for the night.The general direction of their route from the

Lharugo Giachug to this hamlet was south-west. It was wide throughout but generally rugged and stony.

The Tsang-po which rises near the Manasarowar lake is called by different names in various places. In Ngari Khorsum, it is named Tamjan-khamba, in the Tsang district—Nari Chu, and in some parts of the district of Lhokha which extends from Gia La to the Kong-ka Dzong (fort), it is named Tsang Chu or Tsang-po. The general direction of the river is eastwards. The force of its current a little below Khatha is very strong. In its further course, it receives contributions from innumerable streams and water courses which rise from the southern and western slopes of that portion of the range which lies between the Ata Gang pass on the east and the Gia La (pass) on the west. It is said that the river finally inclines to the south, and after joining with the Zayul Chu, nearly half of its dimension, flows into India.

On the 6th, proceeding up the left bank of the river, they passed Zangri Khammedh gompa and Zangri Dzong. Shikhar Dzong is situated about three miles to the south and on the right bank of the river. From Zangri Dzong, the road leaves the river and ascending the hills on the right reaches Daisithi Gompa. Next day, descending 2-1/4 miles and then following the left bank of the river, they reached the gompa of Hon-Ngari Thanjang (Naridachang). It was a large building on an isolated mound. The latter had about 200 houses around it. Grass and fuel were procurable. Here they halted for the night. On the 8th, they crossed the river which is 200 paces wide and very deep. On the right bank of the river is Naiko Dukha (ferry). Proceeding three miles from the ferry, they arrived t Tse-tang (11,480 feet), a large town containing about 1,000 houses, shops, a gompa and a fort, from there a route branches off to Lhasa by way of Samaye. Dechen Dzong is about forty-five miles from his town. They halted there for three nights.

On the 11th, proceeding up the right bank, they passed the temple of Ghyasa (Chense) Lhakang and later arrived opposite the large gompa of Samaye, surrounded by about 1,000 houses and shops.

Next day, they passed the hamlet of Dughio, the gompas of

Chinduchoka and Jera and the *churtan of* Jiambaling. Continuing along the right bank of the river, they arrived at Chitishio Dzong where there were about 1,000 houses, a fort and some shops. This place was well known for its woollen cloth.

On the 13th, they passed the villages of Taishion and Chishio, the large gompa of Ra-medh and Nianga Lhakang temple. Continuing their journey up the right bank of the river, they passed the *churtan* of Kong-Ka, Kong-Ka Dzong surrounded by about 600 houss, and the hamlets of Lhasang and Kina (10,510 feet) where they stoped for the night.

On the 15th October, 1882 they arrived at the village of Jiang-thang. Proceeding 4-1/2 miles further, the route diversed from the Tsang Chu which comes from the west. The general direction of the route from the hamlet of Khatha to this place was to the west and along the bank of the river which is this portion of its course has a very slow current. Turning from here to the south and proceeding for a mile, they arrived at Kam-pa-par-tse stage-house, which they had visited when going to Lhasa some four years ago. Pundit Kishen Singh ended his route survey here as this place was fixed by Pundit Nain Singh. Leaving Kam-pa-par-tse, the explorer and his faithful servant, Chhumbel, arrived at Darjeeling on the 12th November, 1882. In this portion of the route, they suffered severely on account of heavy snow.

Results of the exploration

The explorer helped solve some interesting geographical probloems. Broadly stated, one relates to the Irrawady and the other to the Brahmaputra, based on the evidence which he had secured.

As to the question of the north-watershed of Irrawady, it will be seen that the Zayul district is peculiar in that it is locked in right round by a high and continuous watershed, which is cut through only at one place, i.e., by the Zayul Chu. The district is made up of two valleys; in the eastern runs the Zayul Chu proper, rising at Tila pass; the western is the bed of the Rong-thod Chu, rising at Ata Gang pass. The two streams unite near Shikha and then cut through the range. For want of other names, the ranges round Zayul district are herewith given adopted names compounded of the two districts which each divides. Thus Rong-thod-Mishmi stands between the Rong-thod valley and the Mishmi valley; similarly Rong-thod-Pome; the range south-east of Zayul-valley is given the name of Zayul-Khanung. The ranges themselves were acautally and visually followed by the explorer and his verbal account in addition leaves no doubt that apart from minor defects which only an actual topographical survey could elicit, his delineation is in the main correct. On this evidence, it now stands that the watershed of the Irrawady is the range between Zayul and Khanung.

The Tsang-po rises near the Manasarowar lake from where it has been traced, practically continuously for some 850 miles to Gyala Sindong.

SECTION THREE

KALIAN SINGH
HARI RAM
LALA
NEM SINGH
KINTHUP
RINZIN NAMGYAL
UGYEN GYATSO
MIRZA SHUJA
ATA MOHAMMAD
ABDUL SUBHAH

KALIAN SINGH

Kalian Singh hailed from Milam vilage in the Johar valley in Kumaon. He was selected to continue the survey work in place of the Chief Pundit, Nain Singh who needed rest. Kalian Singh who came to be known as the thired Pundit was the second cousin of Nain Singh.

Pundit Kalian Singh assumed the character of a Bashahri, and taking a few loads of merchandize, started in April 1868 with a party of Basharis or men of Koonoo. He made his way from Spiti, through Indus. Here the 3rd Pundit measured the velocity of the Indus River by throwing a piece of wood into it and then noticing how long it took to float down 300 paces. The velocity turned out to be 2.15 miles per hour. The depth was five feet and breadth about 270 feet in the month of July. From Demchok he went northwards through Churkang and Roksum (Rokjung) to Rudok.

Churkang was found to be a favourite place for holding monthly fairs. Roksum turned out to be a large standing camp where a great annual fair was held, the *Jongpon* (Dzongpon) always attending it in person.

Pundit Kalian Singh found that the fort at Rudok was built on a low rocky hill, rising about 250 feet above the flat ground at its base, having the Buddhist monasteries of Sharjo, Lakhang, Marpo and Nubradan close to it on the east, south and west and with about 150 scattered houses along the foot of the hill. A stream called the Chuling Chu passes by the fort and flowing in a north-easterly direction for about four miles, joins the Churkang Chu, another large southern feeder of the great Pangong lake which is about nine miles from the Rudok fort. The explorer heard that there is a small lake about half a mile north of Rudok. It swarms with wild fowl and is celebrated on account of a place called Kalpee Mhai on its north-eastern shore where the groud is so intensely hot that it smokes and readily burns any wood that may be thrown into it. This place is much resorted to for the purpose of worship. He remained a couple of days at Rudok.

Leaving Rudok on the 22nd July. 1868, Kalian Singh and the party marched back to Roksum, and then turning eastward by a new road, advanced through the districts of Rawang and Tingche to Dakorkor, a large standing camp where an annual fair was held. Several small lakes supply salt to Bashahr, Spiti and other places During the last three marches to Dakorkor, no water of any kind was found and the party were forced to carry a supply in skins. In this arid part of the country, the soil was of a dazzling white colour, a peculiarity which extendes as far as one could see.

Kalian Singh was informed that five days' march to the north there was a large district called Jung Pahiya-Pooyu and that throughout it the earth is of the same white kind, so white in fact that the eyes of people who are unaccustomed to it get inflamed from its glare just as if they were suffering from snow blindness. The district is inhabited by the nomadic Dokpa people It was under Lhasa but did not form part of Ngari Khorsum. It had a separate Sarpon or gold commissioner of its.own. The largest encampment in it was called Thok Daurakpa, said to have at least 200 tents. The district abounds in small tarns. It must be very elevated as the inhabitants eat very little grain. A large river is said to flow from Jung Phaiyu-Pooyu northwards and then to the east towards China. The district takes its name from some high snowy peaks which are probably those at the eastern end of the Kuen Lun range.

The Whor (Hor) country is said to be due north of this district, and from information gathered elsewhere there is little doubt that Whor (Hor) is the Tibetan name for eastern Turkistan.

The explorer whilst marching from Rudok to Thok Jalung saw no high peaks to the north or east, evidence which all tends to prove the existence of a large plain called Chang-tang in that direction.

The Dakorkor camp, which the 3rd Pundit reached, lies about twenty miles to the north of the Ailing Kangri peaks on the right bank of the Ailing Chu and not far from Thok Nianmo goldfield. He arrived just as the annual fair was commencing. About

150 tents were already pitched and the *Jongpon* and *Sarpon* were present, but in spite of their presence a band of mounted robbers came down upon the camp and threatened to loot it. These robbers seemed to be numerous in Tibet. This particular band was said to come from the great Namtso lake district. The men actually began to rob but the *jongpon* told them to stop and he would make each tent contribute a *parcha* (about 5 lbs.) of tea and each agreed to and the collection handed over by the *Jongpon* to the robbers.

The explorer paid his contribution and saw the robbers depart but he came to the conclusion that they might appear again at any time and it would not be safe to take his merchandise with him. Consequently, after consultation with his Bashahri friends, he decided upon sending the greater part of his goods by the Indus so as to meet him at Lhasa or on the great road to that place. One of his men, Chhumbel, who has figured earlier in the book, was despatched for this purpose.

Kalian Singh, starting from Dakorkor, continued his march eastward down the Ailing Chu till it fell into the Hagung lake, a large lake which appeared to have no exit for discharing superfluous water. The Ailing Chu, which feeds it, was found to be 150 paces in width with a rapid current just before it falls into the lake. The shores of the lake had marks which showed that it had once been more extensive. Continuing his journey, the explorer passed the Chakchaka salt lake from which the greater part of the Tibetan salt, which was sent down to Kumaon, Nepal and other places, was extracted. The salt of Tibet is preferred by the people of Kumaon and most hill people for its taste and medicinal value though the salt from the Indian sea-shores is to be had at much the same price. The explorer heard of another salt lake to the east of Chakchaka which, with other similar lakes, probably supplies a portion of that which is generally understood to come from Chakchaka.

The next places of importance seen by the explorer was Thok Sarlang which at one time had been the chief gold-field of the district but had been practically abandoned on the discovery of the Thok Jalung gold field. The third Pundit passed a great excavation, some thirty to forty feet deep and 200 feet in width and two miles in length from which the gold had been extracted. He heard that there was another gold-field to the west but his route took him direct to the Thok Jalung gold-field which he found in much the same state as when visited by explorer Nain Singh.

From Thok Jalung, Kalian Singh passed through the Majin country, partly undulating and partly quite level but all about the same altitude, viz., 15,000 to 16,000 feet above the sea-level. The drainage sloped towards the east and nothing but comparatively low rounded hills were visible in that direction, whilst on the west the party skirted a large plain of a yellow colour, said to be drained by the upper Indus.

The party passed numerous lakes producing salt and borax and after nine days's journey in a south-easterly direction, found themselves at Kinglo, a big camp on the banks of a river called the Chu Tsang-po which is so large that it cannot be forded during summer, This river flows eastwards and falls into the lake called Nganglaring or Cho-Sidhu, said to be about the same size as the Manasarowar. It has a small island in the centre. The lake is reported to receive a large stream from the south, another from the east and a third from the north. Though receiving so many streams, it is nevertheless said to have no exit.

To the south of the lake, there is a well known monastery called shellifuk, the residence of a great Lama. Still further to the south, there are some high snow peaks and district called Roonjor while to the north are the districts called Gyachun and Girke, the latter probably adjoining Phaiyu Pooyu. To the east he heard of another district called Shingwar.

Then the Pundit followed the course of the Tsang-po Chu nearly to its source, crossing one very high range called Nak-chel and another called Riego and finally descending to the Manasarowar lake.The Nak-chel and Riego ranges are evidently off-shoots of the Kailas peak. The Nak-chel peaks appeared to be very high both on the east and the west.

When crossing the range, the explorer saw a very large herd of wild yaks which are called *dong*. They were mostly seen between Majinkinglo and the Manasarowar lake. Great herds of wild asses called *kinags* were seen throughout, sometimes as many as 200 were in sight at the same time where the plateaux were extensive. The Hodgsonian antelope, wild goats and sheep were seen in numbers. Large grey wolves were constantly found but never more than two or three at a time, though packs of them were often heard yelling at night. Many a reddish hare and a kind of fox were seen on every march. Marmots were numerous, their subterranean villages being met with whenever grass and water were at hand. Quantities of geese, ducks and storks were seen on the lakes. Eagles and vultures appeared to be just like those found in the Himalayas and were seen everywhere.

Several salt lakes were passed by and others heard of. He describes the celebrated Chakchaka salt lake as being all but connected with the Hgung lake and stated that around the lakes, and almost at the same level, is an area of about 20 miles by 10. This space is filled with salt, the water having evidently at one time covered it.

Borax fields were seen at Roksum and Chakchaka and many people were working on them. No gold or salt mines were seen or heard of between Thok Jalung and the Manasarowar lake but numerous borax fields were seen, at one of which about 200 men were at work near a camp with some thirty tents. The other fields were not being worked when the explorer passed. The borax generally found its way down to Kumaon, Napal and other places.

Altogether, this portion of the third Pundit's route brought to light the position of a number of gold, borax and salt fields. In marching south from Thok Jalung, he appears to have left the gold bearing rocks and from the information he received it is evident that this part of Tibet contains and inexhaustible supply of gold. While marching from Rudok to Thok Jalung, the explorer heard about many gold-fields in the area.

As to the borax, there appeared to be any amount of it to

be had for digging, the Lhasa authorities only taking a nominal tax of about eight annas (a shilling) for ten sheep or goat loads, probably about three maunds or 240 lbs.

The salt fields appeared to be the source from which the hill population from Nepal to Kashmir drew the greater part of its supply of salt.

Throughout his march, Kalian Singh was at an elevation of over 15,000 feet and yet an encampment was met with nearly every day. Thieves were numerous and threatened the party several times but on seeing the explorer's party well armed, they invariably went off, not liking the look of an English gun. The party arrived at Manasarowar in safety and decided upon wating for the Ladakh *kafila* which was known to be on its way to Lhasa. Whilst there, the Pundit made a carefree traverse of the Manasarowar lake with bearings to the peaks north and south. Though the water was sweet, no exit was seen. At one point on the west, the ground near the Ju monastery was low and looked as if water had perhaps at one time flowed through it towards the Rakas Tal lake, though it is now too much above the lake to admit of it.

The explorer was unable to join the Ladakh *kafila* but made his way by himself the great road to Shigatse where he was stopped. He was unable to advance further. Whilst marching between the Manasarowar and Shigatse, he was also able to take bearings of the mountains on either side of that road.

Chhumbel, who was sent back from Dakorkor, managed to join part of the Ladakh *kafila* and reached Tra-don monastery where he was detained. The Ladakh merchant fortunatly remembered his old friend, Pundit Nain Singh, and on being told that the man was carrying merchandise on the Chief Pundit's account did what he could be protect him and ultimately Chhumbel was allowed to cross over the Himalayas by a southerly road pass Muktinath into Napal.

When Chhumbel found that he would not be allowed to go to Lhasa, he told the Ladakh merchant that an agent of Pundit

Nain Singh had gone ahead, to whom he was to have delivered some goods and requested the merchant to see that they were delivered to the agent. The merchant promised to do this and took charge of the packages. Chhumbel then put his own laggage on a couple of sheep and started off to south. Though it was early in December, he was able to cross Brahmaputra river on the ice which was strong enough to bear laden yaks.

The first day Chhumbel reached the Likche monastery where he found men from Lohba in the Mustang district north of Muktinath. These men had gone beyond, to the north of Tra-don for salt and were returning with it. Chhumbel managed the make their acquiantance and on hearing that he was a Bashahri (Man of Koonoo) going to worship Muktinath, they agreed to take him with them. Their salt was laden on about sixty yaks, each carrying 1-1/2 to 2 maunds (120 to 160 lbs.). The two men were able to manage this large number of yaks as the road was a good one.

From Likche, Chhumbel ascended gradually over a plateau with plenty of grass and shrub, the latter making good fuel even when green. Three easy marches took him over this plateua and landed him at Lohtod, four or five miles beyond or south of the Himalayan watershed. The plateu had a few small knolls on it but was otherwise undulating. The ascent, even to the waterhshed, was very slight indeed. The pass has a slight ascent. He got a good view of Lohtod village from the pass. It consisted of about sixty houses surrounded by a number of scattered ones which he thought might make a total of several hundred. The houses were built of sundried bricks. He noticed a great many fields growing barley, buck wheat, mustard, radish and a small proportion of wheat, though the only trees visible were a few poor willows. This confirmed the easy slope of the ground of Muktinath, which is about 13,000 feet above the sea-level. Next day, Chhumbel reached Loh Montang where the Loh *Gyalbo* (Raja) lived in a stone fortlet near a small town of some 200 houses surrounded by a great deal of cultivation.

From Loh Montang, three days' easy march landed Chhumbel at Muktinath. On the way, he passed a large village called Asrang where the *Gyalbo* resided. At every three or four miles he saw a group of houses, mostly to the west of the road but he met no tents south of the Himalayan watershed. Muktinath (Lohchumik) stands in an open spot with four villages of about fifty houses each, lying a mile to the south of the shrine.

HARI RAM

The explorer Hari Ram hailed from Kumaon. In 1871, he made his way from Darjeeling to Tibet, passing through Sikkim. From the Tista pass, he reache Tashirak in two marches. The pass was covered with snow. It is stuated on the waterhsed of a very hgh range that runs near by east and west. Tashirak is a large standing Bhotia encampment on a feeder of the Arun river which rises in a glacier to the west. It is about 15,000 feet above the sea-level. Marching north, Hari Ram crossed Nila pass and after passing a large monastery reached Shara village (50 huts) in Tinka district, generally known as Tini Dzong. On the 4th September, 1871, he reached the vilage of Lamadong (13,000 feet), with about fifty or sixty houses. Before reaching the place, he had seen no cultivation except that of Indian corn in small quantities but at Lamaong itself there was a good deal of wheat and peas. Other villages in the neighbourhood were well cultivated. All these villages are on or near the Rangthang river, the eastern branch of the Arun river. He had again reached a warmer region.

On them the 6th September, hari Ram crossed the Tinki pass and reached the village of Tashichirang on the bank of the Mo-tre-tung lake (14,700 feet) which is a fine sheet of water about twenty miles in length and sixteen miles in width. He was unable to go completely about it but he could see it fully as he passed along its northern shore. He did not however discover any sign of an outlet. The next day he reached Ningzi, a Sikkim village (50 houses) which boasted of a wonderful number of dogs. He himself saw at least 200.

On the 9th, Hari Ram reached Chajong or Tattapani hot springs, about 15,000 feet above the sea-level, where he took latitude and thermometer observations. Four reservoirs, each about thirty feet in circumference and three feet deep had been built to catch the waters of these springs which appeared to be sulphurous and had a high reputation for their curative properties and were visited by many people. The place was swarmed with antelopes which were quite tame, being neve disturbed, as they were considered to be dedicated to the deity of these hot springs. He crossed the Lagulung pass (16,200 feet) which had quantities of glacier ice close down to it, and passed the village of Sai Dzong which was surrounded by numerous other villages with cultivation. On the 15th September, he encamped at Chota-Tapy or Darcha village on the bank of the Sai Dzong stream which rises in Sikkim. Next day, he reached Balu Kot village of about twenty houses after crossing the Gyaling mountains by a pass covered with snow. This place had a good deal of cultivation and numerous other villages were visible round it. Passing thence through a level and well cultivated country, the explorer reached Shigatse on the 17th.

He paid the usual homage to the Lama of Tra-shi-lhun-po, making an offering of two rupees. He found the city of Shigatse in much the same state is described by the Chief Pundit, Nain' Singh.

The explorer remained in Shigatse till the 29th September and then made his way south-westwards, towards the Ting-ri-Maidan. He passed Shimrang village and crossed the Shabki Chu (river) flowing down into the Tsang-po. A number of villages were seen along and off the road. The harvest was being reaped.

On the 2nd of October, Hari Ram reached the great Sa-kya monastery which is only second is that of Tra-shi-lhun-po. Situated on a low spur, it was inhabited by about 2,500 monls ruled by a great lama called Sakya Gangma (king or above all others). He was looked upon as a diety. His monks were the only ones in this part of Tibet that were allowed to marry. They were called Dhukpas, the other lamas who were not allowed to marry being called Calupas. The town of Sa-kya, lying at the foot of the monastery, was about half the size of the city of Shigatse. Anbout fifty of the shops in the town were kept by Newars from Nepal and the rest by Bhotias. There is a large amount of cultivation around Sa-kya, though it is about 13,900 feet above the sea-level.

On the 3rd October, the eplorer crossed Dango pass and again got into the gorund drained by the Arun river. On the 5th, he reached the Chaio-kar vilage on the bank of Phungtu or Tingri river. The She-kar Dzong (fort) is about eight miles north of the junction of the Ting-ri and She-kar rivers. On the 8th, he reached the town of Ting-ri, 13,900 feet above the sea-level, which is generally known as Ting-ri Maidan from the large oen plain in which it stands. It is also sometimes called Thing-ri-Ghangra. The town had about 250 houses, supplemented with tents on the occasion of a fair.

Four miles above the junction of the She-kar river, the explorer crossed the Ting-ri river by a wooden bridge, seventy-five paces in length, showing that even at that point this great eastern branch of the Arun is a very large stream as might be expected from its draining the great Ting-ri table-land. In the north and quite close to Ting-ri town stands Ting-ri khar (fort) on a low isolated hills. From Ting-ri town, there is a very good road which runs north-west to Jongkha fort and thence by Kerun Shahr to Kathmandu. Officials are however the only persons who are allowed to travel by this route, traders and all others taking the one followed by the explorer to Nilam. Hari Ram did not make any stay in Ting-ri, being afraid that he might be cut off from India by an early fall of snow. He accordingly pushed on as fast as he could. At first he passed through a wide level tract, and then getting into rougher ground reached Thanglang pass (18,460 feet) on the 10th October. It was covered with ice and snow. On the 11th October, he reached the town of Nilam (13,900 feet) which had about 250 houses. It was ruled by a couple of *Jongpons*.

From Shigatse to the Thanglang pass, Hari Ram had passed through a moderately level tract though at a very great elevation, but from Thanglang pass, where he crossed the Himalayan watershed, he again entered very rugged ground.

Between Nilam and Listi Bhansar, the explorer followed the general course of the Bhotia Kosi river, and though the direct distance between the two passes is only twenty-five miles, Hari

Ram had to cross the Bhotia Kosi river fifteen times by means of three iron suspension and eleven wooden bridges, each from twenty-four to sixty paces in length. Near the bridges the precipices were so impracticable that the path had of necessity to be supported on iron pegs let into the face of the rock, the path being formed by bars of iron and slabs of stones stretching from peg to peg and covered with earth. This extraordinary path was at no place more than eighteen inches and often not more than nine inches in width and was carved along the face of the cliff, some 1,500 feet above the river which could be seen roaring below in its narrow bed. It is of course impassible for ponies and yaks but very few sheep and goats even go by it though it is constantly passed by men with loads. There were several other smaller pieces of path between Nilam and Listi Bhansar which were as bad. From Listi Bhansar, the route did not call for any special notice.

Hari Ram, it will be seen, went completely round Mount Everest but his route was so hemmed in by the great mountains that he never got a view of the Everest itself. It seems to have been invariably hidden by the subordinate peaks which are tolerably close to it. Possibly it may have been seen but never continuously so as to enable him to recognise it again and to fix it by bearings with a moderately long base. The Kinchinjunga and Jano peaks were, however, seen from the wst of Taplang Dzong but only a short base could be secured. The explorer was much impressed by Kinchinjunga (28,150 feet). It is known to the villagers near Taplang as Kumbhkaran Langur. The people south of the Himalayas in Nepal call all snowy mountains *langur*, by which they mean the highest points. They call the peaks that have no snow *bhanjung* and the low ground under the *bhanjung* is called *phedi*. Neighter the Bhotias nor the Gorkhas seem to have specific names for the remarkable peaks. The explorer asked all sorts of people but with the exception of Kinchinjunga he never got any name for a peak, though in a few cases they gave that of the nearest village.

Hari Ram's route-survey, it may be said, gave a rough idea as to how the mountain drainage in the region runs. He more especially elucidated the geography of the basin of the Arun or

Arun Kosi river, the great eastern feeder which drains the whole of eatern Nepal. His work also defines the course of the Bhotia Kosi, the western tributary of the Kosi river. Out of his route survey of 844 miles, 550 miles may be said to be over entirely new ground. Hari Ram took latitude observations at eleven points and determined the heights of thirty-one places.

Pithoragarh to Tra-don

On the 1st July, 1893, Hari Ram started from Pithoragarh in Kumaon and reached Askot two days later. At Askot, there resided a leader named Pushkar Singh Rajbar whose people were frequently passing into Nepal and the explorer went to consult him as to which would be the best place to cross the river Kali, telling him that he was a physician on his way to Jumla. Hari Ram learnt from him that as the rains had set in, the ropes by which the river was crossed were put away to keep them from rotting but that if he went to Rathi which was higher up the river, he might be able to get across. He accordingly did so and reached Rathi on the 6th. As there was only one rope by which the river was crossed and men suspended themselves by their hands and feet and bore such loads as were to be carried across their chests, the explorer had no nerve for it; so he had a sling made for himself and was drawn across in it. He stopped at Bargaon (50 houses) in the Don *patti* in Nepal on the 7th July. On the 9th, he reached the hamlet of Maiholi (2 houses) and on the 10th, Shipti village (30 houses) after crossing kotidhar pass (5,793 feet) and the river Tatigar.

The next day, Hari Ram went to Shiri in the Marma *patti*. The villages of this *patti* were all in the valley of the Chamlia river. Cultivation was extensive. The villages were situated where the hills had gentle slopes and the land which was terraced was irigated by small channels from the Chamlia. Fish, which abounded in the river, was caught, dried and stored by the villagers in large quantities for home consumption. It was eaten by all castes. He intended to cross the river here but found the rope broken. A couple of miles further up, he found crossing ropes. He then passed over and halted at Matial.

On the 13th, Hari Ram marched to Karala in the Bungnang *patti*. This march consisted of a difficult ascent to Machania pass. At the summit of the pass, the birch and juniper grew. Lower down, oak, *ringal* (hill bamboo) and *pangar* (horse chestnut) were found. The lands in the *patti* were well cultivated. He halted at Karala (5,326 feet) on the 14th July owing to rain. He crossed and recrossed the Karala *gar* and stopped at Bipur on the 15th.

Two days later, the explorer crossed the Karhi pass and reached Jakhora village. The next day, he crossed the Kansi pass and halted at Sain village in the Bhajangaya *patti*. The road was good. Bhajangaya was an old fort out of repair. It was formerly the residence of a Raja. On the 22nd July, the explorer reached Bargujal *ghat* on the Seti river. The path from Taglakhar to Silgarhi and Doti followed the course of the Seti river, and at this place one had to cross from the right to the left bank by a rope bridge 180 feet long. He passed Majh village and halted at Dogra in Bajru *patti*. Bajru fort, where the Raja lived, was on the sumit of a hill. It was surrounded by oak trees and there was no cultivation near it.

There was a good deal of excitement in this place caused by an order of the Nepal King, Jang Bahadur, for raising troops. Places which formerly supplied 100 soldiers were now required to give 150, and those that were not formerly required to furnish any were now to raise men according to the revenue paid by them.

On the 24th, Hari Ram passed through the village of Maitoli and followed the Kunra *gar*. The hills were covered with oak and rhododendron. Kunragarhi is situated on a woody summit of the ridge to the south of the Kunra *gar*. The Raja resided there. The explorer stopped at Sudap in the Kuna *patti*.

On the 25th July, Hari Ram halted at Jugar village (25 houses) which is, 5,781 feet above the sea-level. Then he descended to the Bhaunera or Bariganga river. It was crossed at this place by means of a rope. To the south of this place is a high peak on a snowy ridge where the Makla Devi temple is situated. It is well known and visited by pilgrims from Kumaon, Garhwal and

Nepal during the full moon in August. He passed through Jili village and halted at Rajtoli on the 4th August.

On the 5th, Hari Ram followed up the Parkhia *gar* up to its source and crossed Parkhialekh (about 8,095 feet) which was on the boundary between Bajru *zila* and Jumla and halted at Kalapora village (about 50 houses) in the Kunrakhola *patti*. On the slopes on either side of the Kunrakhola *gar*, there were several villages with cultivation. On the 7th, he followed the Karnali and Khatiarkhola *gar* and remained at Kalakhata vilage (about 60 houses) at night. On the 9th August, he crossed Kalakhata ridge (about 60 houses) at night. On the 9th August, he crossed Kalakhata ridge (about 14,528 feet) on which birch and juniper grow, and entering a ravine arrived at Lurkon village on the Jawa river.

The Sinjakhola *patti* was considered the most productive in these parts. Rice was the only crop, raised by means of irrigation. Ponies were bred in great numbers in this *patti* and exported to Kumaon and other places.

On the 12th August, Hari Ram arrived at Chaughan (8,016 feet) which is situated on the bank of the Tila river. Chaughan consisted of a collection of mud houses forming a street occupied by some shopkeepers and about forty-five priests of the Chandan Nath Mahadeo temple. There was a custom-house with about 300 sepoys, three Subedars and a Captain by the name of Debi Man Singh Basaniath, who was also the headman in the Jumla *zila*. Chaughan is situated in a plain surrounded by mountains. The whole valley was well cultivated and there were a number of villages scattered ove it. A road from Taglakhar passed through Chughan and Dullu Daelekh to Lucknow.

On the 20th, Hari Ram crossed Morpani Lekh (12,458 feet) and descended to the Laikhola valley and after crossing the Balangur pass reached Tibrikot. He was shown here the civil and criminal code of Nepal which was taken partly from the Hindu *Shastras* and partly from the Indian codes of civil and criminal procedure. It was in the Nepali language.

From Tibrikot, the explorer followed the course of the Birehi river and reached Charka on the 4th September, having passed Barphang and gompas. The river has high perpendicular rocky banks and the people had made a tunnel fifty-four paces long through the rock. Charka was the last village on the river Bheri. On the opposite side of this river was a gompa, to which the first born male child of every family in the village was dedicated as a Lama as is the practice among Buddhists generally. On the 7th, he reached Kagbeni after ascending Diji pass (16,879 feet) and crossing the Kali Gandak river by a wooden bridge. It consisted of about 100 houses and was inhabited by Bhots.

From Kagbeni, Hari Ram made a trip to the famous temple of Muktinath (11,284 feet). There is a spring with sulphurous smell which enters a cistern from which the water runs out in 108 spouts, under each of which every devotee passes. The water collecting in a trough below passes out in two streams which, flowing to north and south of the temple, meet to the west, thus encircling the temple with water. About 600 feet from the temple, to the south, is a small mound with a little still water at its base, smelling of sulphur. From a crevice in this mound at the water's edge rises a flame about a span above the surfcae. This place is called Chume Griarsa by the Bhots.

On the 10th September, the explorer followed the Kali Gandak river. There were forests of cedar below the snow; no other trees were found. Then he passed through Khamba Sumbha village. After two days he reached Changrang village after crossing the Chungi pass (11,000 feet). Changrang consisted of about thirty houses and a fort, the winter residence of the Loh Mantang Raja.

On the 13th Hari Ram reached Loh Mantang. It is situated in the centre of a plain, about 11,905 feet above the sea-level. The plain was irrigated by channels. It was enclosed by a wall about six feet thick and fourteen feet high, having an entrance by means of a gate to the east. In the centre was the Raja's palace consisting of four storeys. In the north eastern corner of the enclosure was a gompa. Drinking water was brought in by means of a canal. Besides the permanent residents, there were always a number of traders of mixed origin who had the privilege of going to Lhasa and they even went to Calcutta for the purchase of goods. The Raja was a Bhot. He collected revenue from all sources of about 10,000 or 12,000 rupees a year, out of which he paid about Rs. 2,500 yearly to Nepal.

On the 19th September, the explorer crossed the Photu pass (15,080 feet). He passed thousands of wild horses grazing on the plain. They were in herds of about 100 each and were not at all shy. On the 21st, he encamped at Chumik-giakdong" a sheep-fold on the stream. Here the river is about 250 feet wide and has a very gentle current. It was crossed by boats made of yak's hides which were sewn at the ends and were attached to sticks at the sides. They were kept dry and thus retained their shape. They were propelled by two or four oars. Two or three men could cross in each.

On the 23rd September, he arrived at Tra-don after fording the Chachu Tsango, two miles above its junction with the Brahmaputra river. Tra-don consisted of about twelve houses and a *Lamasari*. The houses were occupied by men whose duty was a forward property or letters for the Lhasa Government or any other for which they might have received orders. For this purpose they kept ponies, yaks, goats and sheep and their beat lay two or three marches either way. They were not remunerated directly for this service, but escaped taxes. The headman of each station or *ta-sam* received a small percentage of the taxes.

Hari Ram could not go beyond Tra-don towards Lhasa nad returned to Lhomantang on the 28th September. He recahed Kagbeni on the 1st October and started south following the course of the Kali Gandak river and reached Marmali village (about 100 houses) on the 2nd. On the 3rd October, he passed Tukla village and remained at the villag of, Lidi. Near Beni village on the banks of the Kali Gandak river, there was a copper mine from which copper was taken to Pokhra town or converted into vessels or coined. On the 7th, he crossed the Maidi river by an iron bridge and reached Baglung village. It consisted of about fifty-five houses and some shops. There were copper mines on the hill sides. A

Nepali captain was stationed to look after the coining of pice at this place and at Beni and to collect revenue from all sources.

On the 8th, Hari Ram crossed the Kali Gandak river by boat, the current being very gentle. He remained at night at the Raja's residence at Panglang which was one mile from the river. On the 9th October, he reached Kusamchaur. There were copper mines along the hills on the opposite side. On the 11th October, he passed through the large and well cultivated village of Damar (about 100 houses).

On the 12th, Hari Ram went to Purthi Ghat in Gulmi *patti* on the river's edge, about 2,036 feet above the sea-level. It contained about fifty houses and fifteen shops. To the west of this place, about two miles on the hill side, were copper mines which were worked in about 50 places, and it was said there was abundance of copper ore along the hills to the right of the Kali Gandak river between Baglung and this place. Then he passed Astewa Phedi or Astewa Tar in Gulmi *patti* and Ridi Bazar (1,305 feet above the sea-level). Ridi *bazar* contained about fifty shops kept by Newares, a mint where Nepali pice was coined, and a custom-house.

The only copper coin current in Nepal was a mixture of iron and copper made at Kathmandu. Forty eight Kathmandu pice were equal to one Nepali *mohar* and two *mohars* and two annas of the Indian coinage were equivalent to one Indian rupee.

On the 20th October, Hari Ram halted at Tansen (about 4,668 feet) which gives its name to the *patti*. There was a fort here where the governor of the district resided. On the 14th November, 1873, the explorer came to Pilhua village. On the hill sides were forests of *pipal, sal*, banyan and other tropical forest trees. He followed the course of the Kali Gandak river and passes through the villages of Thalitar, Kumalgaon, Tarigaon, Nookot, Bihartar and mukundpur. There was no cultivation in these villages. These were merely sumer residences of the people who during winter months took all their belongings to the plains in the south, where they had their rice fields. Then he journeyed through Kanjoli and Linawar and remained at Kulhua village on the 22nd November.

The explorer remained for the night of the 23rd at the junction of the Nariani, Panchperna and Saonmukhi rivers, where there is a custom-house. The following day, he reached Bhojagaon, a frontier village of Nepal, where there was a custom-house. Then he crossed the boundary, and though disappointed at want of success in Tibet, he felt thankful that he had been able to return to India safely.

In Nepal and Tibet

On the 9th July, 1885, leaving Darbhanga in Bihar, Hari Ram reached Jhanjharpur railway station and from there made his way to Dagmara *thana* in the Bhagalpur district, situated about three miles south of the Nepal boundary. On the 11th, he and his party crossed the Nepal boundary and arrived at Bhagbatpur *thana* which held about 250 Nepali soldiers. The road was good for carts and the surrounding country was well cultivated. Having obtained the passport after making customary presents, they reached Janoli village. On the 13th, they struck the right bank of the Mohoria *khola* and followed its course up to Mohoria pass. They passed Mainagaon and arrived at Tirjuga village on the right bank of the Tirjuga (Tilju) river. The river was swollen and small cannoes were used for crossed it. After Tirjuga, the road passed through dense jungle which affords good grazing ground for cattle.

On the 15th July, they crossed the Baru *khola* and reached Mahuwabas cattle-shed. They halted at Bamangaon on the 16th and went up to the Rautapokhri tarn on a hallow on the ridge. This place is held sacred and in August a large number of devotees resort to it. Then they crossed the Khari *khola* and climbed up to the Bhojiabas vilage and Yari-bhanjang cattle-shed. They passed Morenia, Bijutar and Rampur villages and reached the Yari *khola*, about one mile aboe its junction with the Sun Kosi river. Then they travelled through Jadanpur and Chibu Tar villages and reached Jhabagaon after crossing the Sun Kosi river. They continued and recrossed this river at Jairamghat by a ferry. The bed of the river is rocky, and at places signs of gold washing were found.

On the 24th, the explorer and the party ferried across the Sun Kosi at Majhigaon and reached Bilungtarghat *chauki* through which the military road from Kalthmandu via Okhaldonga *thana* and Halsia Mahadeo temple passes on a Dhankuta. This temple is famous in Nepal. On the 25th, they followed the course of the Dudh Kosi. This river waters an extensive valley which is highly cultivated on both banks and produces sufficient rice for export to the northern-most limits of Nepal. It rises from Dud Kund lake called Humichho by the Tibetans, which is said to be about nine miles in circumference. It is visited in August for religious ablutions. Then they passed Dumri village and ascended the fort of Aisalukharka. There was a copper mine near this fort. On the 3rd August, they halted at Lokhim village. Then they journeyed through the villages of Chochim and Waksa and reached Jubang village. The hills on the westenr side of the Dudh Kosi rive from Waksa to Jubang ae extensively cultivated and large flocks of goats, sheep and yaks find pasture on the slopes of the spurs which run eastwards to the river. Jubang was the first village where Hari Ram found Tibetans. At this village the grass-covered huts of this south gave place to shingle-roofed ones and this style of roofing was exclusively found for some thirty miles to the north On the 7th August, they halted at a hamlet called Paia

On the 8th, Hari Ram and the party passed through the large village of Churia Kharak on the left bank of the Kusham Changbo On the 9th, they reached Nabjia village in the Khumbu *patti*, which was the chief resort of traders both from north and south The villagers were well-to-do. From Nabjia northwards, the valley of the Thami Changbo is very contracted. About two miles north of Nabjia is Khumbu Dzong, the residence of the governor One of the commonest diseases in the locality is goitre and as the explorer succeeded in curing the daughter-in-law of the governor, he was allowed to go north with a trading expedition. They passed Taran village which was the last village beyond which there was no vegetation

On the 3rd September, after wading the Thami Changbo, they ascended a narrow gorge the Pangi *dharamshala* (rest house)

Here the party met snowfall for the first time in this march. At a distance of about 300 paces to the north, the horse-shaped black rock of the famous diety, Takdeo (horse-god), can be seen standing on the summit of an inaccessible spur. This place is considered very sacred by the Tibetans. At Pangji, the explorer came up with a large party of traders with their yaks on the way to Ting-ri and he was glad of their company for crossing the difficult pass.

On the 24th September, starting at day-break and feeling their way over the snow-bed which was extremely dangerous work owing to the numerous clefts on the way, occasionally covered with recently fallen snow, the party, after a toilsome ascent of five or six hours, reached the sumit of the Pangula pass. The height of the pass was estimated to be above 20,000 feet. On the march from Pangji to this pass, the gorge is extremely contracted, and large masses of rock brought down by snow-action from heights on eighter side are to be met with in the valley, poised like capitals on pillars of frozen snow, about thirty-five feet in circumference and about twenty-five feet in height. After a half hour's halt at the summit, the party started northwards down a bed of melting snow lying in a narrow gorge. The route then ran along the snow covered mountain side to the Keprak river to the east and reached Keprak village and *chauki*. Along this part, Hari Ram saw results of huge avalanches which come down from both sides into the gorge, forming natural arcades here and there through which the sluggish stream of Keprak finds its way. The *Gyangpa*, the village official of Keprak was subordinate to the *Dipon* (governor) of Ting-ri. The explorer was detained there but was allowed to go to Ting-ri with the help of the Khumbu governor's son.

On the 8th October, they crossed the Keprak river by a wooden bridge. There was no snow on the mountains north of this point. Descending the northern face of the spur, they entered the grassy plain known as Ting-ri Maidan. It is known as Tingli Maidan by the Nepalese, while the Lhasa people speak of it as Thingri Ghangar. *Ghangar* in Tibetan means plain. On the 9th October, they reached the town of Ting-ri.

The town of Ting-ri (13,860 feet) consisted of about 250 houses. The inhabitants were chiefly Tibetans and a few Gurkhas. The roofs of the houses were all flat. The larger timber consisted of pine logs brought chiefly from Shalak and Nilam. On these logs lighter pine rafters were laid which were then covered with a layer of strong furze, locally alled *dama*. A layer of wet mud was thrown over and well rammed. This provided a water-proof roof. But when the snow lay thick on the roof, it had to be pushed off to prevent the timbers from sagging under its weight. The country immediately around Ting-ri was well cultivated, barley and peas being however the only produce. The inhabitants appeared to be well-to-do. It was intensely cold during winter due to its high altitude, its proximity to the Tingri Changbo river which is frozen in winter and the piercing winds which sweep over the extensive plains. The Daipon, with about 500 Tibetan soldiers, occupied the stone-built Ting-ri fort.

Trade

As Ting-ri lies on the high road from Lhasa westwards, it is the constant resort of traders for whose convenience a big *serai* had been built. The bulk of the goods were carried on mules. From Bhagalpur to Ting-ri, the chief articles carried northwards were tobacco leaf, cotton cloth, broad-cloth, iron brass and copper vessels, corals, rice, oil and Indian rupees which were used to make jewellery. For these, the Khambu men used to go annually in parties to India, taking with them muskpods, yak-tails, antelope horns, blankets, stuffed *munal* and argus pheasants. From Ting0ri, blanket, musk-pods, goats, ponies, *ghee* and yak-tails were exported to Nepal.

Produce

The country northwards from the Mohoria *khoia* to Ting-ri, excepting the Rakhola valley which produces an abundant rice-crop, is extremely uporudctive, the only grain grown being maize. Cotton is grown in small quantities as far north as Aisalu Kharka and here and thre is little *til* (sesamum) is to be seen.

Of the domestic animals, buffaloes are to be met with as far as Aisalu Kharka but fowls, pigs and goats are bred and kept in every village as far north as Jubang. At Jubang and northwards, large herds of yaks, *zobus, zomus,* goats and sheep are found. The yak and *zomu* afford a plentiful supply of milk.

Fauna

South of Khambu, *munal* and argues pheasants are met in large numbers. Musk-deer, *thar* and *gurrel* are found occasionally. In the Ting-ri Maidan, large herds of *kyangs,* Tibetan antelopes, may be seen roaming at will. Flocks of wild pigeons and large ravens are found in the vicinity of Ting-ri.

Flora

On the Moharia range which corresponds to the Shivalik range of the Western Hindustan and in the valley to the north, the *sal* grows luxuriantly. *Tun, dhak, semal* and *Jamun* are also found. On the Mahabarat range, oaks, rhododendrons, mountain pear, cherry and other denizens of a medium altitude grow in profusion. In the valley of the Sun Kosi river, the *sal* is again met with as also the tall bamboo, *pipal* and *semal.* But the trees grow sparsely in this locality. The mountain sides from Dumri to Jubang are well wooded with oak and rhododendrons and occasionally fir with an undergrowth of *ringal.* The higher elevations to the west of Jubang are densely covered with *deodar.* From a few miles north of Jubang to Khumbu Dzong, the lower parts of the mountain sides are thickly wooded with a large species of oak, birch, pine and stunted rhododendrons, with a dense undergrowth of *ringal* jungle. For the four or five miles beyond Khambu, a solitary pine, rhododendron or a Tibetan furze may be seen. After this not a tree is to be seen, and till the suburbs of the Ting-ri are reached the only vegetation met with is a short grass found in the *maidan* and the stunted furze on the hill sides.

On the 25th October, 1885, Hari Ram and party left Ting-ri and after passing Tokchhu village reached the right bank of the Phangju Changbo (Ting-ri Changbo). Then they passed by Chhamda village and after about a mile a hot spring. The water was very hot and had a sulphurous smell. They halted at Dakcho village. The villagers on this march and on the route followed during the next two days to Makpa grew luxuriant crops of barley, peas and turnips which were then being reaped. The valley from Chhamda for about twenty-five miles onwards showed abundant signs of having once been very largely populated but it is said that in the last great war between the Nepalese and the Tibetans most of the inhabitants were killed and the place was almost deserted.

On the 26th October, they reached the Puri village. On the 27th, travelling through Simi and Tokchhu, they reched Makpa where the *gyangpa* of the village examined the passports. On the 28th, they descended and pushed on, for fear of robbers who infested this locality, through the Digurithanka plain to Digur village. The plain which extends some seven or eight miles on both sides of the road on the east of Digur, affords abundant pasture for large herds of cattle, ponies, yaks, sheep and goats which are brought here to graze even from the distant Dok Thol province. The Dokpas dwelt in black tents and when chance came they practised robbery also. A small party of them was sighted but fled away on the discharge of some shots from the gun. The spur bounding the Digun-thanks plain to the north has a russet hue.

On the 29th October, they reached the Palgutso lake which is nine miles by four miles. The explorer was informed that it had no outlet. The water was clear and sweet and small fish were seen in it. The next day they crossed Chharkiu pass and travelling through ups and downs reached Jongkha fort at the junction of the Satu Changbo and the stream from the east. It was about forty paces square and was surrounded by a mud and stone wall, five feet thick and twenty feet in height, with loops-holes all around. Within the fort was a gompa which had about 100 Lamas. There were about twenty shops. Two *jongpons* resided here.

Nubri pass was closed by heavy fall of snow. So the explorer took the road to Kirong. He took leave of his friend, Sunnam Durje, who helped him so much. On the 3rd November, Hari Ram and the party followed the course of the Jongkha Changbo, passed Damdoe poststation and halted at Gunda. The river flows through a very narrow gorge from Damdoe to Rakma. No cultivation was seen. On the 4th November, they reached Tadang hamlet from where a glacier was seen to the north and an immense avalanche hurled down. On the 5th, they passed Rakma and reached Pangsang. At Rakma, cultivation was seen in the open valley.

On the 6th November, 1885, they proceeded to Kirong, a small scattered town, larger than Jongkha fort. It was the residence of two *jongpons*. The houses were all stone-built, gable-roofed and shingle-covered. On the 11th, they forded across the Gundan Chu and reached Thangsia hamlet. Then they travelled through Khimbuk, Paimasena *chauki*, crossed the Rasia *khola* and passed Rasuagarhi fort, Biasiyari, Temuria Bhansar and Birda.

They continued their journey along the Bhotia Kosi river, passed Ungul and Shabru villages and crossed the Shabru *khola*. A little beyond was a hot water spring. Then they passed Dunglang and Bharku villages, and crossed the Trisuli river which rises from Damodar Kund. They continued the journey past Dhonju, Thandi, Gurang, Ramcha and Belrawali villages. The route then kept near the left bank of the Trisuli river past Simri and Naoakot and they reached Kinchak *bazar* (Kinchut *bazar* of explorer Nain Singh). In this market the trade consisted of grain, cotton and woollen cloth, metal vessels, shoes, etc. The houses wer stone-built and roofed with tiles.

On the 18th November, they followed the course of the Samri *khola* and halted at Kakni *pawa*. Then they ascended Samri *pawa* at the pass on a spur. At this pass, in spite of rest-houses there were three provision shops for travellers. They continued past Tharku, Bhagtani, Kalonsia and Charangia *patwas* and halted at Achania village.

On the 21st November, they passed the villages of Belghari, Suporia, Salianbiasi and Saliantar. The country on both the flanks of the road from Kinchak *bazar* to Saliantar was well cultivated and numerous villages wer seen dotting the hill sides all along. The plateau of Salianter, five miles (north to south) by two miles, is elevated about 700 feet aove the Akho and Buria Gandak rivers. On the western side, the face stands like a mural precipice overhanging the Buria Gandak except where a passage to the river has been made along a flight of stone stops carried down from a distance of a quarter of a mile. The pl;ateau is well inhabited and though not watered, the soil yields a very good rainy-season crop.

On the 23rd November, they followed the course of the Buria-Gandak past the villages of Qdari, Pipri and Lodanda and halted at Labubiasi hamlet. The road was impracticable for any but foot-passengers. Then they passed through dense jungle to Khorlabiasi and halted at a *jegate* (chauki). About two miles from there, a glacier was visible to the east from the foot of which a good-sized waterfall issued and plunges down a precipice of which the explorer estimates the height as 2,000 feet. For about half way down, the water is visible in a continuous body but thereafter it descends as a shower of fine spray to the depth below. On the 28th November, they halted at Pangsang village and on the 29th crossed the Dhunga Sangukhola over a natural bridge formed by two huge rocks which about against each other at a height of 40 feet above the water-level. Then they passed through Niak, Ranagaon and Bhudgaon and halted at Birjam which is called Nubri by Tibetans. It was the headquarters of the governor of Nubri *ilaka*. Between Birjam and Niak, the sites of several villages were passed which were occupied by the villagers of the neighbouring mountains in winter. The explorer having reached the northern limit of his route, retraced his steps along the Buria Gandak and in six days arrived at Arughat on the right bank of the river, opposite Salinatar. On the 10th Decmber, they decscended to the *chuki* of Borlanghat where ferry boats carried passengers across the Buria Gandak river. The river lower down has a somewhat tortuous course.

Then they journeyed through Majatar and Satbisitar cattle sheds, Baktiarghat village, Kundutar and Darguntar cattle sheds and reached the *chauki* opposite the point where the Trisuli falls into the Buria Gandak. From Arughat to the junction of the Trisuli, there were numerous villages on hill-sides, east and west of the river but the low ground which had an abundance of pasture was occupied by the hill people with their cattle during winter. In several places Hari Ram saw traces of gold-washing on the banks of the river.

On the 18th December, they crossed the river which is henceforward known as the Trisuli and halted as Bichraltar village.

On the 19th they passed Phachchamtar *chauki*. The explorer saw gold-washing being carried on iat this place. The party continued their journey past Hugdi *chauki*, forded the Hugdi *khola*, ascended Jogimara village, passed the ruined fort of Jogimara and halted at Kaolia village. On the 26th, they halted at the fort of Upardangarhi. This fort is a square with ech side of 100 paces and had a loopholed masonary wall to the height of twenty five feet. In the hot weather, it was a sanatorium for Nepalese soldiers who were sent to it from the Chittawan *ilaka* in the plains.

On the 1st January, 1886, they proceeded along the crest of a spur to Seriabas *thana* and thence through a jungle-clad land to Dabarpani hamlet and beyond to Kalwarpur village. From this place southwards, the inhabitants of the villages are called Tharus, an agricultural sect of lowlanders. They continued their journey past and Gotholi Parsoni village. A ferry boat carried passengers across the Trisuli, both at Goghat and Deoghat lower down. The Deoghat temple is situated at the confluence of the Kali Gandak and the Trisuli rivers. Below the confluence, the river is called the Narayani. At Deoghat, an annual religious fair is held at the beginning of February. This fair lasts about a month and large quantities of goods as well as cattle and ponies change hands. The traders who frequent the fair come all the way from Pokhra, Kathmandu, Batoli and Bettiah. Nearly two miles below Deoghat is the *chauki* of Dharigaon and three miles lower down is the villages of Nariangarh. The explorer and the party left Parsoni on the 8th January and proceeded throgh dense jungle infested by wild elephants to Nariangarh. It was the timber depot where all the timber that floated down the river in winter was examined and duty was levied. Passing through the temporary hamlets of Bancharia, Belua, Langota and Hatali they halted at Simri.

On the 10th January, 1886, they passed throgh the hamlets of Sisai and Sakarbhar to Jitpura village. Then they continued the route through Naiagaon and Pathargaon. After about a mile, the right bank of Rapti was reached. On the 12th January, they proceeded to Kura ghat at the junction of the Rapti and Nariani. The next day they reached sheds opposite Tribenighat on the bank of the Pachnad stream.

Trade

The trade from the direction of Lhasa between Tingri and Kathmandu was chiefly carried over the Nilam Dzong route. There was no trade whatever on the route between Ting-ri and Jongkha fort but the latter formed a convenient *entrepot* for the Dokpas and other Tibetan traders from the north and north west, who brought down in summer salt, goats, blankets, musk-pods and ponies for the Kathmandu market. As the Nilam Dzong route was absolutely impracticable for ponies, the trade in these was very largely forced into the route via Jongkha fort and Kirong. The traders returned with rice, tobacco-leaf, brass and copper vessels and cotton and woollen cloth imported from India.

The Nubri *ilaka* is famous as the tract in which the plant of *nirbisi* is indigenous. Its root has got medicinal value. Large quantities of the root were gathered in the months of July to October and dried in the shade. The root was then chiefly exported north-westwards, while a comparatively small quantity found its way to the south. On the banks of the Nariani river, timber was cut and floated down the river in logs and large stocks were kept at Tribeni.

Of the domestic animals, yaks, *zobus*, goats and sheep with a few fowls occasionally were found in the portion of Tibet between Ging-ri, Jonkha fort and Rasuagarh. In Nepal, to a latitude of about $28\text{-}1/4^0$, along the route taken by the explorer, buffaloes, cows and goats were met everywhere, while further north the country was inhabited by the Tibetans and sustained yaks, *zobus* and sheep.

Fauna

Besides, a few Tibetan antelopes found in the open country west of Ting-ri, the only wild animals seen by the explorer were the golden wolf of Tibet, the marmot and the rate-hare or tailess rat. Tigers and elephants about in the dense *sal* jungles which stretch away east of the Narayni river below Goghat.

Flora

Between Ting-ri and Tashi-rak, not a tree of any kind is to be seen. There is, however, abundance of grass and furze to be met with all along the route. At Tashirak, no furze was seen. From Gunda to a little below Kirong, dense forests were met with at the lower elevations, and of the *betula* and *bhojpatra* on the higher mountain sides, with a thick undergrowth of the mountain-bamboo or *ringal*. As is to be noticed in other parts of the Himalayas, the northern faces of the mountains were generally found to be more luxuriant both in arboreous and shrubby vegetations, due partly to greater depth of soil and partly to less direct influence of solar rays. From Thungsiu, for a couple of miles beyond Ramcha, oak, rhododendrons, wild cherry, the mountain-pear and a tree called *anyar* were found. A dense undergrowth of *ringal* was met all along this part of the route.

Southwards from Ramcha to Naiakot, thense westwards to Arughat and northwards again to Lodanda, the usual tropical specimen met with in the lower belt of the Himalayan vegetation were seen, such as mangoes, plantains, the large bamboo, jackfruit, *semal, tunn, shesham* and some dwarfed *sal* trees. Beyond Lodanda and as far north as Niak, vegetation pertaining to the middle belt was there. Still further north, *khursoo, betula* and *bhojpattra* with an undergrowth of *ringal* jungle were to be seen for some distance upto the mountain sides. In the portion of the Nubri *ilaka* north of Pangsang, atees, with is highly valued for its medicinal properties, is found. The root of this plant is said to be of ashy colour with two tubers very white inside and of a bitter taste. The roots are gathered from June to December and dried in the shade. Another plant of the same kind called *bis* is also seen in the locality. This is probably the *acanitum ferox* and was described by the explorer as differing from *atees*. The plant sends up several stalks emanating from several yellowish-white tubers congregated round the root while the *atees* has but a single stalk. The tubers of the *bis* are also much larger than those of the *atees* and the former do not acquire a proper consistency till November and December. The root of the *bis*, though highly poisonous, is used medically for rheumatism and other diseases. For this purpose, it is encased in a thick covering of cowdung and well baked so as to reduce the virulence of its poison. But the most important plant found in this locality is the famous *nirbisi* which is said to be, as its name signifies, an antidote to poison, *nir* means antidote and *bis* means poison. The tubers brought down by Hari Ram were generally uniform, the heart being white or brown but he avered that in some plants the hearts is of reddish colour and these are much more valuable than the others.

LALA

Lala was a hillman of Sirmur Near Simla.

He left Darjeeling for Shigatse on March 29, 1875 on his first independent assignment. After crossing the Ranjit river, Lala ascended the Namchi village in Sikkim. Then he came down to the right bank of the Tista river. Passing through splendid open forest and several villages, the explorer reached the junction of the Lachung and Lachen rivers. Crossing the Cheungtong and Rama villages, he reached Lamteng at Lachen *chauki*. A Sikkimese official who resided there guarded the road and revied taxes on any merchandise which passed. Between Lachen *chauki* and Shigatse, there was a small trade in mader and planks which were carried on yaks. Lachen *chauki* is about 7,500 feet above the sea-level.

Lala passed through the village of Niuan, situated in an extensive plain. The houses were found full of property but deserted as the residents had gone to their winter residence in the plains, no one being left in charge. The people were so good and honest that no theft occurred and the owners found their property intact on their return in summer. He crossed the Lachen river and reached Thango village on the 20th April, 1875. There also he found the houses full of grain and cooking utensils but left unguarded. The owners had gone to their winter quarters at Lachen *chauki* and would return in the month of May. The jungles were left behind this village and nothing was to be seen but a few stunted trees and occasional patches of grass. Eleven mles from Thango, there are two Sarola takes separated from each other only by the road. The eastern one is about one square mile in extent and rather deep and the western somewhat smaller.

From the lake, the road ascend to the summit of the pass which is known by various names—Sarola, Lachen La, Ta-tsang La and Kangra Lama La. The height of the pass is about 16,500 feet above the sea-level. On the summit of the pass by the side of the road, there were heaps of stones with a number of sticks above them, to which bits of rag and paper were tied with prayers written on them. Devout travellers never failed to make a circuit of them, hat in hand, muttering the usual formula of prayer. About seen miles from the foot of the descent is the fort of Kam-pa, situated in the midest of an extensive plain. Scattered over the plain in little clusters were tents of shepherds. Every tent had its compliment of large dogs which were very dangerous. When about three miles from the fort, three unarmed horsemen galloped up and ordered the explorer's party into Kam-pa fort for due enquiry into their business. They were brought before the *Jongpon*.

The fort of Kam-pa is circular, about 1,500 paces in circumference and is built upon a small mound. The walls, six feet thick, are built of stone. In the middle of the fort is the entrance to a subterranean passage which leads to a small stream of water that washes the base of the mound on which the fort stands. The fort was used as a jail and in it were confined some fifty prisoners, all for minor offences. The *Jongpon* was assisted by three *Nirpas* or waiters and every third day a runner was sent to Shigatse with letters.

On the 15th day, the explorer was ordered to proceed without delay to Shigatse. He passed through Ku-ma, ascended Lasum La and came down to Bhadur plain covered with villages and cultivation. The village of Bhadur consisted of groups of houses. The fields were irrigated and manured, the crops being principally peas and barley. Then he crossed Gampola. In the plains, the explorer saw many herds of antelope. At the Babgialing village dwarfed *maznu* (willow) trees were seen since leaving Thange village.

The explorer arrived at Shigatse about the 15th May, 1875. Finally at the end of October, he was set at liberty.

There were Tibetan soldiers at Shigatse. Each company comprised thirty or forty men. These troops were armed with swords and a gun to every two men. The guns were very heavy. In action, the muzzle was supported on two sticks which were hinged on the woodwork under the barrel. One man placed the butt against his shoulder and took aim while the other touched it off. The armed force and two buglers whose instruments were of brass, about six feet long, straight and with a huge-bell-shaped mouth, which was rested on the shoulder of another man whenever the bugle was sounded.

In November 1875, the explorer left Shigatse and again started his work. He passed the enclosed garden of Kungkayling near the bridge over the Pen-nang Chu. Then he followed the course of the Tsang-po to Jagsa, passing many villages on the road. The river is said to freeze over entirely. Sometimes the country was over-flooded in places about the village of Taktukha but the water did not go far inland.

There was a regularly organised goods and passenger traffic by boat down stream from Shigatse to Jagsa, divided into two stages at the village of Nimo, which is about twenty miles from the mouth of the Pen-nang Chu. The boats used were oblong in shape, flat-bottomed and the boatman drew his boat on shore, dried it and then carried it back on his shoulders to the upper end of the stage again.

A range of snow-clad hills closes in on the right bank of the Tsang-po about three miles to the east of Jagsa and it was reported that there was no road along this bank, the river here entering the hills and falling over many rapids. There is no boat traffic between Jagsa and the iron chain bridge of Chak-sam over the Tsang-po near Lhasa.

From Jagsa, the road turned south-east and entered the district of Rangchung. The explorer passed through Jamchen and Humidolma monastery which had about 1,500 Lamas. From here the road ran through a fertile valley containing several villages up to Chuchen village (*chu* means water and *chen*, warm) built on a mound from the base of which issues a small stream of water whose temperature was 150°F. The water issued in small jets and was conveyed by a short trough to a little pool in whch the sick people bathed. It had a bluish tinge and a strong sulphorous smell.

Twenty six miles from Chuchen, the road joined the road

from Gyantse to Lhasa at the village of Ya-sik on the margin of the Yam-drok Tso. Between Shigatse and Yasik, there was considerable traffic. The explorer met Nepalese merchants taking cloth and brass vessels to Lhasa and many Kashmiris returing from Lhasa with brick tea.

From Ya-sik, Lala traversed along the western side of the Yam-drok Tso as far as the village of Demalang. The Yam-drok Tso is about two miles wide opposite Ya-sik and is only half a mile wide at Demalang. The eastern shore, visible from these two villages, is an expanse of flat land from which the Tungchin peak rises.

From the Kam-pa pass, he passed Jama village on the right bank of the Tsang-po river and reached Kukhang village and a monastery protected by a fort which had a small garrison as a guard for the Governor. From Kukhang he passed through many villages upto Kirtijung with a large *bazar* and fort, about 600 paces in circumference. Its walls, fifteen feet high, were in ruins in many places.

Lala journeyed through Jhanpaling containing about 300 houses and the famous monastey of Samaye with about 1,400 Lamas. It is situated on the left bank of the Tsang-po river and is a renowned place of pilgrimage. Then he reached the *bazar* of Tse-tang. A daily open air market was held there which was well supplied with goods of all kinds from Calcutta, China, Kashmir and Nepal. This *bazar* was also famous for the sale of perfumed sticks (Joss-sticks) that are burnt in temples. In the monastery of Tse-tang, there were about 700 Lamas. There was a fort in Tse-tang.

At Tse-tang, low hills come close down the south bank of the Tsang-po. The hills bordering the plains on the north bank of the river are also low. From here, the river was seen trading away to the horizon, about east by north in a wide valley, the view down which was bounded by a snowy range apparently a great distance off. The explorer was told that after flowing in his direction for about fifteen marches, the river turns south and passing through a wild regioin enters a country governed by the British. This accorded with the generally received opinioin that the Tsang-po enters Assam as Brahmaputra river.

The road continued along the right bank of the Tsang-po river past Tse-tang but the officials warned Lala against going along it unless he accompanied a strong body of merchants for it was beset by thieves and there were wild turbulent tribes armed with bows and arrows to be met with near Tsari. After remaining at Tse-tang for six days, the explorer, thinking he might be short of funds, turned south about the middle of December 1875, intending to follow the route of the renowned Pundit Nain Singh into Assam. For thirteen miles from Tse-tang, the country is fertile, and there were many villages along the road, but thence the country becomes bleak and burren. He passed through Dagyeling village, crossed Yarto Tra La (16,300 feet) and recahed Karkang. Thirteen miles from Karkang is Giarok village with a few houses and some fields. He passed through Sumno village and reached a large lake, six miles long and four miles wide. Near the lake was nice short grass and herds of antelopes and wild assess were seen. Then he travelled through Tangsho having a guard house and a large houe for travellers and Tsona Dzong (12,900 feet) where there was a large *bazar*, a monastery and a detachment of mounted soldiers. There were several springs of warm water, colourless and almost odourless, from which the inhabitants took their drinking water.

Passing through Chukhang, the explorer reached Mantangong or Tawang, with about 300 houses scattered around it. There was heavy *ringal* (dwarfed bamboo) jungle about this place. There was also a large monastery with about 700 Lamas. Several of the buildings in this monastery had gilt roofs.

With regard to the climate and weather at Shigatse, Lala states that during the month of May no rain fell though the sky was cloudy. The rains set in about the middle of June and there was a good deal of it during the months of July and August. In September little rain fell but it was very cloudy. In October it was dry and strong winds blew from the east, commencing regulrly at 11 a.m. rising to their height at about 2 p.m. and gradually declining till about 5 p.m. when they ceased. They rarely blew at night. These winds were extremely cold and in December and January, they increased to such tremendous violence that for three or four hours in the day, while they were at their height, no one stirred abroad as it was impossible to travel at that time.

About the end of March 1876, the explorer followed the same route as that taken by Pundit Nain Singh in 1865-66 as far as the bridge over the Pen-nang Chu at Pen-nang fort but from there he kept to the left bank of the river. Some distance from this fort, the hills come down close to the road and there is one large and very steep hill called Kuriradon, overhanging the river, which was famed as the haunt of robbers, whose mode of attcak was to sling down stones at the solitary traveller, who dropped his load to eascape across the river. Lala travelled in company of fifteen merchants, and except that several men came up and boldly demanded alms, the travellers were not molested. Passing several villages and water mills, the explorer came to Chachin monastery containing about a thousand Lamas. Three miles further on is Malingong village and a bridge across the river. Half a mile from the bridge on the right bank of the river, is the important town of Gyantse. After a stay of couple of days at Gyantse, the explorer returned to Manilagong and travelled along the left bank of the Pen-nang Chu, eleven miles to Changra.

Then he passed through Salu and Pika villages and the Ka-la lake which is about two miles broad. The villages of Ka-la-shar are great fishermen, going out on the lake in their little leather boats and fishing with line and hook baited with paste. They catch a number of fish which are dried in sun. Five miles futrher is the village of Cha-lu. A mile from Cha-lu, a stream opens out into chains of small lakes and it joins Ram lake, three miles from the village. The road then entered an extensive plain. He passed through Tuna village, situated about twelve miles north-north-west of the great snowy peak of Chumalhari or Phan Jammu which is 23,900 feet above the sae=level. After going through Chukya village, he reached the fort and the small town of Phari in the midst of a large plain. From this place a road leads off about north-east into Bhutan.

The fort of Phari is about 1,500 paces round its walls, which were built of rubble stones and were thirty feet high. The town consisted of about seventy five houses surrounding the fort. The inhabitants kept large herds of sheep and yaks and employed themselves exclusively in carrying trade. *Sattu* and wheat flour were imported from Gyantse and rice from Bhutan. Their own flock supplied them with meat, milk and butter.

Leaving Phari, Lala crossed the Ammo river and entered a great forest. He then passed through Kalika which belongs to the country of Dumu or Sikkim. Five miles from Kalika is Chumbi, the summer-residence of the Sikkim Raja. All the houses in this village were roofed with planks. The Raja's palace was not large but the roof was handsomely gilted. There was a small monastery in Chumbi. Then he reached Rincigaon where he left the Ammo river and entered a forest of huge pine trees. He crossed the Jelep La and proceeded via Kalimpong to Darjeeling where he arrived in July 1876 after an absence of one year and four months from the Biritsh territory.

The explorer noted a strange and apparently unaccountable phenomenon connected with Giamsena lake. At intervals of five to ten minutes, a kind of explosion was heard, apparently proceeding from undr the water, some forty yards from the shore. During the four hours he sat by the margin of the lake, these curious and inexplicable sounds were repeatedly heard. The sound was not sharp like the report of a gun nor like the noise of falling rocks but a dull, hevy concussion. The surface of the water was not in any way disturbed over the part whence the sound apparently proceeded. One of the men of the *chauki* or guard-house on the banks of the lake told him that these sounds were caused by the breaking of ice at the bottom of the lake. But on this hypothesis the fragments of ice at the bottom of the lake. But on this Hypothesis the fragments of ice must necessarily have floated to the surface of the water. No ice was visible on the lake except a fringe of shore ice along the margin.

NEM SINGH

In June 1878, Lieut, Harman engaged Nem Singh to give him instructions in the Tibetan language. Nem Singh belonged to Sikkim and was of about thirty years of age. He was a good Hindi scholar and well-read in his own language and Tibetan literature but knew little English. He was employed as a *sardar* (head of a gang of labourers) in the Public Works Department and casually as interpreter at Darjeeling Court. He had trvaelled in the plains of India. Lieut. Harman taught Nem Singh a little surveying. Nem Singh took to it very well and was found sharp and industrious. He was offered the service of an explorer which Nem Singh accepted eagerly. He soon learnt traversing with prismatic compass, to plot his work, use the boiling point thermometer, read the Hadley's sextant and understand maps. The rainy season of 1878 was very wet and for 27 days at a stretch Nem Singh did not get a sight of the sun or stars. Ltd. Harman decided that it was better for Nem Singh to go to work with the imperfect knowledge than lose the season. He was instructed to trace the Tsang-po river from Tsetang downwards as far as he was able to, also to make a circuit of the Yam-drok Tso or Patti lake and to give a good description of the iron-chain bridge voer the Tsang-po river at Chak-sam.

On the 6th August, 1878, explorer Nem Singh left Darjeeling and travelled by the Jelep La to Phari, then by the Yam-drok Tso and the iron chain bridge to Lhasa. He did not make a circuit of the Yam-drok Tso but made some observations and gave an acount of the bridge. He spent considerable time at Lhasa and the monasteries around. He saw the great copper cauldrons in which rice and tea were prepared for the Lamas. These cauldrons measured twenty feet across and six feet deep, built up in masonary and with planks laid across so that the cooks might easily stir up the contents and ladle them out. He paid a visit to the bell-foundry and saw large bells two feet high. He started that the rice from Bhutan, which is considered the best, was not allowed to be sold in the market to the general public but only to Lamas. Nepal rice was sold to the public.

He was very little troubled by rain beyond Phari, getting it only at Rip village and Mimdzong. Snow fell at Chukurgyi monastery and the Lung pass. The country between this monastery and the Cholamo lake was covered with snow. Near Rip village, he entered an undulating country covered with low thorny bushes. For fear of robbers and unable to make good progress, he returned along he same route at great speed. Some of his bearings and astronomical work were not satisfactory and his field-book was not kept up-to-date.

So Nem Singh was sent to Pundit Nain Singh in Kumaon for proper instruction in the use of the sextant and his survey duties. He prosecuted his studies with vigour and was sent on an important journey with a Lama who knew the route. Starting work at Tsetang in October 1878, Nem Singh followed down the right bank of the Tsang-po river and passed Ngari Tratsang monastery, containing about 300 Lamas and Takur-dzong with about forty houses. The Tsang-po at this point flowed in a wide bed about 400 paces in breadth. The current was very slight. The discharge of water was about 15,000 cubic feet per second which agrees with the estimates of explorer Nain Singh. At ten miles from Tsetang, he passd the village of Jamtong or Jang (about 80 houses) where the road from Lhasa joined. The limit of the road is defined by two parallel rows of stones placed close together. At 18-1/2 miles from Tsetang, he reached Sangri monastery and a ruined fort. Then the route left the Tsang-po and went north. At 40-1/2 miles, it joined another road from Lhasa. Then he crossed the Milk Chju and the Lung pass whcih is high and covered with snow, and reached Chukurgyi monastery which had about 300 Lamas.

About eight miles from Chukurgyi, there is the small lake of Cholamo situated on a high ground. It was customary to throw coins and white scarves in the lake. The large and fine fort of Gyatsa Dzong and the Takpo monastery were met at eighty-eight miles from Tsetang. Two miles further, the road met the left bank of the Tsang-po. On the opposite bank, three roads from Tsetang,

Tsari and Kongo met. The Talha Chu was crossed by a bridge. All the bridges over the streams in this region were of the same pattern. The abutments were made of stones and the chasm was spanned by beams, one above the other, each one overlapping the one below till but a small gap remained in the middle which was covered with planks. The shore-ends of the beams were weighed down with big stones.

At 105-1/4 miles, the explorer passed the small monastery of Pare Chote where the Gewa Ring-bo-che was born. He was a small boy of 11-1/2 years when Nem Singh saw him. The Aru monastery is at 111 miles. A mile beyond Aru, he met five Chinese journeying to Lhasa with loads of musk balls which they had collectd in the Lepcha district in the south and near Tsari. Across the Tsang-po, a road goes south to the country where lead mines were worked. It supplied Lhasa and all the surrounding country with lead. The local people paid their revenue in lead. Then he journeyed along the right bank of the Tsang-po river to Gyala Sindong which is about 287 miles from Tsetang. There are many ups and downs along the route and the river was kept in sight nearly all the way. Nem Singh passed the Nang monastery, crossed the Tsari Chu and Kongbo Nga La and then reached Longkar Dzong. On the 23rd October, 1878, he crossed Kyimudong Chu. At this place the Tsang-po river makes a great bend and turns to the north-east for a course of nearly a hundred miles At 171 miles from Tsetang, the route entered an undulating country covered with low thorny scrub; Habitations were very scarce.

At 188-1/2 miles from Tsetang, he reached the forts of Orong and Gacha, where *Jongpons* resided. He met people whom he calls Lepchas. They were called Monbas by the Tibetans who give the same name to the Lepchas of Sikkim. In features, complexion and dress, the former are not distinguishable from Sikkim Lepchas but have a language of their own and do not speak the Rong language of the Sikkim, Lepchas. They were much esteemed for their truthfulness and straightforwrd dealing. A good number of them had come to Orong for trade and had brought with them valuable loads of musk-balls, madder, and *lashin*, also cane, bamboo and baskets of the Sikkimese type, the basket resting on the back and held by a starp across the forehead. Nearly all the musk which is found at Lhasa comes from his Lepcha district which also supplies most of the baskets found about Lhasa.

At 226 miles, there is the village of Mongboding on the eastern boundary of Kongbo district. An ascent of six miles takes one to the small village of Fuchu. There was the important monastery of Chamna with about 500 Lamas. Across the Tsang-po river, on the left bank, was the Chamkar or Temo monastery containing about 400 Lamas. Before recahing the large fort of Gyala Sindong at 287 miles from Tsetang, the ruins of many villages and forests were passed. The river passes through a gorge to the west of Gyala Sindong where Nem Singh closed his work.

The road continued along the right bank of the Tsang-po river for four days and then crossed to the Poba or Lhoba country. The work Poba signified a man of Bhutan. The inhabitants have a peculiar dialect and differ greatly from the Tibetans in custms and religious observances. They are bordered to the south by Gimuchen.

There was a road from Gyala Sindong to Pemako district. There were many villages of Lepchas and the people of Bhutan. Explorer Nem Singh gives the height of Gyala Sindong as 8,000 feet. This shows that the Tsang-po river has fallen 2,000 feet in its course of 250 miles from Tsetang. Nem Singh was tole that the river, after flowing thorugh Gimuchen country, enteres a land ruled by the British.

He describes Phari as a most desolate place without any wood. It is situated in the midst of a vast plain at about 12,000 feet above the sea-level. The ascents and descents from Phari to Lhasa are very gradual and the route extremely easy.

The great iron chain bridge over the Tsang-po river between the Yam-drok Tso and Lhasa was called Chaksamtuka. The small monastery at the souty entrance to the bridge was called called Chak-sam. The bridge was formed of four iron chains, two on each side.

KINTHUP

Kinthup Belonged to Sikkim. He had previously accompanied explorer Nem Singh to Gyala Sindong (Gyala and Sengdam) and had since traversed Bhutan with Rinzin Namgyal, another Indian explorer. He went as companion to the Chinese Lama, whom the late Captain Herman sent to Gyala Sindong to throw marked logs into the Tsang-po river at that place, having previously arranged for watchers to be stationed at 6he junction of the Dihang and Brahmaputra rivers, to ascertain whether the logs came down by that course and so to settle beyond possibility of doubt the identity of the Tsang-po with the Brahmaputra of Assam. The plan failed owing to the bad faith of the Chinese Lama who sold Kinthup into slavery and returned to his own home in China. Kinthup managed to escape and returned to Darjeeling after an absence of four years, having traced the course of the Tsang-po down to Onlow or Olon, nearly one hundred miles lower than any previous explorer had done and within one march of Miri Padam (Domro or Padam) which is about thirty five miles from the nearest plain of India. This man was not a trained explorer and the information he brought was not based on the instrumental route survey. It could only be regarded as a bona fide story of his travels from recollection two years after his return. The acound was translated into English from the original by Norpu, an exployee of the Survey Department and subsequently compiled by Colonel Tanner.

Kinthup crossed the Donkhya (Dongkhya) pass on the 7th August, 1880 and halted for two days at the Cholamo lake to arrange for transport for Gyantse. There the Lachung and Gyantse traders exchanged their goods and the left with the latter on the 10th August, 1880, reaching Gyantse in seven days. He left Gyantse on 23rd August, disguised as a pilgrim and carrying *khursings* (cradle for packs) after the manner of pilgrims. After passing Dongkar where the Lama's nephew lived, he reached Lhasa on the

1st September, 1880, where the Lama feasted his old companions and remained for six days. Then they returned to Chu-shul by boat down the Lhasa or Kyi Chu and reached Ke-desho Dzong on the southern bank of the Tsang-po river opposite Dorjen Thag. Excellent clothes and blankets were made there. The Lama fell ill at Tsetang and lived ther for twenty days. Kinthup meanwhile had to cut grass for the Lama's horse and was very badly treated. From Tsetang, they went to Makmoi and Rongchaker Dzong (about 50 houses). The soil is very productive in this region.

At Lhagyri Dzong, there were about 500 houses under the rule of a *Jongpon*. The place had two gold mines. They halted at a *jikkyop* (rest house for travellers). After crossing the Putrang pass, they reached Rizur on the 16th October, 1880. Kinthup reports that the inhabitants of Lamda (about 40 houses) were chiefly employed in the trade or musk which was brought from Kongbo and sold at Lhasa. The soil yields good crops of wheat and barley. The stream which rises at the back of the Putrang pass followed Kinthup's line of route. Dakpu Dongppa (about 160 houses) was ruled by Dungkhor, a nobleman of Lhasa. The Tsangpo river is half a mile to the north. On the 20th October, passing Ani Gompa (nunnery), with about 50 runs, they spent the night in a cave.

At Nang Dzong, all roads to Kongbo branched off. At Pari Chote village, the Dalai Lama, nam,ed Nga Wang Lobzang, was born. The traders, called Golokpas, visited this placed annually in October qnd November with merchandise consisting chiefly of salt, wool, barley and rice. At this place a Tibetan officer called Dedupa resided whose main duty was to buy rice for the Lhasa Government. Many musk and other deer were found in the hills about there. The Tsang-po river is about one hundred paces from Nang Dzong. After passing a *jikkyop*, the explorer reached the Kongbo Naga La. This pass is very high and dangerous. Wild people and herds of wild sheep called *ragu* or *ragowa* were found on this mountain which remains snow-clad in winter. Constant gusts of wind caused the snow to fly about in summer and it is very difficult to cross the pass during stormy weather.

On the 25th October, 1880, the Chinese Lama and Kinthup reached Don Kargoan (probably Kongkar Dzong of explorer Nem

Singh). Here the Tsang-po river flows in a northerly direction. They passed Tsung Shod and stopped at Kyimdong (about 10 houses) in order to collect provisions by means of begging. There were some lead mines here. The roads to Tsari, Pachakshiri and Lhasa joined here. At Thun Tsung, they found many houses and cultivation. There was a large and beautiful temple here having eight mannificent altars. Both priests and nuns were allowed to preach and live together in this temple. Then they passed through Kum and Bumkyimgog and returned to Thun Tsung where they stayed for four months. The detention was owing to the Chinese Lama falling in love with his host's wife. Finally the state of affairs betwen the Lama and the lady became known to the host and the bad-charactered Chinese Lama had to pay Rs. 25 in compensation, an arrangement which was effected by Kinthup with great difficulty.

They started from Thun Tsung on the 6th March, 1881. After travelling through Jaket (Chake), Gonsa and Dehmu (Temo) where there were about 100 houses and a monastery containing about 350 monks and Chu Lhakang, they reached Guru Chyokhang (Guru Duphuk). This place is named after a hermit who devoted many years to the contemplation of the diety at a time when it was full of monsters, who were turned to religion by this *Guru* (saint) who conveted them into his disciples. Then they passed through Gyala Sengdam (Sindong) where there is a waterfall which drops from a height of about 100 feet, and reached Gotsang Dupu which is situated on a rock where the aforesaid *Guru* remained many years as a hermit. The Tsang-po is about half a mile distant. As there was no road to proceed further, they returned to Gyala. The Tsang-po river was crossed by leather and wooden boats in winter but in summer these boats were incapable of transporting people over it. So the travellers had to swing by a rope which is stretched across. They passed Nyukthang and stoped at Pemakchung. As there was no road ahead, they retraced their steps. The Tsang-po is two chains distant and falls over a cliff called Sinji—Chokyul (Singche Chogye) from a height of about 150 feet. There is a lake at the foot of this fall where rainbows are always visible. Then they passed Chu Lhakang, crossed Dehmu pass and reached Kongbo Lunang where there were about 140 houese with good cultivation and three monasteries.

At Tongjuk (Tong Kyuk), a bridge was built over the stream where the passes were checked. The Chinese Lama went with the gateman to obtain permission from the *Jongpon* while Kinthup stayed at the bridge and hid his three compasses and pistol. On the 14th May, 1881, the servant of the *Jongpon* forcibly took away one compass and the pistol from Kinthup at the instigation of the Chinese Lama. On the 24th May, the Lama pretended to go out on business for two or three days and told Kinthup to wait at the *Jongpan's* quarters. Kinthup waited there for more than two months when he was employed in stitching clothes. The Lama never returned. At length, Kinthup began to suspect that the Chinese Lama had fled. One day as he was tending the hourses of the *Jongpon* at Lhaye with a man who was well acquainted with him, he learnt that the Chinese Lama had sold him to the *Jongpon* as a slvae and had himself gone to his country. After working some months in slavery, on the 7th March, 1882 he succeeded in escaping to Namding Phukpa and passed through Po-Toi-Lung (Po Trulung), crossed the Pok-Tung-Dho Chu (Po Tsang-po) by bridge and ran away with the utmost speed. At this point, the road to Pemako Chung was quite impassible for four-footed animals.

Explorer Kinthup reached Dorjiyu Dzong. Many wild beasts of prey were found there. The road was very bad. He followed the course of the Tsang-po river and passed through Pang-go where there is Tsenchuk Gompa. He passed Panshing, Khing Khing (Keng Keng), Tambu and Rinchenpung and reached Kondu Potrang which had a monastery, fifteen houses and a dzong. From the top of the mountain one could see Zayul country to the north-east, Po-yul to the north-west, hills of India to the east and the hills of Tsari to the south. Then he reached Kondu Potrang. This mountain can be crossed in summer upto the 1st August after which it is closed by snow.

Starting from Tambu and travelling to the west, he crossed the Tsang-po river at about one mile by a cane bridge. At Marpung, he found a monastery with fifteen nuns and thirty priests who were allowed to live together. On reaching Marpung, Kinthup heard that men sent by the *Jongpon* in search of him had come to arrest him. He at once ran away to the monastery and bowed thrice at the feet of the Great Lama and told him what had happened and the cause of his flight from the *Jongpon*. In reply, the Lama asked him his destination and whether he had parents. Kinthup told him that he was in inhabitant of Tsung Chungra and that he was going on pilgrimage and had no parents. He begged the Lama not to hand hhim over to his pursuers. The Lama at once wrote to the *Jongpon* stating that he would pay Rs. 50 to him for the value of Kinthuup's life. It took ten days more to settle the matter. He served under the Lama for four months and took one month's leave on the ppretence of going on pilgrimage. He passed through Yortong (Yandong), Paleng and Biping. He did his things in a jungle and went to Giling (about 50 houses) in pretended search of salt which was found on the flat ground hereabout. He secretly made 500 logs, all one fot long, that he had been ordered to make by Captain Harman. Then he carried the logs on his back and hid them in a deep cave. After that he returned to the Lama and served under him for two months. He again took two months leave, pretending to go to Tsari on pilgrimage but he went to Lhasa instead.

 Explorer Kinthup passed through Yortong (Yordong), Ani Pasam, Pankong Kongma and reached Kungmen Gyalmu where there is a big lake. No trees are to be found higher up. He next crossed the Doshing pass and at its foot found two cattle sheds. At Pheodoshong there were about fifteen houses. The Tsang-po is near it to the north. From Chamna, he retraced his steps and reached Thun Tsung in eight days. He crossed Bimbi pass and reached Podzo Sumdo where the roads to Tsari, Men Chhuna Dzong and Kongbo joined. Here there were many houses and a wide plain. Then he crossed Totsen (Tsoka) pass and reached Totsen (Tsoka) village where there is a big lake and a monastery. Many musk deer, spotted deer and wild yaks were found on this hill. The pass is inaccessible after the months of October and November.

 Kinthup proceeded to Tsari where there is a high pass over

which no woman was allowed to go. The reason assigned is that once a goddess named Drolma who wished to judge the moral bebaviour of men and women laid herself across the path at that summit of the pass. A man came by and found the road blocked by the goddess who was disguised. So he asked here with kind words to get out of the way. The goddess told him that she was too weak to stir and requested him to take pity and find another road, and if not, he could cross over her body. On hearing this, the man took a different road. After a short time a woman passed that way and finding the path blocked asked the goddess to get out of the way. The goddess gave the same answer but the women did not take pity and rudely crossed over here body. So from that date women hae been forbidden to pass over and the name of the pass has been known as Drolma pass. It is snow-clad and no wood is found here. There was a *jikkyaop* where firewood, water, and food were kept for travellers by the Government. Kinthup stayed there for one day.

On his way from Mipa, he came to a place named Kodothang where it is said that the above mentioned goddess Drolma kept her cattle. Even now many stone pitchers were lying there and the supposed foot-marks of cows ere visible on stony rocks. A mile higher up, he passed a *jikkyopp* where a cup of curd was given to every traveler. It was kept there by a man named Dakpu Dungpa, whose daughter is said to have gone over the Drolma pass disguised as man. On her way, shewas overtaken by an avalanche and killed. When the news reached the Tibetan Government, Dakpu Dungpa was ordered to keep a cattle shed at the *jikkyop* and to give a cupp of curd to every traveller. Starting on a level road, he found another *jikkyop*, about the miles further, where every traveller got a cup of wine besides water and firewood, if he liked to cook food. A small lake was also there. Ascending a high hill from this point, he could discern the plains of India. On the journey to Tsari by this route, none was allowed to spit even, as the whole ground was considered as holy and the halting places were kept exceedingly clean.

He next ascended the Shangu pass where he found an inn. Men-Chhuna and Loyul villages and the plains of India are visible from this pass. Great number of wild animals like deer, musk deer and beautiful birds were found there. Descending through a valley, he reached Yume (Yumey) where there was a monastery with fifteen priests. The road which branched off from Tsari joined there. No one was allowed to shoot the wild animals of this place. Ascending Yume pass, Kinthup reached a *jikkyopp* where many marmots were seen.

From Chosam (Chazam), he crossed the Gongma (Kongmo) ppass which was covered with snow. Then he followed a stream issuing from the Karam La pass, at the foot of which there were many houses and a *dzong* with many cattle. The soil is poor. At Dok, he halted in a solitary cow-herd's hut. On the way further, he found many cowsheds. At Ngen Lora, there were about 30 houses. At Lharingbu, there was a ruined *dzong* and a gold mine. The gold diggers lived in three houses with about twenty-five men in each. The roads to Lhasa and Men-Chhuna joined at Ngen Lora.

He reached Lhasa by boat and spent three days at the Romoche monastery. The reason for his going back was want of news from India. A *Kazi* (chief) of Sikkim was at Lhasa, whom he requested to write a letter to the Chief of the Survey of India thorugh Nimsring, interppreter (evidently explorer Nem Singh) at the court of Darjeeling. The contents of the letter were as follows:-

"Sir, the Chinese Lama who was sent with me sold me to a *Jongpon* as a slave and himself fled away with Governent instruments that were in his charge. On account of this, the journey pproved a bad one. However, I, Kinthup, have prepared 500 logs according to the order of Captain Harman and am prepared to throw 50 logs pwer day into the Tsang-po river from Bipung in Pemako, from the 5th to the 15th of the tenth Tibetan month of the year called *Chhuluk* of the tibetan Calculation.".

This leter was sent through the *Kazi's* wife who was going to Darjeeling, to the above mentioned interpreter Nimsring, requesting him to inform the Survey authorities of these facts.

Kinthup returned from Lhasa by a different route, following the road to China. He crossed the Kyi Chu, passed through the foot of the Kong-bu Ba pass and reached Kongbo Giamda, following the course of the stream issuing from the pass. There were shops kept by Nepalese and Tibetans at this palce, a junction of roads from Lhasa, China and Kongbo. Kinthups left the China road and travelled south-eastwarde. At Kongbo Naboib, he found three *dzongs* and many houses. The soil yields rich crops of wheat, barley, oats and peas and supports many cattle. At Nyangtset, there were about twenty-five houses and a monastery. At Tashi Rabla, he found about forty houses on both sides of the stream which he was following, the soil being very rich. At Phuchushergi-Lhakang, he discovered a lake north of the stream which he left here and turned towards the Tsang-po river.

Crossing the Tsang-po, he reached Chamna and retraced his route to Pemako where the roads to Lhasa and Gyala Sindong joined. He reported to his rescuer, the Lama and served under him for nearly nine months at the end of which the Lama set him free. Kinthup bowed thrice before him and bade him good-bye thankfully. He was, howver, again engaged by a man for a month for stitching clothes, in return for which he got salt and food.

After a month he made his way to Bipung where he stayed for ten days and threw all the 500 logs into the Tsango-po. He went to the large village of Pangodudung with a monastery and a *dzong* where water for drinking was fetched from a great distance. Then he entered the populated British area along the Tsang-po to earn sufficient money for visiting Lhasa on pilgrimage and returning to his home. He passed through Korba from where the river is about a mile, and Ma-yum with four houses. A big streama falls into the Tsang-po near Agni (ng) and many Lhobas fished in it. Then he reached Angi where there were about 300 houses. Hanging (Paling), with about thirty houses, was situated on the bank of the Tsangpo and opposite it there were large cultivated fields of rice and *kodo*. Hogs and cows abounded.

At Shobang, there were ten houses. Puging (Rikar) was a large village with about 100 hosues on the oposite side of the Tsang-po which is a mile away. There were pine-apple and plantain trees here. The men and women were living in separate houses. About this part, there were many cotton fields from the yield of which the inhabitants prepared cloth which they sold in the market of Pemako. The Tsang-po flows about two miles away from the village of Keti (Gette) where Kinthup halted. Shimong (Simong), where there were about 140 houses, is situated about a mile from the Tsang-po. Kinthup halted at Mongri village where he had to give a handful of salt to every man and woman in the house for a night's shelter.

Kinthup reached Mabuk or Cobuk, with about forty houses. There were many mango, plantain and *marshat* trees. The soil produces rich crops and many cotton sellers gathered there. He passed Tarpin (Dalbuing), with about eighty houses. The forests around Olon or Onlow abounded with wild animals such as tigers, leoppards, and bears. Damro or Padam, with about 100 houses, is about four miles away from the Tsang-po. It was a well known market place whre traders brought their merchandise for sale. Then he went to Lhasa on pilgrimage and returned to Darjeeling.

Kinthup reached his own country of Tasheding in Sikkim after three years. On reaching home he found that his mother had died during his wanderings. So he stayed there for two and a half months for performing her last rites. On the 19th October, 1884, he re-started from his village and met the explorer and interpreter Nem Singh and Mr. A.N. Paul at the monastery of Namchi. Nem Singh odered him to accompany them to the Lachen and Lachung valleys. He went with him to these places and finally reached Darjeeling on the 17th November, 1884.

RINZIN NAMGYAL

Explorer Rinzin Namgyal started from Darjeeling on the 2nd October, 1884. Passing through Singali Tuant, he reached Megutak cave. Along the route, he saw a number of *munals* and blood phesants. The *munal* is a majestic and beautiful bird of the Himalayas. Then he crossed the Yam-pung la and reached the Dholia pass. No sooner had he reached the pass, clouds spread out and snow began to fall. In darkness, it was difficult to trace the way and he had great difficulty in climbing down. The party reached a knoll where they passed the night. On the 12th, they descended abruptly by a winding path in the Kurmo-thang valley and rested in a cattle-shed near the Kurmo-thang-chu. Then they passed Boktob having three cattle-sheds. This place was frequented by traders of Khangabachen village who used to go further east to exchange salt for *tsod,* a kind of creeper which yields a red colour. The Kurmo-thang valley contains an extensive grassy plain surrounded by pine and rhododendron trees. Next day they visited two lakes; the larger one is named Tso-domdong, as its water bears resemblance to the green colour of peacock's feathers. this lake is an object of great veneration to the inhabitants of the surrounding country. The next day they crossed the Chumbab Kang pass where a fall of snow detained them for four days. Then they reached the cave of Choolung kyak where they rested for the night. It was big enough to give shelter to some fifteen persons. Water, grass and fuel were procurable there. Next day they passed Kema-ram, a cattle-shed.

On the 19th October, the explorer and the party crossed the Yalung river by a wooden bridge and reached Tseram village (5 houses) which is situated in a grassy level plain. The inhabitants kept a number of yaks. The tract abounded in game such as *semus,* musk-deer and *munal.* Four roads to Taplang Dzong,

Gunsa village, upper Yalung and the road followed by the explorer joined there and the place had a customs-post.

Next day, they ascended along Yaluk river and visited the upper Yalung village, the summer resort of the inhabitants of the lower Yalung. The former village contained about forty houses, *churtans (chutens)* and small temples marked with flags. The explorer was astonished to find that all the houses full of property were locked up and left without guard. On enquiry he came to know that the inhabitants had temporarily migrated to their winter residence in the warmer region. A market was held there during summer when traders from different parts of the country gathered to exchange their articles. Glaciers are visible and they covered the head of the river. Cows and bullocks were held sacred and they were never used as beasts of burden. Any peson infringing this custom underwent a severe punsihment.

On the 23rd October, they reached the Yalung snowy peak, about 19,000 feet above the sea-level. Next day they returned to Tseram village. Then they passed through Semaram and Tongak and reached the famous cave of Phukpa-Karmu, which gives shelter to passengers against snow and wind. Next day, with the aid of ropes, they climbed over the Kangla Nangma pass where a road runs to Sikkim via Jongri. On the 3rd November, they arrived at Gunsa village.

Gunsa is a large village situated in an open and flat valley enclosed on all sides by snowy mountains which rise in precipices to a stupendous height. It contained about 150 houses made of stones and wood. Some of them were two storeyed. The Khangbachen river emanates from the Jonsong pass to the north, dividing the village from a monastery surrounded by about forty houses. It flows through a narrow valley from south of the village and joins Yalung river. The stream was bridged over in a number of places with timber to facilitate communication between the village and the monastery. Here they found some patches of cultivation. The produce was wheat, potatoes, barley, *phaphar* and other vegetables. The inhabitants were well-to-do people, generally engaged in trading business. Women of this village spent their time in weaving blankets. The men and women in the village used to go every night from one family to another to interchange visits, when they were treated with courtesy and presented with cups of *mowa* (a kind of liquor) and fruits, etc. Thus they used to pass their night with folk songs and dances. In case of death occuring in the village, their jolliness was stopped for three days as a respect to the departed one. They observed Tibetan customs and kept yaks, goats, and sheep. They were ruled by a headman whose duty was to collect revenue and taxes. The village lands were fenced round to protect them against musk-deer, *burrel (nao)* and *munal* which the villagers were forbidden to shoot. The explorer passed five nights there, enjoying the hospitality of the cultured villagers who were happy in their own circle and environment.

On the 7th November, Rinzin Namgyal and the party crossed Khangbachen river and reached the Nanghola pass whence they saw, seven miles to the west down in a valley, a town called Waloong Zom on the junction of the raods and between two rivers, Yongma and Waloong. It contained some 300 houses and a row of shops on either side of the street thorugh the town. Next day they retraced their steps to Gunsa village.

On the 9th they followed the course of the Khangbachen river and reached the village of the sme name, the summer residence of the inhabitants of Gunsa. The village was situated at the junction of the Thonak and Thongchen rivers and was found empty as the inhabitant had temporarily migrated to the warmer region. It was surrounded by barley fields.

Jonsong pass (about 20,000 feet) is a continuation of the Kinchinjunga range. They passed Khangbachen and Lonak and reached the Jonsong pass on the seventh day from Gunsa. This pass could not be crossed unless some fifteen men helped clear the passage over the snow.

Passing over a moraine, the explorer and the party arrived at the cattle-shed of Chizin Lhe. Thence they returned to the north and reached Chhorten Nyima pass. From there they passed Chizin, a cattle-shed and reached the cow-shed of Shonak. Their stock of provision had run short and they were obliged to live on the flesh of the game. About two miles from Chizin, they saw the footprints of a wild yak. They traced the marks for about four miles and came across two wild yaks. They tried to catch them alive but the beasts escaped. Marching for somedays, living on the flesh of wild animals, they arrived at Zemasamdong at the junction of Lachen and Zemu rivers where they replenished their stock of provision.

On the 5th December, 1884, the explorer and the party reached Lachen or Lomting village which is situated on a small table-land on the west of the Lchen river. It contained about 110 hosues and a small monastery. The villagers were well-to-do people and their trade lay in carrying canes, beams and planks, etc. to Tibet. They had a number of yaks, sheep and goats and made blankets of various kinds, which were sold in Sikkim where they also sold salt, earthern pots, musk, etc. They stopped there for four days.

The explorer reached Darjeeling, via Cheungtong and Tumlong on the 31st January, 1885.

Sikkim • Bhutan • Tibet

On the 1st November, 1885, Rinzon Namgyal left Darjeeling, accompanied by his trust-worthy servants of Sikkim, crossed the Ranjit river, about 1,050 feet above the sea level, by ferry, passed through Kistan village, the monastery of Namchi and Donyer halting place, crossed Pendong ridge and halted at Tami village. On the 4th November, he reached Turko village where they found orange trees. They crossed the Ringphi Chu and the Rangpho Chu which fall into the Tiswta river. The Tista valley in this locality is unhealthy, fever prevailing after the rains. They passed the night at Namphak hlating place.

On the 5th November, the explorer and the party, after passing through an undulating ground, reached the hamlet of Kasair. During this march they observed orange trees flouishing in large numbers, the fruits of which were sold in Darjeeling and other markets. Then they passed through Samdong village, crossed the Tista river by a cane suepension bridge about 400 feet in length and reached Yeungthang.

On the 9th November, they reached Tuman. Next day they crossed the Phobam La (6,680 feet). Then they journeyed through very heavy forest of Reh village and halted on the bank of the Rongni Chu. On the 11th, they followed the course of this river and passing through Pakyong village reached the village of Dikaling. Along the banks of the Roro Chu, copper mines were pretty extensively worked.

On the 15th November, they reched the *bazar* of Chongthapa (2,900 feet) where a fair was held every Sunday. Then they passed Lingtamtho and Koi villages, crossed Pangola, passed Asam village and, desending, crosed Di Chu, which is about 100 feet in width, the banks of the stream sloping down to the water which has a rocky bed. It is boisterous in its flow and falls in the Tista river in the plains. The upper portion of the Di Chu valley is covered with dense forests, giving shelter to all kinds of large games.

On the 3rd December, the explorer and the party crossed the Song la (7,400 feet) and going down very dangerous slopes they reached Assam-dokyul village, consisting of trading herdsmen. Butter and *chud* were the principal articles taken from there to Tibet and bartered for salt, blankets, etc. The plant *chud* is found growing wild in these parts entwined round the trunks of trees and is a very important articles of trade. A rich red dye is extracted from it when dry. This dye was in great demand throughout Tibet.

On the 4th December, they crossed the Chang Chu, the Sa La on the Gyi-mo-chi ridge and arrived at Bindu-kha village with about twenty houses. It is situated in Bhutan territory. According to the custom in Bhutan, both sexes shave the hair on their heads. This custom was adopted by the villages. On the 6th, they crossed the Bue Chu by a wooden bridge, ascended through a thick forest to the cattle-sheds of Athong and Bakling. Bakling was a place of some importance as hundreds of heads of cattle were kept there and a brisk trade in butter was carried on with Paro. The cattle were of good breed and of large size. Many purchasers used to come to the place.

On the 7th December, they ascended through a thick forest and struck the road leading from Sip-chhu to the Tula La. Following this road, they reached Longchok cave where they rested for the night. The road was frequented by robbers. On the 8th, they crossed the Guachhau Pass (9,950 feet) and then gained the Tule La (Tug La). Game abounds in this locality and the explorer observed the rhododendron and a species of bamboo growing in great luxuriance. Then they descended over a very precipitous path to Baklia cattle-shed and reached the right bank of the Ammo Chu which was spanned by a cane bridge about 150 feet in length. *Am* signifies mother, hence Ammo Chu is spoken of as the mother of all its tributaries. The *shao* stag, musk-deer, wild sheep or *burral*, goat, *munal*, pheasant and other game abound in the uper regions of Ammo valley, while in its southern or lower portion, the elephant, tiger, bear, wild pigs and *thar* equally abound and often proved destructive to the cultivation. Then they crossed the Dul Chu which joins the Ammo river after many fine waterfalls varying in height from 50 to 100 feet. They halted at Sangbe Dzong.

On the 10th December, they passed over a very precipitous path and crossed the Sum Chu by a wooden bridge. The banks of the Sum Chu are rocky and precipitous. They passed Doring cattle-shed and continued they journey through snow to Tegong Donkhim (rest-house). On the 14th, they gained the Tegong La (12,000 feet) on the Chumalhari ridge. The dwarfed rhododendron grows on this ridge. The silver fir occupies the ground on both sloppes and attains great age and dimensions, some trees being about thirty feet in girth and of magnificent appearance. A splendid view of the surrounding peaks is obtained from this pass.

They descended till they reached the Ha Chu which takes its name from the tribe who inhabit this part of Bhutan. The Hachu valley is broad and open and roads run its whole length on either side. It was thickly populated but owing to extreme cold, the inhabitants temporarily migrated to warmer region with all their cattle during winter. They stayed at Pudung village at night. This valley was under the immediate control of the *Jongpons* residing at Tumphiong and Batte Dzong, who were in their turn subject to the Paro Chief.

On the 15th December, 1885, the explorer Rinzin Namgyal and the party reached the deserted village of Piadongkha. Game abounds in this locality and a road leads to Paro over the Sang La. The pine *(pinus excelsa)* thrives here, its timber being employed in building houses and bridges. Its chipped pieces when lighted afford light in the dwellings. On the 16th December, they travelled to he Batte Chu and reached Batte Dzong (8,850 feet). The fort is perched on the summit of an almost inaccessible rock. The explorer reached Chebi village on the 20th December. It contained ten houses built of stones and a monastery. The houses as a rule were long and large enough to afford accommodation to several families. Cereals were not extensively cultivated but the people devoted much time to raising vegetables and looked after the fruit trees which were numerous. The hill tops were generally bare but pine and fir occupied the slopes and valleys. On the 21st Decem,ber, they marched to Giabasurthong village, crossed the Giaba La (9.800 feet), descended to Wanakha village and reached Tashigong village containing about 150 souls.A fine view of the upper valley of the Wang river is obtained from here.

On the first day of the Tibetan new year, all the inhabitants of the valley and the adjacent parts make holiday and witness the dancs and feast of the Paga monastery. On the 23rd December, they travelled through dangerously precipitous ground to Dokhang Sampha wooden bridge over the Wang river. After paying toll tax, they crossed it and struck the main road between Buxa Duar and the Tashi Chu. There was a temple near the junction of roads. They ascended the Sema La and then descended to the large village of Kapcha with a fort and a monastery. To the east were seen several hundred houses scattered about two miles away.

A road leads from Kapcha to the Tarka La (Taka La). The *Penlop* of Tarka Dzong had been murdered a few years ago and his Government usurpped, but his seven surviving sons, with many of his faitufhul adherents, fled to Tsongsa nad lived there for many years. When the sons attained manhood, they determined to regain their father's property and to avenge his death. With this end in view, they stealhily entered the Tarks Dzong one night and set fire to the houses. The usurper, along with many followers, fled precipitately, leaving the fort in the hands of the seven sons of the murdered predecessor. All this was transpiring at the time of the explorer's arrival at Kapcha village, not far from the scene of these disorders and it was this disturbance that barred his entrance into Tarka.

Like the Government of Tibet, that of Bhutan was divided between Deb Raja, the secular head on the one hand and Dharma Raja, the religious one on the other. The former exercised political authority with the help of his powerful barons, while the latter was supposed to be absorbed in the contemplation of all the concerns the spiritual welfare of his subjects. Deb Raja was supposed to be an incarnation of the preceding deceased Dharma Raja and was selected in infancy by the chief monasteries of Bhutan.

The most powerful chieftains of Bhutan were the *Penlops* of Tsongsa, Paro and Tarka (Taka) and the *Jongpons* of Thimbu, Punakha and Angduphorang.

On the 24th December, 1885, the explorer crossed the Tanakpho Chu by a wooden bridge and continued the journey. The road was undulating till he arrived at Chukha Dzong. Next day he and his party prepared to cross the bridge at Chukha, 250 fet long. At first they were refused permission to cross it. On the 7th January, the Thimbu *Jongpon,* the first miniser of the Deb Raja, arrived at Chukha and permitted the explorer to travel on to Buxa Duar. Chukha has warm climate. Game abounds here. A road leads from his village to Tarka pass.

The explorer and the party crossed the bridge at Chukha on the 11th January, 1886 and reached Maruchom village having over twenty houses, Between Chukha and this place, the Wong Chu flows between high preciptous banks, dangerous in the extreme and, in conseuqence, the road is carried not along the bank but about one mile away from the river westwrds. On the 14th January they proceeded on their journey and gained the summit of the Singchhu La (5,700 feet). Descending, they arrived at Buxa Duar. Rinzin Ramgyal again approached the Thimbu *Jongpon* who granted him the passport to travel throughout his jurisdiction without molestation but said that it was beyond his power to grant him the passport to travel throughout his jurisdiction without molestation but said that it was beyond his poer to grant him the passport to travel in Eastern Bhutan. The *Jongpon* wrote to Deb Raja asking for his boon for the explorer but the reply came back after fifteen days asking the explorer to report to the Deb Raja personally.

The explorer engaged the services of a Lama to guide him through Eastern Bhutan. With the Lama guide he and his party left Buxa Duar on the 9th February and travelling by bullock cart, rail and steamer, arrived in Gauhati on the 21st February from where they marched to Dewangiri where they arrived on the 26th. At Dewangiri, Rinzin Namgyal found only Bhutanese with a sprinkling of Nepalese.

The same day, they reached Chugi-hot. This place was the winter resort of numerous families from Bhutan who used to bring horses and articles of commerce to sell and barter for the produce of the plains. On the 27th, they proceeded along the Chugi Chu and followed its course. This valley, varying from 200 feet to half a mile in width, is covered with good pasture for cattle. Proceeding further, they gained the summit of the Tungka La (7,900 feet). A monastery named Tungka Gompa has been erected on the pass. Provisions were procured at Tungka Gompa after which they reached the right bank of the Kongri Chu and halted for the night. The vale of the Kongri Chu is broad and pretty level and affords pasture to numerous herds of cattle. Fish is plentiful in the stream and cultivation is carried on extensively on both the banks.

On the 1st March, 1886, Rinzin Namgyal and the party arrived at the junction of the Kongri Chu with the Diri Chu (1,590 feet) and in consequence of the low elevation and forested area of the entire vale, fever prevailed there. Then they crossed a large chain-bridge, about 300 feet long, over Dangma Chu which flows with a rapid current. They passed the village of Kenga with a monastery. The Dangma Chu or Manas is a large river and finds its way to the Brahmaputra below Gauhati. It is hardly fordable below Tawang and is the largest river of Bhutan. Cultivation is extensively carried out round Kenga.

Eastern Bhutan, lying to the east of about 91° longitude is divided into two parts known as Kurted and Kurmed (Upper and Lower Kuru). The people speak a language called Chingmi which is entirely different from that spoken in Western Bhutan. Kurted is the portion lying north of a line drawn from Tashingong to Thungsi La, and Kurmed the portion south of the same line. The former possesses lofty snow-clad mountains and peaks and is extremely cold and unfavourable for cultivation while in Kurmed the climate is less severe and the people are given much to cultivation and bartering and are as a rule industrious. The women take part in all active duties equally with the men.

On the 2nd March, 1886, the explorer and the party reached the Kenga La (5,650 feet). A monastery stands near it. Then they passed the ruined village of Tongla Kenga. They forded the Sindu Chu and halted on the left bank of the Kuru Chu. Next day they crossed the bridges over the Shonga Chu and reached Saling village after crossing the Saling Chu by a bridge. The Shonga valley is well watered and green but being at a low elevation it is hot and feverish. It is covered with pine and fir trees of magnificent growth.

On the 13th March, they left Saling and followed the course of the Shonga Chu till they reached Singur village (9,800 feet), situated in a grassy plateau surrounded by magnificent specimen of the silver fir called *dungshing* by the local people. Game abounds in his locality and the explorer noticed immense herds of yaks and cows grazing in the neighbourhood. The people do little cultivation but tend their immense herds of cattle and barter butter for other commodities. The population of this place was about 200.

Then they gained the Wandong La (12,490 feet) from which a fine view was obtained of the country lying to the east and northeast. They halted at Laba rest-house. Firewood was abundant here. On the 15th march, they crossed Thungri La after a stiff ascent. There is a temple *(mendong)* at the pass. On the walls of this *mendong* the religious formula *"Om mane padmi hom"* was chiselled. They descended through a fine forest of silver firs and reached the Manichhukhor temple. Then they passed Orha Mendong. They party proceeded to the Orha La and the explorer, taking only a guide along with him, went to the village of Orha in order to procure provisions.

Orha is a very large and important village, possessing a fort and two monasteries and about 300 souls, situated on an extensive, open, grassy plateau and watered by the Orha Chu. Cultivation is carried on extensively through the climate is cold. Cattle, horses, mules, assess, goats and sheep were seen in large numbers and altogether the village might be said to be rich and the people prosperous. Trade was also conducted on an extensive scale, the people taking their articles as far as Dewangiri in the south and into Tibet across the northern frontier. The manners and customs of these people slightly resemble those of Tibet. On the 16th March, they crossed the Tangsbi Chu, passed Tangsbi village and halted near Tang-Chu. Crossing it, they arrived at the large bridge at Bioka. Then they travelled to the large village of Angduchholing 8,900 feet near Bioka Dzong.

The fort of Bioka Dzong would appear to be one of the most important in Bhutan. The *Jongpon* of it appeared to be a very powerful chief, his rule extending over the entire country known as Pumthang, embracing the tract of basins of the Pumthang river and the Tang Chu as fr as eight miles below their junction. Bioka Dzong (9,300 feet) is built on an eminence overhanging the river. Its walls rose to the great height of 150 feet and were occupied by the chief and the retainers. There was no water in the fort but a well-built covered way had been constructed to a spring near the river bank from which the wter supply was obtained. In the neighbourhood, numerous monasteries existed, attended by proportionate number of priests. It might be said that the chief interest of Pumthang centred at this village of Angduchholing, being better populated than any other part through which it flows.

The climate of Pumpthang is most salubrious and disease is hardly known to exist there. Splendid forests of pine and fir adorn the lower ridges, spurs and even the valleys, while game of every description roamed at large under their shade, with little or no fear of molestation, for the people were averse to taking life even of wild animals. Trade was also carried on extensively by the people of this part and they also cultivated *phapar*, wheat, buck-wheat and potatoes. Women employed themselves chiefly in the manufacture of cloth and blankets.

Recrossing the Pumthang river, they reached its junction with the Tur Chu. The valley of the Tur Chu is very green and abounds in good pasture as a result of which numerous herds of cattle are taken there to graze. Then they passed through the villages of Shugtag, Sangalakhang and Doram and reached Shabjethang temple where they stayed for the night.

On the 10th April, they crossed the Nashi Chu and reached the village of the same name. The pine grows upto this point but not higher. They passed a small tank called Chozho, the usual halting place for travellers. They stayed at a cave for the night. On the the 11th April, they passed the junction of the Kurmathang Chu with the Pumthang and reached Chhampa village, a place of some importance where barter trade was carried on.

On the 12th April, they continued their ascent along the Pumthang river and reached Lhabja cattle-shed beyond which fuel was not procurable. Moving upwards they reached Phukbakha cave (15,400 feet) and halted there for the night. Two miles beyond Lhabja, a road crosses a pass and enters Tibet. Owing to heavy fall of snow, they were detained at the cave for four days. It was miserable as the accommodation was scant and the low roof prevented them from standing.

The morning of the 17th April broke bright and clear and they ventured to scale the pass and reached a small frozen lake called Lorcha Cho with a circumference of about a mile. It is the source of the Pum thang river. After about three miles more of stiff ascent, with much difficulty they gained the summit of Monlakachung pass (17,500 feet) where the eye ranged over a sea of snow, the wind adding not inconsiderably to their almost unbearable trials. The pass is situated on a lofty range trending in an easterly direction from the peaks of Kinchinjunga to Chumalhari and Kulha Kangri. This elevated watershed is confined between the upper sources of the Kosi and Manas rivers and presents one unbroken wall of snow and ice, extending for nearly two hundred miles from the eastern frontier of Nepal to Eastern Bhutan. Having taken observations of the many peaks visible, the explorer and the party began to descend into Tibet which is not so steep and after travelling about five miles through deep and fresh snow reached Suphuk cave where they halted for the night. A small lake, the source of the Yura Chu, lies about a mile east of the cave. Great masses of glaciers lie on either side of the pass.

On the 18th April, they followed the course of the Yura Chu till they came to the rest-house on the side of the pass, where goods were collected prior to being conveyed across the frontier. They continued their journey to the hot springs of Jhagpachachu where they halted for the night. There are about fifty hot springs at this spot, the water of which varies in temperature from the tepid to almost boiling heat and possesses a strong smell of sulphur. In the centre, a tank had been constructed and the water from these springs was conveyed there by cuttings in the soil. The people from all parts come there for bathing in these waters and a rst-house has ben erected at the spot. They had faith in its curative properties.

On the 19th April, 1886, the explorer and the party travelled along the course of the Yura Chu. Crossing the Gunsa Chu, they passed Yura Dzong (14,650 feet). The headman of this fort was called Deva who was under the *Jongpon* of Tuwa Dzong where they reached on the 1st May. Then they passed Seh village containing about eighty houses, overlooking which is the large monastery of Sangkar Guthok with about 100 prietsts. The head Lama was an intelligent priest and supposed to be learned in Tibetan religious lore. The monastery contained several hundred volumes of Tibetan writings besides numerous richly adorend images and a large quantity of wooden types which were used in the printing of their books. Seh village is situated on the right bank of the Yura Chu which flows here through a fine grassy valley, rich in pasture and surrounded by lofty snow-clad mountains.The villagers numbering about 300 appeared prosperous and even rich in the possession of large herds of cattle, yaks, horses, mules and assess, which roamed happily over the valley. The yak was the most favoured among the people for its fine milk, long hair and being the best beast of burden in high altitudes. Cultivation was carried on pretty extensively. A hot spring about a mile north affords the luxury of bathing in warm sulphorous water. A road leads from here to Lhasa, Shigatse and Phari through the Monda pass.

On the 4th May, they crossed Lhobrak pass. On the 7th, they arrived at Lhobrak Kharchu, a place held in great veneration by the people who go there for worship and carry away the sacred water which percolates through a rock and drops on the floor beneath. Crossing the bridge over the Tashiyangsi Chu, they spent the night in a cave. On the 12th May, they crossed the Dozam La and reached a grassy flat where they halted. On he 13th, travelling through an undulating ground they reached the Dozam Chu and followed its course. On the 15th, they marched over undulating country and came near Men-chhuna Dzong. Two days more of marching brought them to Tawang (Men-Tawang) and five days more to Odalguri, along the route traversed by the famous explorer Nain Singh. From there, they found their way to Gauhati on the 31st, 1886, and by steamer and rail arrived at Darjeeling on the 3rd June.

UGYEN GYATSO

The Explorer Ugyen Gyatso left Padamtain on the 10th June, 1883, halted at Namchi and reached Yangong monastery where his uncle had been the Chief Lama. The 15th June was a Tibetan holiday in honour of Buddha Menlha, the medicinal diety of Tibet. So the explorer gave a feast to the monks. All the villagers between Rungpo and Rungum attended that day and were feasted royally. He left Yangong monastery on the 22nd June, crossed the Rungam river and the Seuntan (Singtam) pass and halted at Lingtam Gorrh. Heavy rains impeded his progress. The party had to bridge the Mun Chu before crossing it and took refuge in a cave called Ralaltakpuk. On the 29th June, they crossed the Tista river in full flood, passed through Ringim monastery, Myang and Chakung, making their way by a road infested with leeches and snakes, and reached Cheungtong monastery.

On the 6th July, the explorer arrived at the outpost of Lachung where he made necessary arrangements for yaks and ponies for transport. Then the party proceeded to Samdong, crossed the Donkhya pass (18,100 feet) and reached Gonpu Thatsang. Following the course of the Arun river, they passed Lung-dung village and the nunnery of Dsa-lung-nya-gon where fine carpets were prepared.

A short march next day brought the party to the hot springs of Kusi (Ko-so) where they rested for the necessary opperation of a bath. There wre two large *Kunds* or wells and several smaller ones, one of which was so hot that beef could be boiled in it readily. The ground all round was too hot to trend on with naked feet and water boiled with a harsh noise. This village was the centre of the local carpet industry. On the 26th July, they crossed the Ketsu pass (14,500 feet) and passed through Kampa Dzong and Gonpu-tha-tsang (Ta-tsong) and halted at the Langoi *dok*. The next day's march involed the crossing of three easy passes of Lamo

La, Kesar La and Selung La. Between these passes were open level plains with a certain amount of marshy land and many *doks*. On the 30th July, the party crossed Lama La (16,800 feet) and reached Kyil-khordub (Kinga takdup) where there was a rock-cut cave or hermitage of considerable celebrity.

From She-kar monastery, the explorer travelled over open gravel covered plain with occasional fields of barley cultivation past the village of Kab-shi.

On the 31st July, the party crossed the Pongong pass (16,200 feet) after a steep ascent and reached the bank of the Nyang river or Pen-nang Chu. From this pass the explorer looked down the great and fertile valley of the Nyang river and could see the town of Gyantse across the intervening gravel-covered plains, surrounded by gardens and orchards. He visited the great temple at Gyantse which overlooks the town. He followed the course of the Nyang river towards Shigatse. His road passed through succession of villages surrounded by barley fields. On both sides of the river are stupendous mountain chains. He passed through Dong-tse monastery, Pehsi temple and Norpu-kyang-dsin. As the explorer approached Shigatse, villages and cultivation became more frequent and he describes the country he passed through as consisting of plains and widely extended fields, well-watered by the Nyang river. A few miles further they came to the outer walls of Tra-shi-lhun-po which has been fully described by Pundit Nain Singh.

On the 14th August, 1883, the explorer continued his exploration eastwards from Shigates. He first followed the course of the Tsang-po river along its southern bank, passing through well-cultivated country bordering the river. To his south, lateral valleys slopes downwards to the Tsang-po river. Some of the valleys, the valley of Lhan in particular, were of geat fertility and beauty. At Tag-tu-kha, fifty miles from Shigatse, there was a ferry which makes the point to which the river is navigable from Shigatse.

On the 20th August, the explorer crossed the river Tsang-po with difficulty. Rains were continuous and the river was in flood.

On the 22nd August, the party left the marshy swamp of Tsa-thang and reached the Yam-drok Samding monastery. The rest of the month was occupied in exploring the very remarkable system of the lake Yam-drok Tso. Due to rain and thick mist, he could not get a cler view of the lake.

The Du-mo lake (14,300 feet) impressed the explorer greatly. Its deep and still water embosomed among mighty cliffs, the silence which hung over the stupendous crags which encircled it, broken only by the hoarse roar of the falling masses which ever and anon thundered down the mountain sides into its depths, were associated in his mind with traditions of demons and genii who were supposed to inhabit the lake and whose good-will was daily propitiated by the people living around. All this struck his superstitious mind with unwonted awe. The level of Du-mo lake was 500 feet higher than that of Yamdrok Tso and it was said to be gradually rising. Then he returned southwords with a view to exploring the Lobrak valley and unknown lakes in that direction.

On the 2nd September, Ugyen Gyatso sighted the lake of Pho-mo-chang-thang from the Yeh pass which overlooks it. Pho-mo seemed to present a strong contrast to the gloomy glamour of Yam-drok and Du-mo lakes. To the south, the explorer describes the snowy peaks of Kulha Kangri and Mau-da as piercing the vault of heaven like thye dazzling spires of crystal *churtans*. The name Pho-mo (i.e. male and female) is derived from two islands in the lake.

On the 3rd September, the explorer crossed the Man-da pass (17,450 feet) and descended to Man-do village and followed the course of the Lhobrak through a valley filled with villages and cultivation. He visited the celebrated shrine of Seh-guru-chhoi-wang built after the model of the famous monastery of Lha-lung

On the 5th September, Gyatso followed the Lhobrak valley into Bhutan. He ascended the Tun Pass (16,850 feet) and reached the grassy plateau which embosoms the sacred lake of Tong-Tsho Pama-ling. It is a beautiful flat country which gently slopes upto the foot of the mountains carpeted with equisitive verdure, lovely flowers and bushes of different shrubs. At the head of the lake is the monastery of Tong-tsho Pama-ling. Looking from it to the south east, the view embraced the crystal surface of the thrice holy lake flanked by a range of bellowy mountains overtopped in the distance by the lofty snows of Kulha Kangri. After visiting the celebrated cave, consecrated to Guru Pema and surrounded on three sides by glaciers, to the north-west of the lake the explorer passed over an elevated plateau nearly 15,000 feet above the sea-level to find his way back into Lhobrak valley and reached the celebrated monastery of Seh-sang-khar-gu-thong.

Crossing the Roi-pa pass (15,800 feet) and the Kha-na pass through heavy mists and fog, Ugyen Gyatso descended into the well-populated and highly cultivated lateral valley of Mug. This country generally possesses the aspect of Sikkim and is reputed to be the most populated and fertile district of Tibet. It was harvest time when the explorer passed through this valley and the air was full of songs of the reapers. This shows the prosperity of the region. He passed through Lung-hah and Thing. Then he crossed the Lhobrak and Tamshul rivers by great stone-bridges. The latter had a guard house at its eastern extremity. A large bell was suspended from the top of the narrow gateway of this house which was struck when the door opened. On either side, a fierce Tibetan mastiff was chained to guard the passage. The use of these magnificent Tibetan dogs as guards has been often referred to by the explorer. They are rough-coated, shaggy and untameably fierce. He reached the town of Lakhrang Dzong.

On the 15th September, he left Lhakhstang to explore the valley of the Tamshul Tsang-po upwards. He next crossed the Dsa-kar pass (14,500 feet) and passed the village of Lu. The valley here was very rich in cultivation and the explorer writes a pleasant reminiscence of the luxuries of the turnips and cheese. At Na-shi, he found another monastery. The Tam-shul river appears to be bridged at frequent intervals. The upper part of the Tam-shul valley is well-cultivated, with many villages and wide grassy plains flanking both banks. He crossed out of the Tam-shul valley by the Shar Khalep pass into the great desert-plain bordering the Trigu lake.

From Tam-shul, Gyatso went straight northward to the village of Hai-do, gradually ascending a gravel-covered plain and passing the monasteries of Rimon, Tasha-choilang and Noo-chok. Cultivtion was scarce here. He crossed the Shar Khalep pass (16,800 feet) and at the foot of it encountered wide, flat, stony plains, showing a marked distinction in characteristics from the Sikkim-like country he had left behind. From the foot of the wind-swept Shar Khalep pass to the border of the Trigu lake, only one halting place was found. It was a favourite haunt of robbers who infested these plains. Next day, he found himself on the grassy plain which immediately borders the Trigu lake. There are hot springs in the neighbourhood. He ascended the Che (Cheya) pass (17,000 feet). Here again, after reching the head of the Yarlung river, he encountered signs of cultivation and civilized humanity. *Mendongs* were frequent and flocks of sheep and goats were scattered over the plains. Then he made his way northwords through a valley which increased in fertility and richness. The Yarlung valley is famous throughout Tibet. At Cho-di-kong, he mentions willows as being abundant on the river banks. Severe floods had at time depopulated and laid waste the valley.

At Gyanthang gompa, he left the valley. From Tse-tang, the explorer turned east along the valley of the Tsang-po from the north and passed through a wealthy district adoining the river. In order to reach the valley of Wokar or Hokar (Oka) through which the river Mik Chu joins the Tsang-po from the north, the explorer crossed a pass called the Kola La, the descent from which brought him immediately in the valley. At the head of the Wokar valley is the Magula pass leading to the great high road from Tibet to China. Dense forests clothe the hill-sides and the open part of the valley is filled with cultivation, chiefly barley.

The explorer describes that there is complete freedom accorded to the women of Tibet. He was constantly indebted to the kindness of the gentle sex for shelter and food and he relates how on a particular occasion, having experienced an undignified repulse from the premises of a wealthy Tibetan gentleman, he accidentlly met the man's daughter-in-law immediately afterwards and related his grievance with a good many uncomplimentary remarks about her relative. The girl laughed and took him straight back to the house from which he had been ejected and treated him with the most flattering personal attention. She was very fair and he gives it as a result of much varied experience that fair ladies always indicate true kindness of heart.

From Zinchi, Gyatso returned by the northern bank of the Tsang-po river to Samaye, visiting the Sangri-khama monastery on the way. He tells of the scenery about here that must almost rival Kashmir woods and gardens. The walnut trees especially attracted his attention. Above all, there were excellent roads like the roads about Darjeeling.

Passing the Ka-pa-tu (Gerpa) where there was a ferry, he passed over sandy plains adjoining the river till he reached the temple of Samaye which has been well described by Pundit Nain Singh and Pundit Kishen Singh. On the 7th October, the explorer crossed the Tsang-po at Tsonka ferry in order to visit Mindo-ling. Here the river is more than a mile broad. He went to the village and the monastery of Tsong-du-tsang which he describes as a large and flourishing place full of trees and gardens. From Mindol-ling, he returned by the same road to the Tsang-po and visited the Ta-thang monastery *en route* where he was nearly torn to pieces by dogs. Passing the Man-dsu ferry, he made his way westwards along the southern bank of the Tsang-po to Lhat-tse, after a harmless encounter with robbers on the road. He then went to the cloth market of Kedesho Dzong from which he turned southward to the Thib valley. The Tsang-po frequently overflows at this piont of its course and the valley is inundated for some distance up the course of the river.

Leaving Thib, he crossed the Tsang-po near the mouth of the valley and visited the monastery of Dorjethang. At this point, the river is about 800 yards wide, very deep and full of fish. There was a road leading to Lhasa via Phurin and Nango-so-na over the Thungo pass and this the explorer determined to follow. As far as Phurin, he found the road good and easy to ascent. After this, he describes it as passing over rough gravel impeded by thorny bushes. The stream was constantly crossed and recrossed by bridges until Kyepa-thi dok (14,840 feet) was reached. Two and a half miles further, the Thungo pass (16,330 feet) was crossed and a flattish, open, grassy plain was found at its summit. After crossing this plain, a second pass was surmounted from which the city of Lhasa could be seen stretched out below as in a looking glass. Behind it, northward, were the hills of Pen-pa-go. Monasteries and vilages lay thickly scattered around. Approaching the river Kyi Chu, the monastic palace of Tse-Chhog-ling (Tse-chog-ling), one of the residences of the King, was passed on the left and the river itself barred the road to Lhasa. At this point where the explorer crossed on the 9th October, 1883, the river is 500 paces broad.

On the 19th October, 1883, Ugyen Gyatso packed up and started again from Lhasa. He was hard up for money and managed to get Rs. 125 by giving a promissory note on Darjeeling. Through the agency of his friend, the explorer engaged a Mongolian monk to accompany him on his return journey to Darjeeling. He passed through Chiri and Dong-kar, crossed Til Chu Sampa and followed the right bank of the Kyi Chu. Barley cultivation and orchards were frequent all along the road. On the 21st October, he continued his route from Netang along the banks of the river which became preciptious and rocky, the road overhanging the river in some parts. He passed Jang (Jang-me) village where there were many houses and cultivated fields of barley and gardens of willow trees. That night he halted at Tsa-bu-na.

Next day he travelled through Chu-shul, and a little beyond the village of Jagang he arrived at the north bank of the Tsang-po. After passing a wide plain, he reached the vilage of Toitsa. His route thereafter lay over the Kam-pa pass (14,950 feet) to Tamalung on the banks of Yam-drok-Tso or Palti lake. It is frozen in winter so that Tia-gang on the opposite bank is easily accessible.

Following the eastern margin of the lake, he reached the Phu-chu pass (15,500 feet). A severe snow storm caught his party on the pass and impeded his progress. The force of the wind on such occasions is severe. It is impossible to face it. The road constantly crossed small but rough spurs running down from the hills on the north-east. The track leads to Ton-nomgyaling (fort) until Tang-do is reached when these north-easterly passes carry travellers into the Yem-drok Kamoling or the great grassy plain to the east of the lake. Between Tang-da and Shab-Shi, he found the flanking hills covered with snow. At the tail-end of the lake, he found great difficulty in crossing the stream which drains into it from the grassy plain of Yam-drok Kamoling where herds of ponies were pastured. The ponies lived in a semi-wild state. Still tracing out the edge of the lake, he passed through Kha-mi-do (Mi-do) and over the Gyanju pass to the plain of Nyamalung.

Then he passed across a deserted plain. From Ka-bu pass, he descended again to another dreary, deserted expanse of plain covered with a coarse stiff grass. He passed Sha-ri and reached Tag-lung (Tra-lung) once again. From it, a long day's journey brought the explorer to the grassy plain at the western extremity of the Phomo-chang-thang lake. The route passed through Trashichodzong monastery and barley fields. Then he crossed the Dug (Tug) pass (16,900 feet) and reached Tso-kong dok.

The Dokpas of these parts are of Horpa caste. They lived in black tents. Inside their tents, boxes were arranged round the sides with a small shrine in the centre of the tent. They were wealthy and prosperous and the explorer could count about fifteen to twenty *doks* or tent villages round the Mho-mo-thang lake. This part of Tibet has the reputation of being the coldest tract in the country. The snow frequently lies deep for fifteen or twenty days at a time, preventing all traffic across the plains which are about 16,400 feet above the sea level. In summer and early autumn, these plains are covered with a short stunted green grass. The explorer crossed the Labtse-Kyaro pass (16,600 feet) in the valley drained by an affluent of the Niru Tsang-po which itself drains into the Nyang river about a day's march from Gyantse. He passed Rob-sang dok and Niru-toi villages and halted at De-lung dok where he camped in a sheep fold.

On the 3rd November, 1883, the explorer crossed the Rob-Sang pass (16,400 feet). At Tag-tsa dok at the foot of the pass, he found large flocks of sheep and herds of yaks and a little further on he sighted the Chumalhari range to the south. He passed through Rangmo dok and Ramah at the northern foot of the Yamtse pass. then he came to Men-gong at the head of the Bam (or Kham) lake. A monastery called Lab chhyi (Lap-chi) is perched on a hill on the north of the lake. It is said to be the branch of Lab Chhyi (Lap chi) monastery of Mount Everest (or Lab Chhyi kang). Passing through the village of Ramme (or Hramme) and the monastery of Lha-wang-po-shyag-cheen, he reached the village of Shur where he encamped for the night.

On the 6th November, he reached Lhegin (or Shegyu). He crossed the Gang pass (15,000 feet) and descended to the Chhukia village and travelled to Phari Dzong on the 10th November. The explorer reached Takarpu dok at night where they hid in the jungle for fear of robbers. Next day, the party followed the course of the Ammo river, constantly crossing and re-crossing by bridges. He tells us that the grass of the open valley is particularly good and that the people of the upper and lower Tomo gather together in the summer months for the purpose of cutting and stacking it. Halting at night at Galing in upper Tomo, the party went to the lower Tomo. The lower Tomo is a flourishing valley in which villages are many and cultivation abundant. There are roads on either side of the Ammo river.

Passing Eu-sakha, Gyatso sent word for his nephew who was a Lama of the Pemionchi monastery in Chumbui to meet him. The explorer could not visit Chumbi or pay his respects to the Sikkim Raja on account of his poverty-sticken condition. With the assistance of his nephew, he passed Chumbi the same night and reached the cave of Ridong. Here two or three days were spent in obtainig porters and resting the footsore animals. The gravel plains of Phari seem to be specially tiring to travellers who were out their shoes over them and lame their animals. On the 16th November, he descended to the Dhang sheo cave. Then he made his way past the Thsoloima lake formed by the drainage of the Cho pass, seing occasional *doks* on the right and left to a place known as Simoighyptsuk. On the 17th November, he crossed the Cho pass (14,500 feet). Pursuing his journey over well known country with many halts, the explorer reached his own monastery of Pemionchi onthe 6th December where he duly entertained his brother Lamas. On the 15th December, 1883, he reached Darjeeling.

Thus ends one of the best records of Tibetan travel that has been achieved by Lama Ugyan Gyatso in a record time of 6-1/2 months.

MIRZA SHUJA

The explorer Mirza Shuja reached Kabul and proceeded to Badakshan in October 1868. Crossing the Hindu Kush by the ordinary route to Bamiyan, he made his way into Badakshan, following the course of the Korcha river. There are Buddha images and frescoes on the famous rock cave in the Bamiyan valley in Afghanistan. The remains which are nearly 1,500 years old are situated about 250 kilometres north-west of Kabul in the snow-clad region of the Hindu-kush mountains and include two of the highest images of the Buddha in the world.

The Mirza reached the Oxus at Iskasim and marching up the stream nearly due east, he arrived at the Punja fort in Wakhan. From Punja, the explorer followed the southern branch of the Oxus river. On the 14th January, 1869, he started from Punja and suffered severely from cold in crossing the Pamir steppe as snow was falling every day. He reached the water-parting between Wakhan and Eatern Turkistan where the rivers were frozen. The source of this southern branch of the Oxus river was found to be a small fronzen lake caloled Pamir-kul (height 13,300 feet). Then he followed the tributary of the Yarkand river upto Tashkurgan, the capital of Sinkur. He was now in the territory of the Alalik Ghazi. He arived at Kashgar on the 3rd February, 1869 and returned to Yarkand and the Karakoram pass.

The Mirza observed latitudes at the chief places on the route by meridian altitudes of the sun and stars and the route survey was made by taking bearings with a prismatic compass and measuring distances by pacing. He executed a route survey of 2,179 miles, fixing the heights of 28 points by boiling-water observations and taking 48 latitude observations at 14 places.

ATA MOHAMMAD

The explorer Ata Mohammad, 'the Mullah' made his way to Jalalabad. He crossed the Kabul river on the 28th September, 1873, and proceeded up the valley of Kunar. He recahed Chitral on the 31st October and spent the winter there. On the 22nd March, 1874, he left Chitral and crossed the Baroghil pass and reched Sarhad in Wakhan on the 8th May, 1874. This pass forms the water-parting betwen the Sarhad and Chitral rivers and is considered to be the lowest depression in the chain that separates India and Afghanistan from northern Asia. He then proceeded over the Little Pamir to Tashkurghan and Yarkand and then by Karakoram pass to Leh. He merely made a route survey with compass without attempting observations for latitude or height for various reasons.

* * *

ABDUL SUBHAN

The explorer Abdul Subhan started from Kashgar on the 17th March, 1874, passed through Tashkurghan and reached Punjah in Wakhan. From here he followd the course of the Oxus river in the direction of Kulab. He reached Iskashim; thence turning northwards, he continued his journey along the river for about one hundred miles, passing through Gharan, Shingnan and Roshan countries. He descriebed the ruby mines.

APPENDIX

KAILAS • MANASAROWAR

Kailas and Manasarowar are the holiest places of pilgrimage for Indians. Kailas is the natural *Shivalaya* (abode of Shiva) where Lord Shiva lived with his consort, Parvati and spent his time in the peaceful atmosphere of the Himalayas in meditation, singing hymns and performing his *tandav* dance to the glory of the almighty God. From time immemorial, our sages and devotees have been visiting these holy places to purify themselves by the glimpse of Kailas and the dip in the holy waters of Manasarowar. The Hindu and Buddhist legends are full of their stories.

Apart from the religions point of view, Kalas and Manasarowar posses unique natural beauty and grandeur of their own. The snowcapped Kailas peak (21,850 feet) sparkles in the sun's rays as a beautiful white-washed temple and manasarowar looks like a sea of blue water. It is a lake with a circumference of forty-five miles, situated amidst extensive undulating pasture-lands of Chang-tang (the heart of the pastoral life in Tibet) which are carpeted with velvet green grass during the summer season, when hundreds of jet-black, wild yaks, antelopes, *kiangs* and other animals graze in peace. The Manasarowar is full of myriad of white swans, ducks and other migratory birds in this season. They lay and hatch their eggs in the reeds along the edge of the lake with the least disturbance as the Tibetans do not kill birds.

Manasarowar falls on the great caravan road of *Jong-lam* from Lhasa to Gartok. In the region of Manasarowar and Rakastal in Southern Tibet, with Gurla Mandhata south of them and holy Kailas to the north, three great rivers, Iindus, Sutlej and the Tsang-po (Brahmaputra) rise within a few miles of one another. To enjoy the natural scene and beauty of these holy places, one should linger about them and avoid hurry and hustle.

APPENDIX

The Route of Pilgrimage

Four centuries, Indian pilgrims had been visiting Kailas and Manasarowar. There are three main routes over the three Himalayan passes of Niti (16,628 feet), Untadhura (17,590 feet) and Lipu Lekh (16,750 feet). For the sake of *parikrama* (circumambulation), the pilgrims usually started from Milam, the last Indian vilalge on this route, crossed Untadhura pass and returned to India through Lipu Lekh pass after visiting Kailas and Manasarowar. They reached Kailas in about two weeks. Milam is the biggest village in Pithoragarh district of Kumaon, from where the traders used to go to Gyanima, Gartok and other trading centres in Ngari Khorsum in Western Tibet for barter trade. After making necessary arrangements for transport, food and clothing, the pilgrims started from Milam. On the first day, they halted at the southern foot of the Untadhura pass. In one day they halted at the southern foot of the Untadhura pass. In one day they had to cross the three joined high passes of Untadhura (17,590 feet), Jayanti (17,000 feet) and Kingri Bingri (18,300 feet) after a steep and difficult ascent, for fear of being caught in blizzards, and spent the night at Chhirchan camp on the other side. This crossing was never attempted during a rainy day. On the 3rd day, they reached Tokpu camp; 4th day—Thazang; 5th day—Chhinku which falls on the direct route to Kailas via Tirathpuri. But the Pilgrims preferred to go via Gyanima *mandi* to replenish their stock of provisions. On the 8th day, they reached Gyanima after crossing the Guniangti and Durmiangti streams on the way. They halted there for one or two days for making necessary arrangements. From there they reached Tirathpuri, situated on the bank of the Sultej, in two days. There are caves, hot water springs and a gompa there. After three days' march from the place, they reached a camp on the bank of the Indus river, just below the Kailas peak. Then they ascended along a deep stream issuing from the Kailas range and reached Landi Gompa (1st gompa of the circuit). Next day they reached Darfu (2nd gompa). Here they left the stream and ascended Gorikund on the ridge north of the Kailas peak. Then they returned following another stream and reached Chhundulpu (3rd gompa). The next point was Darchin village (4th and last gompa of the circuit). Usually the pilgrims started from Darchin and after completing the circuit through the above mentioned four gompas returned to it.

From Darchin, the pilgrims returned and passed around the Rakastal lake and reached Manasarowar in one day. On the 2nd day, they turned south and then to east and halted on the bank of the Karnali river. They followed the Karnali river and on the 3rd day reached Taklokot *mandi* at the junction of three rivers. There are many villages on the banks of the Karnali river with good cultivation of barley and peas. The temple of Khojarnath is about six miles away. After one or two days' halt, the pilgrims proceeded towards India and crossed Lipu Lekh pass by an easy ascent, descended by a gradual slope and halted in a *dharamshala* on the bank of the Kali river. The valley of the Kali river is heavily forested with *deodar* and other trees. After the days, marching from Darchin, the pilgrims reached Garbiang village of Pithoragarh District in Kumaon.

General Information

As the change in climate is abrupt from the low and hot plains of India to the severely cold high table-land of Tibet (average height about 15,000 feet), many pilgrims suffered and some died for want of proper information and lack of proper arrangements for food and clothing. Colonel Kenneth Mason has written in his book entitled. "The Abode of Snow" that every mountaineer travels on the shoulders of those who have gone before. In other words, the mountaineer takes advantage of the past experience and adds a little for those to follow. Based on the past experience, the following general information is given for the guidance of the future pilgrims to make the pilgrimage a pleasure trip.

Clothing : Just as a Tibetan highlander looks odd in his woollen gown, long boots and woollen head-gear in the low land of India, an Indian with his loose garments of *dhoti* and *kameez* will not only look queer but he cannot also possibly survive in the freezing cold and the piercing winds of Tibet. Not to say of two or three baths per day, he cannot even wash his face frequently with cold water as it will crack the soft skin and blood will come

APPENDIX

out. We should always appreciate the mode of life of other people based on climatic and other factors, however, different it may be from ours. So the pilgrims should equip themselves with the following clothing :—

1. Thick woollen wind-proof bush-shirt. Great-coat is cumbersome and not fit for long marches.
2. Woollen *chooridar* trousers as worn by the hill people. These are wind-proof and very comfortable for sitting crosslegged on the ground.
3. Woollen cap.
4. One light woollen shawl or scarf.
5. One or two pairs of thick boots with strong rubber soles.
6. Four pairs of woollen socks. These keep the feet warm and are very comfortable for long journeys.
7. Sleeping bag made of feathers or cotton wool. The latter is cheaper. Blankets are heavy for transport.
8. Hold-all.
9. Kit bag for keeping provisions.
10. A small *durrie* or tarpaulin.
11. Sun goggles.
12. A long and strong walking-stick.

The females may use light boots, woollen sweater and tight woollen *kameez*. Pilgrims who can afford it, may take tents which are useful for travelling in uninhabited regions.

Food : Veteran mountaineers like Shifton, Younghusband, Murray and others found the local food in the Himalayan region quite nourishing and palatable. They used this instead of importing tons of food-stuff from Europe for their parties. Appetite is strong in high altitudes while travelling. In addition to *chapati, prantha, rice, barhi,* dried vegetables, *dal,* meat, butter, ghee, honey, milk, etc., we require some ready-made food-stuff to ward off the pangs of hunger during marches, mid-day halts and just on reaching the camp at the end of the day before some substantial food can be prepared. *Sattu* is nourishing and tasteful when mixed with hot tea, *gur*, sugar or salt. *Gur-papri* (fried *suji* or wheat flour mixed with *gur* and dried fruits) is a nice snack with hot tea. Tea is very useful while travelling in high altitudes. If quenches thrist and is a good stimulant. A kettle should be kept handy. Whenever the traveller feels thristy or hungry, tea should be prepared and taken with *sattu* or *gur-papri*. Pulses and meat are difficult to cook in high altitudes and pressure-cookers should be used.

Unfortunately since the occuppation of Tibet and Lhasa by China in 1951, no Indian pilgrim could visit the holy places.

GLOSSARY

Oriental language words occuring in the book have been spelt phonetically with the help of vowel sounds. Tibetan words have been divided in different parts such as Kam-pa-par-tse. Where there is a double spelling. the first one is the same as adopted in the book; the second one which appears within brackets is the correct orthography. Ng has been used for the Hindi letter. ङ which has no English equivalent as in Ngari Khorsum. Tse for च as in Shigatse and Dz for ज as in Dzong.

The following abbreviations, denoting the particular language to which a word belongs, are noted against each word except those of nomadic dialect or of doubtful origin :—

(A)	denotes	—	Arabic
(C)	"	—	Chinese
(H)	"	—	Hindi
(M)	"	—	Mongolian
(N)	"	—	Nepali
(P)	"	—	Persian
(S)	"	—	Sanskrit
(T)	"	—	Tibetan
(Tur)	"	—	Turkish
(U)	"	—	Urdu

A

Abra (T), a rat without a tail found in the tableland of Tibet.
AK, the short name of the explorer Kishen Singh who was enlisted as Krishna in the Survey of India. The first and last letters of the word Krishna have been inverted.
Ala (T), good, excellent, as in Alado, Alagak

Ama (T), mother
Amban (C), governor
Amur-bhaino (M), literally *amur* means health and *bhaino* means is' or 'are.' ("Are you in a good health(", the Mongolian way of salutation.)
Ani (T), nun
Ani gompa (T), nunnery
Anna (H), Indian coin 1/16 of a rupee (now not in use)
Anyar (N), the *andromeda* or *ovalifolia*, a kind of tree
Arki (M), a kind of spirit distilled from sour milk.
Ata (H), wheat flour
Atees (N), The *aconitum heterophyllum*, a kind of medicinal herb.

B

Ba or *pa* (T), pertaining or belonging to, as in Nangba, Chiba, Gaba, as in Ta-sam-pa
Bacha (M), white saltish coat over the surface of the land in Mongolia
Badi (H), dried paste of cucumber and *urad dal*
Baga (M), small, as in Baga Tsaidam
Baghur (T), black yak-hair tent used by nomads
Bam (Bum) (T), a disease in which red blotches appear on the leg
Baral (bharhal or *burrel)* (N), wild mountain goat
Bazar (H & N), marketing place
Beli (M), chief or ruler higher in rank than a Besi
Besi (M), chief or ruler higher in rank than a *Jhasa*
Bhachug (T), cow
Bhaimbu (Bhompo) (T), a religion that existed in Tibet before Buddhism was introduced
Bhanjang (N), mountain range of contracted extent
Bhansar (N), chief custom-house
Bhojpatra (bhoj) (N & H), a kind of birch
Bhongu (T), donkey
Bhu (T), boy
Bhuthog (T), soda
Biasi (N), winter reesidence
Bil (N), the creeping cedar, *juniperus religiosa*

GLOSSARY

Bis (H & N), the *aconitum ferex*, a poisonous herb
Bodh Kai (T), Tibetan language
Bul (Butok) (T), a kind of soda used in washing and mixing in boiling tea to extract its essence and for other purposes
Bulag, a spring of water, as in Dugbulag
Bumo (T), girl
Bure, a kid of silk
Burha (N), a respected elder of a family. It is used in Johar valley of Kumaon also.

C

Cha (Chha) (T), salt, as in Cha-chu
Chadamo, this side, as in Bangbura Chadamo
Chaga (M), an oasis on the border of a desert
Chak (T), iron, as in chak-sam
Chaka (Chhaka) (T), salt-mine, as in Chiakla chaka
Chongju saiwang (Chongju serbang) (T), a religious procession on the 30th of second month in Lhasa after Tibetan festival
Changma (T), A species of a willow
Chanja (Chhangja) (T), an old Tibetan silver coin equal in value to about six annas of the Indian money
Chapati (H) Indian bread
Charas (H), an intoxicating drug
Charpa (T), rain
Chauki (H & N), custom-post
Che (chhe) (T), chief, large, as in Chujacheti, Ramoche
Cheka (Chheka) (M), mare milk rendered acidic by addition of sour milk
Chen (chhen) (M), Mongolian weight equal to about 2 dr. avoir
Chenkang (T), platform in the temples and halls where idols and scriptures are kept
Chenpo (T), big
Chhak (M), a forest tree in Mongolia
Chhang (T), beer made from barley
Chhingba (chhingpa) (T), a kind of felt used for making clothes and tents
Chhingde, a kind of brown bear
Chho (Tsho) (T), lake

Chi (Chhi) (T), a horse belonging to a great man
Chiakla (T), A respectable Tibetan family belonging to Ta-chien-lu
Chiakpo (Chakpo) (T), to be thrifty
Chianku (Changku) (T), wolf
Chiba (Chhiba) (T), a sect of Tibetan Buddhists
Chickyal (Chicke) (T), a Tibeten coin 1/2 of *tanka*
Chigeb (Chikyap) (T), a chief officer who exercises magisterial power as well as collects revenue
Chikha (T), spring
Chiomo (Chomo or *Jhomo)* (T), a goddess, as inChomo Lhakang, Jhomo-Lha Ri
Chionga Chiopa (Chonga Chopa) (T), lterally *chionga* means 15th and *Chiopa*, offering. Tibetan new year festival
Chipa (Chhipi) (T), a small quadruped, marmot
Chi pon (T), master of a stable
Cho (Tsoe) (T), The Tibetan antelope, *antilopus hodgsoni*
Choga (Tur), a loose garment or long overcoat reaching the feet
Choi, a grass which yields yellow colour
Chotra (N), a species of *barberry, berberis aristata*. A valuable medicine. *rasot* is obtained from the decoction of its bark and wood.
Chu (T), a stream, a river or water, as in Dichu
Chuchan (T), hot spring, as in Dam Chuchan
Chud, a kind of creeper which yields red dye when dried
Chugpo (T), rich
Chuktu (T), a kind of Tibetan carpet
Chumi (T), spring
Chung Chung (T), small
Chungja, a middling kind of tea
Chura (Churu) (T), strong cheese which is prepared like gruel and taken with *tsampa*
Churtan (Chorten) (T), a kind of temple within which images, religious books and other objects of veneration are kept.

D

Daba (Dhab) (T), a monk, a scholar, a disciple
Dag (Dhag) (T), a rock, as in Dag Karpo

GLOSSARY 261

Dal (H), pulse

Dalai Lama (M), literally *Dalai* means broad ocean, *Lama*, high priest. The Mongolian ruler Altan Khan, who embraced Buddhism, gave the title of "Dalai Lama" to the incarnations. This term by which the great Lama of Tibet is known to outsiders is never used in Tibet where he is called Gyalwa Rimpoche.

Daloi (C), property chief officer, a commandant of Chinese soldiers. This officer also exercises magisterial authority.

Dam (Dham) (T), a swamp, as in Lingdam

Dama, Tibetan furze

Dau (T), buck wheat

De (T), evil spirit

Demo (T), brown bear found in northern Tibet

Deo (H & N), deity

Deodar (S), a species of pine, *pinus deodara*

Dhag (T), rock

Dhak (N), *butea frondosa*

Dham (T), mud

Dhama (T), brass drum and pipe

Dhangmo (T), cold

Dharmashala (H), charitable rest-house

Dhep (T), book

Dho (T), stone

Dhong or Dhong kyer (T), town

Dhosol (T), coal

Dhoto, a place to which corpses are removed to be cut into pieces and thrown to kites and crows

Dhrapo (T), monk

Dhu (T), boat made of wood

Dhunga (N), stone

Di, literally means mixed, confluence of streams, as in Dichu

Dia Pon (T), a high military officer of the rank of general

Do (T), fair, junction of two rivers, as in Kegudo

Doag Kai (T), dialect spoken by the nomads inTibet

Dok (T), short form for Dokpa, meaning nomad

Dokpa (T), a nomad

Dolam (T), road

Domo (Dom) (T), bear
Dong (T), a wild yak
Dong (Dongba) (T), a village as in Margen Dongu, Urong Dongu
Dongkhim (Dogkhim) (T), rest-house in the nomad lands
Dorje Phamo (T), the name of a goddess. The only incarnate woman in Samding monastery
Dri (T), female yak
Dudh kund (N & H), literally dudh means milk, kund - small lake, milky lake
Dug (M), a Mongolian weight
Dukha (Dhukha), literally du means boat and kha, mouth or source. A ferry, as in Samba Dukha
Dum (Damu), a brick of tea
Dumba (U), a sheep with big fat tail
Dung (Dhung) (T), conch-shell
Dung-bura (Dunga-buwa) (T), literally dung means conch shell and bura (Buwa), to blow. Blowing of conch-shell, as in Dungbura Chamado
Dung shing (T), silver fir
Dunkur (Dunkhor) (T), Tibetan Government officer
Dzo (T), cross-breed female yak
Dzong (T), residence whether fort or otherwise of a governor of a district who is called Jongpon

G

Gang (T), ridge, also ice, as in Rinchingang, Ata Gang
Gaon (N & H), village
Garhi (N), fort
Garpon (T), Chief or Commissioner of Gar in Western Tibet
Gebis, a structure containing images built on top of building
Gegen (T), teacher
Gegu (T), monitor of monks in monasteries in Tibet
Getha, famous woollen cloth manufactured at Gyantse
Ghang (T), snow
Ghangar (Ghangari) (T), snow mountain
Ghat (H & N), a mountain pass, a place where river is crossed
Ghee (H & N), clarified butter

GLOSSARY

Ghur (T), tent

Giachug (T), one stage when travelling in Tibet

Giakhong (T), literally *gia* (short form of *gyani)* means Chinese and *khang* means house. Chinese house or barrack

Gilong (Gelong), a monk of strict celebate life

Gio, (T), village headman

Gisi (Geshey) (T), a religious scholar

Goa (T), gazelle

Gol (M), a river, as in Nichi Gol

Gompa, (T), a monastery

Gonchen (T), a large monastery

Gunkha (T), winter

Gur (H), a coarse kind of sugar made into cakes or balls of different *sizes* by boiling cane-juice

Gur papri (H), fried *suji* or wheat flour mixed with *gur* and dried fruits

Gurrel (N), Himalayan chamois, *nemorhadus goral*

Guru (H), saint or teacher

Gyalbo (T), a king

Gyan, a high or prominent place, as in Gyantse

Gyangpa, chief village official

Gyapi (T), pagoda

Gyatiu, a riding mule

Gyukchu (T), stream

H

Hap (T), a mouthful of water, as in Hapchu Kang

Hara (M), black, as in Hara Nor

Harmo (M), a fruit tree

Haze (Deze), a kind of fox

Himalaya (S), literally *Him* means snow and *alaya,* abode. Abode of snow. In Nepal and Kumaon, the words, *Himal, Himala,* and *Himanchal* are also used.

Hindi (H), an Indian language

Hindu (H), the inhabitants of India, professing belief in Vedic religion

Hindustan (P), India, originally the country on the eastern side of the Sindhu (Indus) river was called Hindustan by the Persians.

Hu-Hu (C), the Mohammedans in China
Humba (M), tamarisk

I

Ikhi (M), large, as in *Ikhi Tsaidam*
Ilaka (U & N), district, jurisdiction

J

Jadwar (N), poison-antidote, herbal plant, called *nirbisi* in India,
Jalno, a temporary judge of Lhasa Court to collect arbitrary taxes during New Year festival in Tibet
Jam, a bridge, as in Giokjam
Jam Pon, a custodian of bridges in a district in Tibet
Jamun (H), a fruit tree
Jang (Jhang) (T), north, as in *Jang* Tulung
Jangkhu (T), green
Jegati (N), post
Jha (T), tea
Jhasa (M), a chief or ruler
Jhema (T), sand
Jhio (Gyawa) (T), a lord, as in Jhio Sakya Muni, Gyawa Rinpoche
Jikkyop, a rest-house for travellers
Jing (M), A Mongolian weight
Jobo (Jhobo, Jopho) (T), a male of cross-breed between a bull and a female yak or between a male yak and a cow
Johsar (Lohsar), New Year festival
Jomo (zomo) (T), a female of cross-breed between a bull and a female yak or between a male yak and a cow
Jongpon (Dzongpn) (T), a Tibetan expression which literally means the fortmaster, collector of taxes under the Lhasa Govt. who was to bear rule for a period of three years. His duty was to guard the road, levy taxes equal to one-tenth the value on any merchandise which passes through his post and to decide cases of a civil or criminal nature
Joukar (Yungkar), a kind of white mustard
Jungchong Pon, title of a commercial representative of the Lhasa Government

K

Kacha (H & N), made of sun dried bricks or mud, as in *kacha* building
Kafila (A), a caravan
Kai (T), a dialect, as in Bodh Kai, box to measure grain 2 *kai* =1 mound
Kalas (H), a spire
Kali (H), the name of a goddess
Kang (Khan) (T), a house as in Romkang, Chenkang
Kankar (H), gravel
Kar (Karpo) (T), white, as in Dongkar, Dag Karpo
Karma (T), Tibetan coin, 1/3rd of *nagtang*
Kauli (C), a kind of grain
Kazi (U), a chief or landlord in Sikkim
Kha (T), source, mouth, also snow, as in Nag Chukha
Khadi (H), hand-made cloth with hand-spun yarn
Khamar, coloured silk
Kham Kai (T), dialect spoken in eastern Tibet of Kham
Khangpa (T), house
Khap (T), needle
Khar (T), fort, castle
Khark (Kharak) (N), cow-shed
Khatak (T), a thin cloth made of silk or from the bark of a tree, varying in size from a few inches to about a yard square, bestowed as an offering or as a mark of greeting
Khola (N), stream
Khor or *khorlo* (T), literally means a circle, a cylinder used by the Tibetans while repeating their prayer
Khorchen (T), a large *Khor* or *Khorlo*, a temple having a large *khorlo* or *khorchen*
Khua (M), the bank of a river, as in Maurusen Khua
Khukri (N), the famous short, heavy, curved knife used throughout Nepal in place of a sword
Khurshing (T), a cradle for packs
Khurso (N), a species of oak
Khuthul (M), a pass
Kiang (Kyang) (T), a wild ass
Kiang Khor (Kiang chak) (T), the method of successive prostration full

length on the road, each prostration beginning where the preceding one ended

Kiaring Kuring (T), irregular, as in Tso Kiaring Kuring
Kodo (T), millet, a small grain known as *manduwa* in India
Koko (khoko) (M), blue as in Koko Shili, Koko Nor
Konchok (T), god
Kosi (N), stream or river
Kowo (T), a boat made of hides
Kulath (H), a kind of pulse
Kund (H & N), a pond or small lake
Kupa (T), string
Kutung (Kudhung) (T), tomb, a hollow monument of metal in shape like a *chortan* raised over the dead body of a lama after his death
Kyi (T), source, as in Kyichu
Kyime (T), female
Kyoka (T), male
Kyopo (T), poor
Kyuwa (T), male yak

L

La (T), pass, a hill, as in Nub Kong La
Lama (T), a high priest or religious teacher in Tibet
Lamathologa (M), literally *thologa* means head, round like a lama's head
Lambardar (U), the owner or headman of a village or villages who is responsible to the government for payment of revenue
Lango (T), bull
Langur (N), snow mountains
Lapcha (Lapche) (T), piles of stones surmounted by flags erected on top of passes for good luck
Leu (M), A Mongolian weight
Lha (T), a diety, as in Lhakang
Lhakang (T), *Lha*, a deity and *kang*, house, a temple
Lhasa (T), the capital of Tibet, literally *Lha* means god and *sa*, land
Lho (T), south, as in Lhoyul, Lhokha
Li (C), a measure of length, equal to about 300 yards
Libun, a species of turnip

GLOSSARY

Ling (T), a continent, an island, a division
Linga (T), a grove of willow and poplar trees
Lobtruk (T), student
Loma (T), leaf
Lung (T), a valley, as in Khamlung, Talung

M

Ma (T), red, as in Machu, Chumar
Maidan (H & N), a plain of some extent
Manduwa (H), a kind of coarse grain
Mane Ringbo (T), literally mane means consecrated stone or stone walls and *ringbo*, long
Mangpo (T), large quantity
Mantra (S), sacred formula
Mar (T), butter
Marpo (T), red
Masur (H), a kind of pulse
Matar (H), peas
Me (T), lower, as in Po-me
Mel (T), fire
Mi (T), man
Mide (T), a kind of brown bear whose feet resemble those of a man and which is very dangerous
Miscal, a Tibetan coin, 2/3 of a *nagtang*
Mitra (H), a friend, correspondent of a Johari trader in Tibet
Mo (T), female, woman
Molam Chemo or *Chhemo* (T), literally *molam* means prayer and *chemo* or *chhemo*, great. The month of asking blessings, i.e., the first month of the Tibetan year
Mowa, a kind of liquor
Munal (N & H), a majestic and beautiful species of pheasant found in high Himalayas, *lophophorus impeyanus*
Muni (S), a holy man, a saint, as in Sakya Muni
Musk (H), strong perfume obtained from the male musk-deer
Musk deer, a hornless deer, found in Central Asia, which produces the valuable perfume called musk. It is found in the belt between the forested and snowy regions of Central Asia.

N

Na (T), a wild goat, burrel
Nag (T), black, as in Nag chu, Rinag
Nagpang (T), black board
Nagpo (T), black
Nagtang (T), a Tibetan coin of equal parts of silver and alloy, valued at a half rupee of the Indian coin
Nagtsa (T), ink
Nagul (T), silver
Nala (H), a stream, a rivulet, a water course
Namado (M), the other side, opposite of *chadomo,* as in Dungbura Namado
Namaga (M), a swamp, as in Chokang Namaga
Namda (Namad) (T), a kind of coarse woollen cloth used in making saddle-pad and felt
Nang (T), within the limits, as in Pen-nag-chu, cham-chu-nang
Nangba (T), one of the two sects of Buddhists inTibet. The other sect is called Chiba or Baimbu. The Nanga sect is sub-divided into Ningma, Sakia, Guba and Gilukpa.
Ne (Neh) (T), a species of barley
Newar (N), the trading sect in Nepal
Nhen (Nyen) (T), a wild rocky-mountain sheep
Ning (T), heart, as in Tso-Ning-Nub-Kong pass
Ningpa (T), old
Nirbisi (N & H), literally poison antidote, a plant of aconite species, somewhat like ginger in its leaves but of a sweet scent
Niugu (T), pen
Niung niung (T), small
No, wild goat
Nor (M), lake, as in Hara Nor, Tengri Nor
Nub (T), west
Num (T), oil

O

Obo (M), a place of worship where flags are erected
Onbo (ngonpo), blue, as in Tso Onbo

P

Padam (H & N), a kind of fir tree
Pahar (H & N), hill or mountain
Pakka (H & N), built of burnt bricks or stones
Palki (H & N), palanquin
Paranta (H), fried *chapati*
Parcha, brick tea - 5 lbs. in weight
Pasm (U), soft wool
Patti (H & N), a fiscal division of territory subordinate to a revenue collector
Pauhung (T), an old Tibetan silver coin equal in value to about 6 annas of the Indian coin
Pawa (N), charitable rest-house
Pekang (T), mustard
Phanpar (Phapar) (N), a kind of grain grown in the Himalayas
Phedi (N), winter residence, low ground
Phingba (T), a kind of coarse woollen cloth used for making tents
Pipal (H), *ficus religious*, a large shady tree considered as sacred in India
Po, fragrant show-match
Pokhari (N), small tank
Pon (T), a petty ruler
Pugu (T), child
Pundit (H), learned men. The explorers Nain Singh, Kishen Singh, Mani Singh and Kalian Singh were given the title of "Pundit" in the Survey of India Records.
Purik nambu (T), woollen manufacture of Gyantse
Pyjama (P), literally a dress of lower limbs, trousers

R

Rabdun (T), literally rab means ford and *dun,* seven, as in Chu Rabdun
Raindiar (N), the most magnificent species of pine, *abies webbiana*
Raja (H), king or chief
Rak (T), brass
Rakshas (S), a demon
Rakshas (S), a demon
Ram (T), indigo, a kind of grass which yields blue colour

Ri (T), a peak, a hill, as in Rinag, Jomo La Ri
Rians (N), a species of oak, *quercus dilatata*
Rigong (T), a rabbit or hare
Ring (Rim)-po-che (T), a title of dignity with which the Lamas and *gyalbos* and sometimes gentlemen of ordinary rank are addressed and spoken of
Ringpo (T), long
Rito (T), a place of retirement for religious contemplation
Romkang (T), a cemetery, literally *ro* means dead body and *kong*, house
Rong (T), a ravine, a defile, also a warm country, as in Rongbacha, Urong, Dongu
Rupee (H), Indian coin

S

Sa (T), earth
Sakhang (T), hotel, restaurant
Sakya or *Jhio Sakya Muni* (T), the Sakya Muni of India, also a subdivision of the Nangba sect of the Buddhists of Tibet which takes its name from a large monastery in Lhasa
Sal (H), a kind of tree, *shorea robusta*
Sama (T), peas
Sampa (T), bridge
Sando, a disease among animals in Tibet
Sang, incense, as in Lhasang
Sange Kuthog (T), *sange* literally means Bodh or Buddha, *Ku*, image and thog, 1000. A sacred place near Saitu
Sangun (N), bridge
Sar (T), new, as in Khansar, Dongsar
Sardar (P), a chief or headman
Sarkari Khajana (H), Government treasury
Sarpa (T), new
Sarson (H), a kind of mustard
Sattu (H), parched grain which is ground into flour and made into paste
Semal (H), a kind of tree, *bombax hepta phyllum*
Semus (Semo) (T), hedgehog
Ser (T), hail

GLOSSARY

Sera, hail
Serai (U), inn, a lodging place for travellers
Serpo (T), yellow
Shan, a kind of tree
Shanyi (T), lead
Shenka (T), width
Sheo (T), lower ground, as in Bhagang sheo
Shian-U (T), magisterial officer of a district
Shiar (Shar) (T), east, as in Shiar Gang
Shibdag (T), a protecting god
Shing (T), wood
Shingnag (T), forest
Shingoha (shingcha), root of a plant exported to China for colouring silk, also said to be used as medicine in China
Shiva (S), the third of the Trinity of Gods (Brahma, Vishnu and Shiva), which are all one in Brahma. Shiva is the Destroyer and Preserver of Life
Shivalaya (S), the abode of Shiva
Sho (T), curd
Shokang (T), Tibetan coin, 2/3 of *naktang*
Shugshine (T), a bark of plant used for making paper
Shug shing (T), tree wood for making paper
Shugu (T), paper
Siga, a village held as a grant, as in Parisiga
Sua, a kind of barley
Swadeshi (H), home-made articles

T

Taichun, a kind of pulse
Tamima (T), an ingot of silver equal to about 156 rupees of the Indian currency
Tandav (S), vigorous Shiva dance
Tang (Thang) (T), a plain, as in Batang, Li-tang
Tanka (T), Tibetan silver coin
Taru, a bush and its fruits
Ta-sam (T), a staging place where officials halt and change horses
Tengri (Thinkari) (M), blue as the sky, as in Tengri Nor

Teu, (M), Mongolian weight equal to about 3 cwt. avoir
Tha (T), horse
Thabu (M), five, as in Thabu Tsaidam
Thain (C), literally the sky, a Chinese official
Thana (H & N), police-post
Thanthu (C), man with white turban
Thapka (T), rope
Tho (T), lake
Thock (Thog) (T), roof, as in Don Thok, Ru Thog, Garthok
Thunje chomo (T), prayer wheel
Till (H), *sesame*, a kind of oil-seed
Tinpa (T), clouds
To (T), upper, opposed to *me*, as in Po-to
Tola (H), an Indian weight equal to 180 grains
Tonkha (T), autumn
Trapu (T), thin
Tsa (T), salt
Tsaidam (M), a place of trade or market, as in Baga Tsaidam
Tsampa (T), barley flour
Tsang-po (T), a large river
Tsawa (T), root
Tse (Tsai) (T), peak
Tshapo (T), hot
Tso (T), lake
Tsod (T), a kind of creeper which yields red colour and is used for dyeing
Tunn (H), *cedrela toona*, a kind of tree valuable for its timber

U

U (T), a lake, as in U-Tsang
Urad (H), a kind of pulse
Utang (M), red, as in Utang - Miris

V

Vakil (U), lawyer

GLOSSARY

W

Whang (C), a chief or ruler higher in rank than Beli
Woma (T), milk

Y

Yak (T), a species of ox found in Tibet and domesticated there, covered all over with a thick coat of long silky hair, that of the lower parts hanging down almost to the ground. It is a very useful beast of burden in high altitudes. The female yak supplies milk to the highlanders.
Yarka (Yerka) (T), a kind of small bells
Yarkha (T), summer
Yi (T), a wild cat
Yul (T), place, province, country, as in Zayul, Lhoyul
Yultha, a cotton cloth

Z

Zamindar (P), a landlord
Zhang (T), Copper
Zingo (T), rich
Zoba (Zo) (T), cross-breed male animal between yak and cow
Zomu (Zomo) (T), cross-breed female animal between yak and cow

ROUTES FOLLOWED BY INDIAN EXPLOR

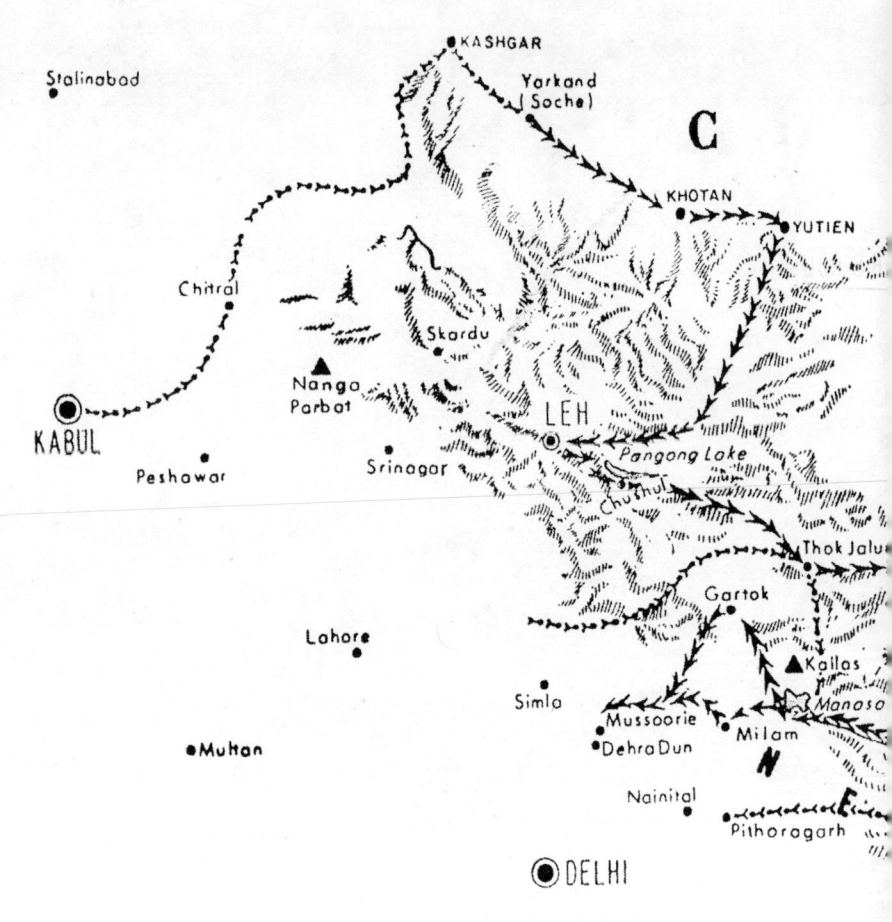